T0248197

THE
TOP TEN
of everything
England

THE

TOP TEN
of everything

England

The Best of the Three Lions
from Adams to Zaha

C L I V E   B A T T Y

First published by Pitch Publishing, 2022

Pitch Publishing
9 Donnington Park,
85 Birdham Road,
Chichester,
West Sussex,
PO20 7AJ
www.pitchpublishing.co.uk
info@pitchpublishing.co.uk

A CIP catalogue record is available for this book
from the British Library.

ISBN 978 1 80150 477 5

Typesetting and origination by Pitch Publishing
Printed and bound in Great Britain by TJ Books, Padstow

CONTENTS

INTRODUCTION

The history of the England football team goes all the way back to November 1872 when the Three Lions played their first ever match, against Scotland in Glasgow. *The Top 10 of Everything England* revisits every aspect of the country's fortunes on and off the pitch in the subsequent 150 years in dozens of ranked lists which are sure to spark debate and discussion among fans everywhere.

The book features a colourful cast of past and present internationals, including the most inspirational skippers from Bobby Moore to Harry Kane, the most prolific goalscorers, the great managers, the toughest defenders and the biggest stars in the England Women's team. It also looks back at the Three Lions' most memorable moments over the decades, including the most iconic matches at the World Cup and European Championship, famous victories in friendly games, the most celebrated derby wins against arch rivals Scotland, the finest goals scored by the likes of Bobby Charlton, Gary Lineker and Wayne Rooney and the most appreciated own goals kindly gifted by the opposition. Additionally, a host of miscellaneous categories rank England's best (and worst!) kits, the wittiest chants belted out from the Wembley stands, the most striking player tattoos, the official squad songs which made it into the charts and the bizarre incidents which left supporters perplexed and bewildered.

Under the superb leadership of current boss Gareth Southgate, England have become a major force on the international stage in recent years, reaching the semi-final of the 2018 World Cup in Russia and the final of the European Championship in 2021. Most fans of the Three Lions, though, will know only too well that the country's football story is as much one of pain and humiliation as joy and ecstasy. So, inside these pages, you will also read about England's most humbling defeats, the players who committed the worst gaffes and blunders, the dodgy refereeing decisions which cost the team dear, the scandals which made front-page news headlines and the bungling managers who the fans couldn't wait to see sacked. Yes, Steve McClaren, I'm talking about you!

Now, there may be times reading this book when you find yourself nodding in agreement and thinking, 'Yes, the author is spot on here; Victoria Beckham is very much the Queen of England WAGS, leagues ahead of Cheryl, Louise Redknapp or Christine Lampard.' However, at other moments you may find yourself sighing and wondering, 'What numbskull wrote this? He hasn't even got Micah Richards in his list of ex-England "Top 10 Pundits". Incredible! Micah's the funniest man on TV!' All I can say in response is that the selections I have made are my own personal choice, based on over 50 years watching England play since I first sat down in front of the TV as an eight-year-old and feasted on the coverage of the 1970 World Cup from faraway Mexico – still, in my opinion, the greatest football tournament ever staged (even if it ended extremely disappointingly for England, whose reign as world champions was ended by West Germany).

Anyway, whether you agree with my picks or not, I very much hope that you find *The Top 10 of Everything England* a fun, informative, thought-provoking and entertaining read throughout.

Clive Batty, August 2022

Want to know how Jesse Lingard feels about being recalled to Gareth Southgate's squad? Or how Marcus Rashford's latest anti-poverty campaign is developing? Then you need to follow your favourite England stars on social media site Twitter:

1) Marcus Rashford (@MarcusRashford); 5.5m followers
Sample tweet, 'Write to your MP via the link below, it's quick and easy. We need long-term solutions. The issue of child hunger is worsening.'

2) Harry Kane (@HKane); 3.6m followers
Sample tweet, 'The first time a Three Lions game has been refereed by a woman and it should be the first of many.'

3) Raheem Sterling (@sterling7); 3.2m followers
Sample tweet, 'Great to lead the lads out at Wembley tonight.'

4) Jesse Lingard (@JessieLingard); 2.9m followers
Sample tweet, 'Nothing puts a smile on my face quite like representing my country! Great to be back with the boys!'

5) Luke Shaw (@LukeShaw23); 2.4m followers
Sample tweet, 'Proud to be part of the team. One final push! See you all on Sunday.'

6) Trent Alexander-Arnold (@TrentAA); 2.3m followers
Sample tweet, 'Amazing feeling to be back in an England shirt.'

7) Harry Maguire (@HarryMaguire93); 1.9m followers
Sample tweet, 'Last Euros as a fan. This Euros as a player. Huge honour – can't wait to get started.'

8) Kyle Walker (@kylewalker2); 1.7m followers
Sample tweet, 'You can't buy that winning feeling! Well played boys, a big 3 points towards qualifying for the World Cup.'

9) Jordan Henderson (@JHenderson); 1.7m followers
Sample tweet, 'Harry Maguire has been a colossus for England. Without him, the progress made at the last two tournaments

would not have been possible. To be booed at his home stadium, for no reason? What have we become?'

10) Jadon Sancho (@Sanchooo10); 1.7m followers
Sample tweet, 'Top performance from the boys! Always a honour to represent England.'

TOP 10 RIVALS

The countries England love to beat the most:

1) Scotland
The rivalry between England and Scotland stretches all the way back to 30 November 1872 when the two sides met in the world's first ever international match, at the West of Scotland Cricket Ground, Partick, Glasgow. That encounter ended 0-0 but there have been many more exciting clashes since, with arguably the heyday of this passionate derby coming in the 1970s when the annual battle to be Britain's top dog was heightened by differing fortunes on the international stage: Scotland qualifying for two World Cups in 1974 and 1978 while England stayed at home. The intensity of feeling reached fever pitch in 1977 when the Scots won 2-1 at Wembley in the British Home Championship, and their supporters celebrated by storming on to the pitch, digging up the turf and tearing down the goalposts. The most significant match between the two sides since then was won by England at Euro '96, the home fans at Wembley celebrating in a slightly more low-key way with a few rousing bursts of the Baddiel and Skinner hit 'Three Lions'.

2) Germany
Forget the two world wars; purely in football terms the rivalry between England and Germany is on an epic, almost Shakespearean, scale. It all started, of course, with the 1966 World Cup Final at Wembley which England deservedly won, although the Germans felt Geoff Hurst's second goal of his famous hat-trick should not have stood. If they held a grudge, the Germans have certainly used it as a powerful motivating force on numerous occasions, ending Bobby Moore and Co's reign as world champions in 1970, beating the Three Lions on penalties in

tournament semi-finals not once but twice, and thrashing England at the 2010 World Cup in South Africa. However, England have also had their moments during this period, famously tonking the Germans 5-1 in Munich in 2001, beating them 2-0 at Wembley in the last 16 of Euro 2020 and, best of all, triumphing 2-1 in the final of the Women's Euros in 2022.

3) Argentina

England and Argentina have only met 14 times in total, but those encounters have been so littered with controversial incidents that the rivalry between the sides is now considered one of the fiercest in world football. The 1966 World Cup quarter-final at Wembley sparked the bad blood, England manager Alf Ramsey describing the opposition as 'animals' after a brutal clash which saw the Argentinian captain Antonio Rattín dismissed. The South Americans gained revenge in 1986, beating England 2-1 at the World Cup in Mexico thanks in part to skipper Diego Maradona's notorious 'Hand of God' goal. Then, at the 1998 finals in France, they won a dramatic match on penalties after David Beckham had been sent off. Becks, though, got his own back four years later, with the winning goal against Argentina in a group game at the World Cup in Japan.

4) Italy

Right from the start there has been an edge to England-Italy matches, with only the second encounter between the two countries in November 1934 being so violent it was dubbed 'The Battle of Highbury'. England won that game 3-2 and have enjoyed some other good friendly triumphs against the Italians, but it's a different story in competitive matches. In five meetings at the finals of the World Cup or Euros Italy have won three and drawn two – although one of those draws was the final of Euro 2020 which, agonisingly for the Three Lions, the *Azzurri* turned into a victory after a nail-biting penalty shoot-out.

5) Brazil

Although the rivalry between England and Brazil is intense, it is based on mutual respect and is perfectly summed up by the iconic image of Three Lions skipper Bobby Moore and footballing legend

Pelé embracing at the end of their nations' clash at the 1970 World Cup in Mexico. Brazil won that match 1-0 and, disappointingly from an England viewpoint, have emerged victorious in three of the four encounters between the sides on the world stage, with the other being a 0-0 draw at the 1958 World Cup in Sweden. For their part, England have had to make do with just four friendly wins in 26 matches in total, the last coming at Wembley in February 2013.

6) Poland

For the 'Boomer' generation the word 'Poland' conjures up images of eccentric goalkeeper Jan Tomaszewski hurling himself across the Wembley turf to defy the England forwards in a 1973 World Cup qualifier which Sir Alf Ramsey's men had to win to reach the finals in West Germany. However, they only managed a 1-1 draw, sparking a rivalry with Poland in which, in the years since, England have enjoyed the upper hand. Indeed, in 17 competitive meetings between the sides since that dark evening in north-west London, the Three Lions have remained undefeated, notching up 11 wins and six draws. All the same, probably best not to mention the Poles to your grandad.

7) Wales

Apart from in the 1920s and 1930s, when the two sides were evenly matched and won eight games apiece, England have had much the better of their meetings with Wales. However, the men from the valleys are gritty fighters and have often made life difficult for their bigger neighbour, notably in January 1973 when a 1-1 draw at Wembley in a World Cup qualifier contributed to England's failure to reach the finals in West Germany the following year. More recently, the Welsh took the lead against England at Euro 2016 through star man Gareth Bale before eventually succumbing 2-1. Even so, the Welsh had the last laugh, as they reached the semi-finals while England were knocked out by little Iceland in the last 16.

8) Sweden

For a mid-ranking football nation, Sweden have a surprisingly good record against England, incredibly remaining undefeated in 12 encounters over 43 years between 1968 and 2011, a run which included draws at the 2002 and 2006 World Cups and a famous 2-1 win in Stockholm at the 1992 Euros. England, though, have reversed the trend in more recent years, beating the Swedes at the 2012 Euros in Kiev and then winning the biggest clash between the two nations in the quarter-final of the 2018 World Cup in Samara, Russia.

9) Croatia

Born out of the break-up of the former Yugoslavia, the modern Croatia didn't play an international match until 1990. England locked swords with the proud Balkan nation over two Euros in the next decade, winning an exciting encounter in Portugal in 2004 before being knocked out of the qualifying tournament for the 2008 finals after suffering two losses to the Croats. Worse was to come in 2018 when Croatia fought back from a goal down to win the teams' dramatic World Cup semi-final in Moscow. Gareth Southgate's men then got a measure of revenge later that year, beating the Croats at Wembley in the UEFA Nations League, and they again got the better of Luka Modrić and Co at the same venue in the delayed Euro 2020 tournament.

10) Republic of Ireland

The Republic of Ireland have been a thorn in the Three Lions' side ever since they won 2-0 at Goodison Park in September 1949 to become the first nation from outside the United Kingdom to defeat England on home soil. The rivalry between the two neighbours, though, reached a peak in the late 1980s and early 1990s when the Irish, managed by English 1966 World Cup legend Jack Charlton, were unbeaten in four competitive matches against England, most famously beating the Three Lions at the 1988 European Championship in Germany. After rioting by England fans caused a 1995 friendly in Dublin to be abandoned the two sides didn't meet for another 18 years, but happily three meetings in recent years have been trouble-free.

TOP 10 HARDMEN

The England players who loved getting 'stuck in' to the opposition:

1) Norman Hunter

As one of the toughest players in the game in the 1960s and 1970s, the Leeds defender was known to fans as Norman 'Bites Yer Legs' Hunter. He lived up to his moniker with some crunching challenges which would often leave opponents writhing on the grass. Hunter was a non-playing member of England's 1966 World Cup-winning squad and appeared 28 times for his country, although his international career is usually remembered for a tackle he failed to make against Poland in 1973 which contributed to the Three Lions' failure to reach the World Cup finals the following year. 'I was a defender and I should have put the ball in the Royal Box,' he lamented afterwards.

2) Wilf Copping

The original Three Lions hardman, Wilf Copping was an ex-miner who played for Leeds and Arsenal in the 1930s and also won 20 caps for England. A combative midfielder, Copping attempted to intimidate opponents by not shaving on matchdays and liked to say, 'The first man in a tackle never gets hurt.' Dubbed 'The Iron Man', he was one of seven Arsenal players who featured in 'The Battle of Highbury' clash between England and Italy in 1934, earning the man of the match award for a typically aggressive display in the centre of the park.

3) Peter Storey

Dubbed 'the bastards' bastard' by Chelsea hatchetman Ron 'Chopper' Harris, Peter Storey was a tough-tackling defensive midfielder who helped Arsenal win the Double in 1971 and also won 19 caps for England in the latter part of Sir Alf Ramsey's reign. 'The trick was to get in as early as possible, hit them hard, give them a good wallop, make them feel as if they'd been in a car crash or hit a brick wall,' was his own colourful description of his approach to dealing with the opposition. Often in trouble on the pitch, Storey remained a rebel in later life and served several prison sentences for a variety of offences.

4) Nobby Stiles

The diminutive Stiles was an effective destroyer in England's midfield at the 1966 World Cup, his most important contribution to the Three Lions' success coming in the semi-final when his close marking of the dangerous Eusébio was a vital factor in the hosts' 2-1 win against Portugal at Wembley. Earlier in the tournament, Stiles was criticised for a bad tackle which injured

France's Jacques Simon, with some voices at the FA calling for him to be dropped. However, England boss Alf Ramsey defended the Manchester United midfielder, insisting the challenge was mistimed rather than malicious and threatening to resign if there was any interference in his team selection.

5) Stuart Pearce

Known throughout the football world as 'Psycho' for his robust tackles, the Nottingham Forest left-back was described by his former team-mate Roy Keane as 'a man amongst boys'. Pearce, who represented England 78 times, demonstrated mental as well as physical toughness in his international career, recovering from the disappointment of missing a penalty in the semi-final shoot-out against West Germany at the 1990 World Cup to score with spot-kicks against both Spain and Germany at Euro '96.

6) Terry Butcher

One of the bravest players to represent England, Ipswich and Rangers centre-back Terry Butcher was never afraid to risk injury by diving in where the boots were flying. Capped 77 times between 1980 and 1990, his commitment to the Three Lions' cause was best illustrated by the famous picture of him with blood dripping down from a head wound on to his white England shirt during a match against Sweden in 1989.

7) Martin Keown

A long-serving defender with Arsenal, Aston Villa and Everton who also won 43 caps for England between 1992 and 2002, Martin Keown was a brilliant man-marker who excelled at neutralising the opposition's star player. Throughout his playing career he delighted in inflicting 'the reducer' – a hearty challenge on an opponent in the early part of a game which would signal to him that he was in for an extremely tough afternoon.

8) Jack Charlton

A tall and gangly centre-half who was nicknamed 'The Giraffe', Jack Charlton was a member of the successful but often ruthless Leeds United team of the 1960s and early 1970s. Most celebrated for his solid defending during England's 1966 World Cup triumph, Charlton was not afraid to court controversy and once landed in hot water after revealing he had a 'little black book' containing the names of players who had fouled him in the past and who he intended to exact revenge upon.

9) Bryan Robson

By some distance the finest footballer on this list, Bryan Robson was an energetic box-to-box midfielder with West Bromwich Albion and Manchester United who won 90 England caps between 1980 and 1991. As well as scoring and making goals, 'Captain Marvel' was also fabled for his committed tackling – although, sadly, he suffered numerous injuries as a result of his wholehearted approach to the game, limping out of all three World Cup finals tournaments he participated in with the Three Lions.

10) Tommy Smith

The Liverpool enforcer was unfortunate to only win a single cap for England, in a disappointing 0-0 draw with Wales at Wembley in 1971. 'The Tank', as he was dubbed, was known for his uncompromising challenges in the heart of the Reds' defence, leading legendary Anfield boss Bill Shankly to once say of him, 'Tommy Smith wasn't born, he was quarried.' Opponents agreed, Jack Charlton remarking, 'When you tackled Tommy, it was like running into a brick wall – it shook every bone in your body.'

TOP 10 JOYFUL ENGLAND NEWSPAPER HEADLINES

The newspaper headlines that England fans might consider framing:

1) 'The World Beaters!', News of the World, 31 July 1966

After England won the World Cup in 1966 the *News of the World* captured the mood of the nation, its front-page headline being accompanied by pictures of skipper Bobby Moore collecting the Jules Rimet Trophy from The Queen and then kissing it on the Wembley turf.

2) 'Golden Boys', Sunday Mirror, 31 July 1966

The *Sunday Mirror* also produced a memorable headline for its coverage of England's triumph, but opted for a picture of the squad celebrating their success on the balcony of the Royal Garden Hotel in Kensington.

3) 'Kane You Believe It!', Daily Mail, 8 July 2021

After England beat Denmark 2-1 to reach the final of the delayed Euro 2020 tournament the *Mail* couldn't resist punning on the name of skipper Harry Kane, scorer of the winning goal in the semi-final at Wembley.

4) 'England! Top of the World!', Evening Standard, 30 July 1966

The London evening paper was one of the first in the country to report England's historic victory in 1966, a sub-heading proudly pointing out the key contribution of players from the capital – 'All West Ham goals, Hurst hat-trick, Peters 1'. A later edition of the same paper was headlined 'Champions of the World' in red lettering and showed Bobby Moore holding aloft the trophy while perched on his team-mates' shoulders.

5) 'Gazzacadabra', The Planet on Sunday, 16 June 1996

The Planet on Sunday was a British tabloid Sunday newspaper that launched on 16 June 1996 with the intention of highlighting environmental issues, but never appeared again. At least the subs on the sports desk came up with a decent back-page headline celebrating Paul Gascoigne's starring role in England's 2-0 win over Scotland at Wembley during Euro '96.

6) 'Spot on!', Daily Star, 4 July 2018

A rare penalty shoot-out win for England, against Colombia at the 2018 World Cup in Russia, merited front-page headlines for virtually all the newspapers. The *Daily Star* kept it pretty simple, illustrating its lead story with pictures of the England players celebrating together in a huddle and goalkeeper Jordan Pickford making a vital penalty save.

7) 'Gay England Attack Stuns Scots!', News of the World, 3 April 1966

A headline which today would surely have eyebrows being raised at breakfast tables across the land referred to a vibrant England attacking display in a 4-3 win at Hampden Park just three months before the start of the 1966 World Cup.

8) 'Blitzed', Sunday Mirror, 2 September 2001

For some newspapers the temptation to invoke World War II terminology when England play Germany is just too strong to resist, but the *Sunday Mirror's* headline on this occasion had some justification as Sven-Göran Eriksson's men routed the Hun – sorry, the Germans – 5-1 in Munich in a crucial World Cup qualifier.

9) 'Semi Gods', Sunday Mirror, 8 July 2018

The Sunday tabloid toasted the Three Lions' progress to the semi-finals of the 2018 World Cup in Russia with this snappy headline, alongside a picture of England players celebrating Harry Maguire's opener in the quarter-final against Sweden.

10) 'By George, We Did It!', Daily Mail, 30 June 2021

Following England's excellent 2-0 victory against old rivals Germany at Euro 2020 the *Mail* pictured a thrilled Prince George celebrating with his parents at Wembley, below a suitably punning headline.

TOP 10 WORLD CUP QUALIFYING VICTORIES

England have reached the finals tournaments of all but three of the World Cups they have entered, recording some memorable wins in the qualifying stages:

1) Germany 1 England 5, 1 September 2001

Having lost 1-0 to Germany in the last match at the old Wembley a year earlier, England needed to win the return in Munich to give themselves a decent chance of qualifying automatically for the 2002 finals. However, Sven-Göran Eriksson's men got off to a terrible start when giant striker Carsten Jancker put the home side a goal up after just six minutes. England soon equalised through Michael Owen and just before half-time went ahead with a brilliant goal, Steven Gerrard firing in a rocket from outside the area. In the second half England, playing with a verve and freedom unseen for some years, turned on the style, Owen completing his hat-trick with two further goals before Emile Heskey rounded off a magical evening with a rare strike 15 minutes from time.

2) Croatia 1 England 4, 10 September 2008

Four days after a somewhat laboured 2-0 win against Andorra in Barcelona, England put on a much more impressive show in Zagreb to the delight of new boss Fabio Capello. In just his second start for the Three Lions, Arsenal winger Theo Walcott grabbed the headlines with a superb hat-trick, all three of his goals coming from firm, low shots that gave Croatian goalkeeper Stipe Pletikosa little or no chance. England's other goalscorer on a memorable night was Wayne Rooney, with a low side-foot from 12 yards, while sub Mario Mandžukić was on target for the home side late on.

3) England 2 Italy 0, 16 November 1977

Playing their final qualifier of a campaign which had begun under Don Revie but now saw caretaker boss Ron Greenwood at the helm, England knew that only a win against Italy at Wembley would keep their slim hopes of reaching the 1978 finals in Argentina alive. The Three Lions took the lead after just nine minutes when Kevin Keegan met Trevor Brooking's cross with a superb glancing header into the corner. The same pair combined for England's second goal nine minutes from the end, Keegan supplying the West Ham midfielder with a cute pass which he knocked in with aplomb. The victory put England top of the group but the following month Italy beat Luxembourg 3-0 in Rome to claim the one qualifying spot on goal difference.

4) Hungary 1 England 3, 6 June 1981

Having lost in Switzerland a week earlier, England needed to win in Budapest to maintain their hopes of going to the 1982 finals. They got off to a good start when Trevor Brooking scored with a bobbling shot on 18 minutes, but were pegged back just before half-time after a mistake by goalkeeper Ray Clemence allowed the Hungarians to equalise. On the hour skipper Kevin Keegan set up Brooking for a left-foot piledriver from the edge of the box which wedged in the hoop holding up the corner of the net. Keegan then rounded off an excellent victory 15 minutes from time, converting a penalty after he had been fouled. Five months later a tense 1-0 win against the same opposition at Wembley ensured England would be on the plane to Spain along with group winners Hungary.

5) England 5 Croatia 1, 9 September 2009
Fabio Capello's England clinched their place at the finals in South Africa with an emphatic victory over Croatia at Wembley. Frank Lampard got the evening off to a good start, smashing home an early penalty after winger Aaron Lennon had been chopped down in the box. Lennon then crossed for Steven Gerrard to head in and double England's lead on 18 minutes. On the hour, Lampard made it 3-0 with a firm header from 12 yards before Gerrard added a fourth with a flying header from Wayne Rooney's looping cross. Croatia pulled a goal back through Arsenal striker Eduardo, but Rooney restored England's four-goal advantage and rounded off a terrific night's work with a tap in.

6) England 2 Portugal 0, 25 October 1961
England only needed a draw to book their passage to the 1962 finals in Chile, but they left nothing to chance by scoring twice inside the opening ten minutes at Wembley. First, Burnley winger John Connelly pounced on a loose ball to score from six yards, then his club-mate Ray Pointer drilled in a rising shot into the top corner. Portugal's 19-year-old superstar Eusébio hit the post twice in the second half, but England held out for a fairly comfortable victory.

7) Hungary 0 England 4, 2 September 2021
England's serene progress to the 2022 finals in Qatar continued as they trounced a hardworking Hungarian side in Budapest. All the goals came in the second half, Raheem Sterling opening the scoring on 57 minutes with a neat finish from Mason Mount's cross. The Manchester City star was bombarded with missiles as he celebrated, but England refused to be provoked and soon added a second, skipper Harry Kane heading in Sterling's cross. Hungary goalkeeper Péter Gulácsi was at fault for the Three Lions' two other goals, spilling a Harry Maguire header from a corner and then allowing a long-range effort from Declan Rice to creep under him.

8) Poland 0 England 2, 31 May 1997

Having lost 1-0 at home to Italy earlier in the year, Glenn Hoddle's England desperately needed to win in Chorzów to maintain pressure on the *Azzurri* for the one guaranteed qualifying place for the 1998 finals in France. Facing a fired-up Polish side backed by a partisan crowd, England got off to a fantastic start when Alan Shearer converted Paul Ince's slide-rule pass on five minutes. Shearer had a golden opportunity to double England's lead just before half-time but struck his penalty against the foot of a post. However, it mattered little as Teddy Sheringham rounded off an impressive victory at the death, shooting home from close range after Rob Lee had rounded the Polish goalkeeper and set him up with a simple chance.

9) England 1 Austria 0, 8 October 2005

England gained a vital win in their bid to reach the 2006 finals in Germany with a rather scrappy win over Austria at Old Trafford. The key moment came midway through the first half, when Michael Owen was fouled in the box. With skipper David Beckham having missed his three previous spot-kicks for the Three Lions, Frank Lampard took over penalty duties and promptly sent Austrian keeper Jürgen Macho the wrong way. On the hour Beckham was sent off after collecting two quickfire yellow cards, but England held out to secure a victory which, after results later that same day, guaranteed them an automatic place at the following year's tournament.

10) Denmark 1 England 4, 15 May 1957

England, including a 42-year-old Stanley Matthews making his last appearance for his country, took a giant stride towards qualification for the 1958 finals in Sweden with a convincing win in Copenhagen against a Danish side they had beaten 5-2 at Molineux six months earlier. However, Walter Winterbottom's team suffered a scare when the Danes scored after 25 minutes – a goal cancelled out by Johnny Haynes's equaliser just before half-time. England had to wait until the last 20 minutes before their superiority was reflected in the scoreline, thanks to goals by Manchester United striker Tommy Taylor (two) and Bristol City forward John Atyeo.

TOP 10 SIR ALF RAMSEY QUOTES

The best quotes from Sir Alf, the only England men's manager to win a major trophy:

1) 'You've beaten them once. Now go out there and bloody beat them again.'
Talking to his players before the start of extra time in the 1966 World Cup Final against West Germany

2) 'I think England will win the 1966 World Cup. We have the ability, strength, character and, perhaps above all, the players with the right temperament.'
Shortly after being appointed England manager in 1963

3) 'We still have to produce our best football. It will come against a team who come to play football and not to act as animals.'
After a tempestuous World Cup quarter-final victory against Argentina in 1966

4) 'I'd sooner anybody beat us than the bloody Scots.'
After England lost 3-2 to Scotland at Wembley in 1967

5) 'I said that it would take a great side to beat us because we are a great side.'
His post-victory verdict in 1966

6) 'We have nothing to learn from these people.'
After Brazil won the 1970 World Cup in exciting style

7) 'I have to make a living just like you. I happen to make mine in a nice way whereas you make yours in a nasty way.'
Speaking to an increasingly critical press pack in 1973

8) 'I have said it many times since taking over as manager: I want a squad, not a team, with players ready for action when I call them.'
Outlining his philosophy before the 1966 World Cup finals

9) 'We must now look ahead to the next World Cup in Munich where our chances of winning I would say are very good indeed.'

Anticipating the 1974 World Cup in West Germany – which England failed to qualify for – after being knocked out of the 1970 tournament

10) 'Sorry, it's my day off.'
Politely refusing to be interviewed the day after England won the 1966 World Cup

TOP 10 GOALSCORERS

The players who have found the net most often for the Three Lions:

1) Jimmy Greaves
A quicksilver striker who always carefully picked his spot when shooting, Jimmy Greaves hit 357 league goals for Chelsea, Tottenham and West Ham – a top-flight record. He was equally prolific for England, scoring an amazing 44 goals in just 57 appearances including a record six hat-tricks. However, he missed out on the biggest moment of his career when he was not selected for the World Cup Final against West Germany in 1966. Nonetheless, many would agree with Gary Lineker, who described Greaves as 'quite possibly the greatest striker this country has ever produced' after the legendary goal-getter died in September 2021.

2) Wayne Rooney
Harry Kane may have him in his sights, but for now at least Wayne Rooney remains England's all-time top goalscorer with 53 goals in 120 appearances. As an 18-year-old with Everton, Rooney starred at Euro 2004 for the Three Lions, earning comparisons with Brazil icon Pelé from boss Sven-Göran Eriksson. However, a combination of injuries and loss of form saw him rarely at his best in later tournaments, much to the frustration of England fans who had often seen him perform brilliantly in qualifying campaigns and for his second club, Manchester United.

3) Bobby Charlton
As an uncapped winger with Manchester United, the 20-year-old Bobby Charlton survived the Munich air crash in February 1958, making a goalscoring England debut two months later in a 4-0

win against Scotland. He went on to become, arguably, the Three Lions' greatest ever player, famed for his long-range passing and blockbuster shots with either foot. A key member of Alf Ramsey's World Cup-winning team in 1966, Charlton won 106 caps and scored 49 goals – a record for the national team which stood until Wayne Rooney broke it in 2015.

4) Harry Kane

Unless disaster strikes, England captain Harry Kane looks set to become the Three Lions' all-time top goalscorer some time in the near future – indeed, if he keeps scoring at his current rate he will set a benchmark that will prove extremely tough to beat. The Tottenham star scored on his international debut against Lithuania in March 2015 and has gone on to reach his half century, including six goals at the 2018 World Cup in Russia to win him the Golden Boot.

5) Gary Lineker

A master poacher, Gary Lineker's international reputation was forged in the heat of Mexico where his six goals at the 1986 World Cup won him the Golden Boot. He took his tally at the finals to ten – an England record – with four more at the 1990 tournament in Italy, and two years later ended his 80-cap Three Lions career with 48 goals, just one short of Bobby Charlton's then-record.

6) Nat Lofthouse

A magnificent header of the ball, Bolton centre-forward Nat Lofthouse scored twice on his debut for England in a 2-2 draw with Yugoslavia at Highbury in 1950 and went on to claim 30 goals in just 33 appearances for the Three Lions – a phenomenal strike rate of 0.91 goals per game. After scoring another brace against Austria in 1952 Lofthouse was dubbed 'The Lion of Vienna', a nickname which stuck with him for the rest of his career and even became the name of a pub in Bolton.

7) Michael Owen

A teenage prodigy who burst on to the international scene at the 1998 World Cup when he scored a wonderful individual goal against Argentina, Michael Owen bagged 40 goals in 89 appearances for England and, but for a series of injuries, might very well have become his country's all-time leading marksman. No fewer than 27 of those goals came in competitive internationals – a tally only bettered by Harry Kane and Wayne Rooney.

8) Alan Shearer

The top scorer in Premier League history with a total of 260 goals for Blackburn Rovers and Newcastle United, Alan Shearer is also one of England's finest marksmen. The powerfully built centre-forward with gunpowder in his boots found the net 30 times in 63 internationals, enjoying a superb tournament at Euro '96 when his five goals in five games won him the Golden Boot and helped propel hosts England to the semi-finals of the competition.

9) Vivian Woodward

An amateur player in the immediate pre-World War I period with Tottenham and Chelsea, Vivian Woodward was a prolific goalscorer who notched 29 goals in just 23 appearances for England. He twice scored four goals in a game, in tour matches against Austria (1908) and Hungary (1909), and also banged in an incredible 57 goals in 44 matches for England Amateurs.

10) Tom Finney

A brilliant winger who was happy to play on either flank, Tom Finney provided England with much more than mere goals but still managed an impressive 30 in 76 appearances between 1946 and 1958. 'The Preston Plumber', as he was dubbed after an early apprenticeship, represented his country at three World Cups in the 1950s – a record which still stands, although it has been equalled by several England players.

TOP 10 PEOPLE CALLED 'ENGLAND'

The men and women who can proudly say, 'England is my name':

1) Mike England

A legend of Welsh football, Mike England won 49 caps for his country between 1962 and 1974, before going on to manage the national team for most of the 1980s. A tough centre-half, he spent most of his playing career with Blackburn and Tottenham, with whom he won four major honours including the FA Cup in 1967 and the UEFA Cup in 1972.

2) Paul England

An English actor and director, his first film was back in the silent era when he played lovestruck miner Norman Druce in the romantic drama *Just a Girl*. He later had roles in *Charlie Chan in London, The Invisible Man Returns* and *The Trial of Madame X*, which he also wrote and directed.

3) Audie England

A US actress who has appeared in more than a dozen films, she is best known for her roles in the erotic science fiction movie *Venus Rising* (1995) and the romantic comedy *Free Enterprise* (1999), in which she appeared alongside *Star Trek* icon William Shatner.

4) Anthony W. England

A former US astronaut who was a member of the backup team for the Apollo missions of the 1960s and 1970s, England was a part of the Shuttle programme a decade later, logging nearly 200 hours in space.

5) Lee England Jr

Now signed to Quincy Jones's management company, Lee England is an American violinist who has shared the stage with the likes of Stevie Wonder, Beyonce and Jay-Z. Wonder if he can play 'Sweet Caroline'?

6) Paul England

The Australian racing driver's big moment came in 1957 when he appeared at his first and only F1 grand prix at the Nürburgring in Germany. Unfortunately, a faulty distributor meant he had to drop out on lap four of a race which was won by Argentinian legend Juan Manuel Fangio.

7) Odette England

An Australian-British photographer whose work has been exhibited around the world, Odette England is also the artist-in-residence at Amherst College in Massachusetts. Maybe she'd like to pop over the pond to take some nice pics of Harry Kane and Co?

8) Roye England

A passion for modelling led Australian-born Brit Roye England to establish the Pendon Museum in Long Wittenham, near Didcot, Oxfordshire shortly after the end of World War II. Highlights of the museum include scale models of railways and scenes of rural life in the Vale of White Horse in the interwar years.

9) Sandhurst England

Sandhurst England was a 19th-century Australian cricketer, but we are not exactly talking Don Bradman here. While working as a teller for the Bank of New Zealand he played just twice for Wellington in 1879, top-scoring for his side with 29 in his final appearance. A decade later, after returning to Australia, he was honoured by the Royal Humane Society of Australasia after rescuing a young boy from a flooded quarry.

10) Lynndie England

A former US Army Reserve soldier, Lynndie England was prosecuted for mistreating inmates at the notorious Abu Ghraib prison in Baghdad during the Iraq War. Photos that were publicly released showed her forcing a prisoner to crawl and bark like a dog on a leash and smiling while naked detainees were placed in a human pyramid. In September 2005 she was sentenced to three years in prison, serving 17 months in a military facility in California before she was released on parole.

TOP 10 PREMIER LEAGUE PLAYERS WHO HURT ENGLAND

The overseas Premier League stars who got the better of the Three Lions:

1) Luis Suárez

After Liverpool's Luis Suárez scored 31 goals to win the Golden Boot in the 2013/14 Premier League season, England knew who the dangerman was when they faced Uruguay in a group game at the 2014 World Cup in Brazil. However the Three Lions were unable to contain the prolific striker, who gave the South Americans a first-half lead in São Paulo with a header from Edinson Cavani's cross and then, after Wayne Rooney had equalised, grabbed the winner late on when he smashed a powerful shot past Joe Hart to all but eliminate England from the tournament.

2) Niko Kranjčar

In their final qualifying match for the 2008 European Championship, England only needed to draw at home to Croatia to earn a place in Austria and Switzerland. However, they went down to a shock 3-2 defeat, the evening starting badly when Niko Kranjčar put the visitors ahead after just eight minutes. There appeared to be little danger when the Portsmouth midfielder tried his luck from 35 yards, but his shot bounced right in front of Scott Carson, hit the hapless goalkeeper on the chest and flew into the net.

3) Clint Dempsey

While with New England Revolution, Clint Dempsey scored a consolation goal for the USA in a 2-1 defeat to England in Chicago in 2005. Five years later, and now with Fulham, he was again on target against the Three Lions at the 2010 World Cup in South Africa, scoring with a low shot from 25 yards that Rob Green in the England goal somehow managed to fumble over the line to gift the USA a surprise point in a 1-1 draw.

4) Gianfranco Zola

Chelsea striker Gianfranco Zola was one of the most talented players of the early Premier League era, and demonstrated his class with the winning goal for Italy in a World Cup qualifier at Wembley in February 1997. Controlling a long pass with his left foot, the little Sardinian quickly swivelled to fire in a powerful right-footer which beat England goalkeeper Ian Walker at his near post.

5) Dan Petrescu

England's group game with Romania at the 1998 World Cup in France appeared to be heading for a draw when Chelsea wing-back Dan Petrescu struck in the 90th minute, controlling the ball on his chest while holding off his Blues team-mate Graeme Le Saux before shooting through the legs of goalkeeper David Seaman to earn his side three valuable points in Toulouse.

6) Dietmar Hamann

Liverpool midfielder Dietmar Hamann ensured England's World Cup qualifying campaign got off to a miserable start when he scored the only goal of the game for Germany at a rain-soaked Wembley in October 2000. After a foul on Michael Ballack 30 yards from goal, England were slow to form a defensive wall and Hamann took full advantage, firing in a low shot which David Seaman could only palm into the net.

7) Harry Kewell

On an evening to remember for their fans, Australia beat England for the only time in their history at Upton Park in February 2003. Star of the show for the Socceroos was Leeds winger Harry Kewell, who scored the second goal in an eventual 3-1 win when he outmuscled Rio Ferdinand before calmly rounding England goalkeeper David James and then shooting into the empty net.

8) Nicolas Anelka

Nineteen-year-old Arsenal striker Nicolas Anelka announced his arrival on the international stage by scoring both of France's goals in a 2-0 friendly victory at Wembley in February 1999. The mercurial Zinedine Zidane set up the youngster's first goal on 69 minutes with a clever flick which Anelka converted with calm assurance. Then, just seven minutes later, the fleet-footed forward was lurking in the six-yard box to turn in Christophe Dugarry's low cross.

9) Eden Hazard

England's magnificent 2018 World Cup campaign ended on a disappointing note when they lost 2-0 to Belgium in the play-off for third place in St Petersburg. Leading by an early Thomas Meunier goal, the Belgians wrapped up victory eight minutes from time when Kevin De Bruyne put Eden Hazard clean through. A master in one-on-one situations, the Chelsea midfielder never looked likely to miss and duly slotted a low shot past Jordan Pickford.

10) Per Mertesacker

Four days after going down 2-0 at home to Chile in November 2013, England lost at Wembley again – this time to old rivals

Germany. The only goal of the game was scored by gangly Arsenal defender Per Mertesacker, who rose above a flat-footed England defence to meet Toni Kroos's right-wing cross with a powerful header beyond the reach of Joe Hart.

TOP 10 INTERNATIONAL MATCHES PLAYED IN ENGLAND BUT NOT INVOLVING ENGLAND

Dozens of international matches have been played on English soil without an English player in sight – and not only at tournaments such as the 1966 World Cup or Euro '96. Here's the pick of the bunch:

1) Portugal 5 North Korea 3, World Cup quarter-final, 23 July 1966
In one of the greatest World Cup matches ever, minnows North Korea stormed into a three-goal lead against Portugal inside the first 25 minutes at Goodison Park. However, star striker Eusébio soon pulled one back for the Portuguese with a powerful shot, and then notched with a penalty just before half-time. In the second half, another Eusébio piledriver levelled the scores before the 'Black Panther', as he was dubbed by the British press, put Portugal ahead with a second spot-kick. Ten minutes from time a José Augusto header confirmed victory for the Portuguese, who would go on to play England in the semi-final three days later.

2) Germany 2 Czech Republic 1, European Championship final, 30 June 1996
After surprisingly beating Portugal and France in the knockout rounds, the Czech Republic met England's conquerors Germany in the final of Euro '96 at Wembley in front of over 73,000 fans. Germany had previously beaten their opponents 2-0 in a group game at Old Trafford, but it was the underdogs who scored first, Czech winger Patrik Berger converting a penalty on the hour. A quarter of an hour later substitute Oliver Bierhoff equalised with a downward header from a free kick, and it was the Udinese striker who grabbed the 'Golden Goal' winner in extra time with

a deflected shot which Czech goalkeeper Petr Kouba allowed to slip through his hands.

3) West Germany 2 Soviet Union 1, World Cup semi-final, 25 July 1966

A one-sided match at Goodison Park saw the Soviet Union reduced to nine men in the first half through injury and a sending off. With no subs permitted, West Germany unsurprisingly won comfortably thanks to goals by Helmut Haller and Franz Beckenbauer, although they suffered a late scare when Russian winger Valeriy Porkujan netted from close range two minutes from time.

4) Wales 0 Scotland 2, World Cup qualifier, 12 October 1977

Following crowd trouble at a previous international, Wales were ordered to play their vital home World Cup qualifier against Scotland at least 200 miles from Cardiff. The Welsh FA opted for Anfield, which was packed to the rafters on the night by both sets of fans. After a tight first half, Scotland took the lead through a Don Masson penalty – controversially awarded when striker Joe Jordan handled the ball from a long throw but the French referee ruled that it had struck Wales defender Dave Jones's arm. There was no debate, though, about Kenny Dalglish's superb header from Martin Buchan's cross which wrapped up a 2-0 win for the Scots and booked their passage to the finals in Argentina.

5) Italy 1 Spain 1 (Italy won 4-2 on penalties), European Championship semi-final, 6 July 2021

In an enthralling encounter at Wembley, Italy took the lead on the hour when Federico Chiesa finished off a swift counter attack with a superb curling shot. Spain hit back ten minutes from time with a goal from substitute Álvaro Morata, the Juventus striker side-footing home after a neat one-two with Dani Olmo. With extra time producing no further goals, the match was settled by penalties, Chelsea midfielder Jorginho clinching Italy's place in the final with a typically nonchalant spot-kick.

6) Russia 3 Czech Republic 3, European Championship group stage, 19 June 1996

Anfield was only half-full for this Euro '96 group game, but the fans who were there witnessed a classic as Russia fought back from two goals down at half-time to lead 3-2 with just five minutes to play. However, Vladimír Šmicer, who three years later would play his club football on this ground after signing for Liverpool, scored a late equaliser with a low shot from the edge of the box which enabled the Czech Republic to advance to the quarter-finals at the expense of Italy.

7) Italy 0 Argentina 3, Finalissima, 1 June 2022

A crowd of over 87,000 flocked to Wembley for the 2022 *Finalissima*, a special match between reigning European champions Italy and South American top dogs Argentina. With Lionel Messi pulling the strings, Argentina were easy victors over an Italian side still nursing their wounds after failing to qualify for the World Cup. Messi set up Inter Milan striker Lautaro Martínez for the opener on 28 minutes, and former Manchester United winger Ángel Di María made it two just before half-time. Right on full time another fine run by the brilliant Messi ended with sub Paulo Dybala shooting low into the corner to wrap up a great win for the South Americans.

8) Republic of Ireland 0 Holland 2, European Championship qualifying play-off, 13 December 1995

A crowd of 40,000 turned up at Anfield to see the Republic of Ireland and Holland compete in a play-off to decide the last qualifier for the Euro '96 tournament in England. The Dutch were the better team on the night and took the lead on the half hour thanks to a smart finish by Patrick Kluivert. Two minutes from the end, the Ajax striker confirmed victory for his side with a clever dinked shot over Ireland goalkeeper Alan Kelly. Having seen his side narrowly miss out on the finals, Ireland boss Jack Charlton decided to step down after nearly a decade at the helm.

9) Brazil 3 Argentina 0, friendly, 3 September 2006

A prestigious clash between the two superpowers of South American football attracted a colourful crowd of nearly 60,000 to Arsenal's Emirates Stadium, but it was the Brazilian fans who went home happier after their heroes romped to a 3-0 victory. A delightful piece of skill by Robinho set up Elano for the opener after just three minutes, and the same player scored again midway through the second half from a cute pass by Kaká. Brazil saved the best for last, Kaká pouncing on a mistake by 19-year-old Lionel Messi to run over half the length of the pitch before slotting home.

10) Northern Ireland 1 Portugal 1, World Cup qualifier, 28 March 1973

Northern Ireland were forced to play all three of their home qualifiers for the 1974 World Cup in England because of the 'Troubles' afflicting the province, hosting Portugal in the first of these games at Coventry City's Highfield Road. On his first start for his country, Nottingham Forest midfielder Martin O'Neill gave Northern Ireland a first-half lead before Portugal legend Eusébio equalised late on from the penalty spot – the last of his 41 international goals.

TOP 10 KITS

The classic kits in which the Three Lions looked especially stylish:

1) Away, 1966–72

Memories of England's World Cup triumph in 1966 are inextricably linked with the kit Alf Ramsey's men wore on the day of the final against West Germany at Wembley: red shirts with a crew neck, white shorts and red socks. Unsurprisingly, the sleek outfit remains a fave with England fans more than half a century on and there are howls of protest when the team fail to wear a red change shirt for important matches – as happened against Germany in the Euro '96 semi-final.

2) Home, 1980–83

Admiral's second home shirt for England broke with tradition by introducing a broad blue and red panel across the shoulders of the white shirt. Combined with royal blue shorts and white socks topped by a red and blue stripe, the overall look was strikingly different. Fans rushed to buy replicas but there were plenty of critics too, including BBC commentator Barry Davies who wondered 'quite why the England shirt should have the colours of the Union Jack' when the Three Lions first wore it in a friendly against world champions Argentina at Wembley in May 1980.

Still, four decades on, it remains one of the most sought-after England shirts among collectors.

3) Away, 1990–92
This Umbro two-tone pale blue shirt with a navy blue collar was taken to the 1990 World Cup in Italy but was unused by Bobby Robson's men. However, it became massively popular with fans after New Order singer Bernard Sumner wore it in the video for 'World in Motion' – the chart-topping England song for the tournament. The cult shirt eventually got a run-out for a European Championship qualifier against Turkey in İzmir in May 1991 but, sadly, was then mothballed and replaced with an utterly hideous shirt in the same colour.

4) Home, 2001–2002
In an obvious reference to the cross of St George, Umbro placed a thick red stripe down the left side of this stylish white shirt. It was a bold move, which happened to coincide with an equally adventurous managerial appointment – Sven-Göran Eriksson becoming England's first foreign boss. The clean design, which looked especially attractive when paired with white shorts, was worn by England in one of their most famous victories of recent times – the dramatic 5-1 rout of Germany in Munich in September 2001.

5) Home, 2020–2022
This Nike kit was held back six months due to the Covid-19 pandemic, but drew a positive response when it was eventually unveiled in September 2020. The white shirt featured a midnight-blue crew neck and a jagged red and blue stripe running down both the sides, creating a 'lightning bolt' effect, while the emblem, Nike logo and player number were all centralised on the upper chest. Paired with navy blue shorts and white socks with five thin red and blue stripes, the tasteful kit was worn at all seven of England's games at the delayed 2020 European Championship – a competition Gareth Southgate's men came within a whisker of winning.

6) Away, 2006–2007
Having previously sported a red shirt with silver numbers and names, England upgraded to gold for this Umbro design. In a

bid to increase the profile of the emblem it was increased in size and also bordered by gold. The glitzy kit proved lucky for the Three Lions, who were undefeated in the five games they wore it, including a 2-2 draw with Sweden at the 2006 World Cup in Germany.

7) Home, 1990–1993

England fans of a certain age have fond memories of this home shirt as it was worn by the Three Lions at all seven matches they played at the 1990 World Cup – a tournament which revitalised the team's fortunes after two decades of stagnation. The Umbro-designed outfit consisted of a smart short-sleeved white shirt with a navy blue winged collar, navy blue shorts and white socks with a navy blue turnover. A kit synonymous with Gazza's tears, Lineker's goals and Waddle's woeful penalty miss.

8) Home, 2010–2011

Graphic designer Peter Saville, famed for his album covers for the likes of Joy Division, Pulp and Suede, was employed by Umbro to create this sparkling white shirt, which also featured tiny red, blue, green and purple crosses on the shoulder to symbolise the multi-cultural diversity of contemporary England. Paired with navy blue shorts and white socks, the Three Lions looked the business in this outfit and enjoyed some good results while wearing it, including a 1-0 win over World and European champs Spain in November 2011.

9) Home, 1987–1989

England may have flopped badly at the 1988 European Championship, but at least Bobby Robson's men looked the part in Germany in this attractive white shirt which included a fashionable crew neck with a plastic snap fastener and a rhombus shadow stripe to combat the growing counterfeit market. The asymmetrical blue and red panels on the edges of the short-sleeved version were another eye-catching feature of a shirt which the Three Lions wore over 20 times.

10) Away, 1959

England have only worn a royal blue shirt on three occasions, most recently for a friendly against Peru in May 1959. Made by Umbro, the shirt was accompanied by white shorts and white socks with a red and blue hoop around the top. Although stylishly attired, the Three Lions crashed to a depressing 4-1 defeat in Lima, the only consolation being a goal for 19-year-old striker Jimmy Greaves on his international debut. Since then, only England goalkeepers have appeared in royal blue.

TOP 10 UNCAPPED ENGLISH PREMIER LEAGUE PLAYERS

A bunch of players who can count themselves unlucky never to have worn the Three Lions on their chest at senior level. What do England managers know – eh, lads?

1) Mark Noble

Before his retirement at the end of the 2021/22 season, West Ham's Mark Noble had made more Premier League appearances than any other uncapped Englishman. It is a bit of a mystery why he never had a senior call up, as he represented England from under-16 to under-21 level, captaining the higher age group in some of his 20 appearances. A workmanlike midfielder who always gave his all, it's possible that a lack of goals from open play – over half his total of 55 in the Premier League came from the penalty spot – counted against Noble in the eyes of a succession of England managers since he made his Hammers debut in 2004.

2) Steve Bruce

Now better known as a manager, Steve Bruce was formerly an extremely successful defender and captain of Manchester United, with whom he won three Premier League titles. To the surprise of many observers, though, international honours eluded him apart from a single England B cap against Malta in 1987. However, in November 1994 Bruce was offered the chance to play for England in a friendly against Nigeria by Terry Venables, but turned it down. He later recalled, 'I was close to 35 and I said, "I'm sorry, I would rather not have had an international career than just have a sympathy cap."'

3) Kevin Campbell

No English player has scored more goals in the Premier League without winning a senior cap than Kevin Campbell, the powerful striker finding the net 83 times for Arsenal, Nottingham Forest, Everton and West Brom between 1992 and 2006. Campbell did collect four under-21 caps and played once for an England B side but the nearest he got to full international honours was when he was put on standby by Graham Taylor for a friendly against Spain in September 1992. 'I was not disappointed at all not to play for England,' he said in 2021. 'There were a lot of good players in that era so it was difficult to get into the team.'

4) Charlie Austin

Despite playing for relegated QPR, Charlie Austin was the fourth-highest scorer in the Premier League in the 2014/15 season with 18 goals – only Harry Kane among English players fared better. The prolific striker caught the eye of England boss Roy Hodgson and was named in his squad for matches against the Republic of Ireland and Slovenia, but didn't feature in either game. 'I never had an explanation,' he later told talkSPORT. 'I wasn't there for a jolly up. I felt I showed enough at club football to get a call-up and enough to be rewarded with a cap.'

5) Marc Albrighton

After starting his career with Aston Villa, Marc Albrighton was an ever-present as outsiders Leicester City won the Premier League in 2016. His pinpoint crosses from the left set up numerous chances for Foxes strikers Jamie Vardy and Shinji Okazaki, leading boss Claudio Ranieri to opine, 'Albrighton embodies the spirit of Leicester.' Surprisingly, however, he never featured in England manager Roy Hodgson's squads, although he did win eight caps for the under-21s, scoring on his debut against Lithuania in 2010.

6) Paul Warhurst

A versatile player who could perform equally well in defence, midfield or up front, Sheffield Wednesday's Paul Warhurst enjoyed a golden spell as a striker for the Owls midway through the 1992/93 season, scoring a dozen goals in as many games. England manager Graham Taylor promptly selected him for a World Cup qualifier away to Turkey, but injury prevented Warhurst adding to the eight under-21 caps he had won two years earlier.

7) Steve Ogrizovic

After the legendary Peter Shilton retired from international football in 1990, England tried out various goalkeepers in the following seasons but, surprisingly, Coventry City's Steve Ogrizovic never got a chance between the sticks for the Three Lions. An FA Cup winner with the Sky Blues in 1987, the giant stopper went on to play in a record 601 matches for the club before retiring in 2000. Despite being repeatedly overlooked by England, he once turned down a chance to play for Yugoslavia, the birth country of his father.

8) Troy Deeney

Watford's record Premier League scorer with 47 goals, bustling striker Troy Deeney also helped the Hornets reach the FA Cup Final for just the second time in their history in 2019, blasting home a last-minute equaliser from the penalty spot against Wolves in the semi-final at Wembley. A regular scorer in club football for over a decade, Deeney might well have earned an England call-up but for his volatile temperament and the black mark he carried for serving a three-month prison sentence for affray in 2012.

9) Kevin Nolan

Among uncapped English players, only Mark Noble has made more than Kevin Nolan's 401 Premier League appearances. After making his name with Bolton, the attacking midfielder enjoyed a couple of excellent seasons with Newcastle, winning the Championship Player of the Year award in 2010 and then scoring a personal best 12 goals (in just 30 games) in the Premier League the following campaign. It wasn't enough to earn him an England call-up, however, although he had previously won two caps for the under-21s.

10) Ben Mee

A consistent player who has racked up over 300 appearances for Burnley, centre-back Ben Mee has been unfortunate not to take the next step up after winning two caps for the under-21s in the 2010/11 season. Gallingly, he has seen two of his central defensive partners at Turf Moor, Michael Keane and James Tarkowski, earn full international recognition with England while arguably performing better than either. Now aged 33, his chances of ever playing for his country would appear extremely slim.

TOP 10 WORLD CUP QUALIFYING DEFEATS

On three occasions (1974, 1978 and 1994) England bitterly disappointed their fans by failing to qualify for the World Cup, so it's no surprise that defeats from those disastrous campaigns feature prominently on this list:

1) Norway 2 England 1, 9 September 1981
England had beaten Norway 4-0 at Wembley a year earlier, and were expected to make light work of their mainly part-time opponents in the return in Oslo. All was going to plan when Bryan Robson latched on to Kevin Keegan's header to give Ron Greenwood's men a 14th-minute lead, but poor defending gifted the Norwegians two goals before the break. Unable to find a way past an obdurate defence in the second half, England slumped to a third defeat in seven qualifying games, putting their chances of reaching the finals in Spain in grave peril.

2) Poland 2 England 0, 6 June 1973
Sir Alf Ramsey's team got off to a dreadful start in Chorzów when a free kick from the left flicked off Polish midfielder Jan Banaś, and possibly England skipper Bobby Moore, before going in off goalkeeper Peter Shilton at the near post. Moore was also culpable for Poland's second killer goal just after half-time, losing possession to star striker Włodzimierz Lubański, who ran on to rifle a low shot past Shilton. A bad day for England got even worse when Alan Ball was sent off for violent conduct 13 minutes from the end. The defeat meant that England had to beat the Poles in the return at Wembley to qualify for the finals, but they were held to a frustrating 1-1 draw.

3) Norway 2 England 0, 2 June 1993
Embattled England manager Graham Taylor switched to a back three to counter Norway's direct style, but the gamble backfired

as his team suffered a disastrous defeat. Norwegian midfielder Øyvind Leonhardsen opened the scoring with a mishit shot from a quickly taken free kick just before half-time, and Lars Bohinen added a second early in the second half following a swift break which exposed the lack of cover for England's struggling defence. The result virtually guaranteed Norway a place in the finals in the USA, with England and the Netherlands left to slug it out for the second qualification spot.

4) Italy 2 England 0, 17 November 1976

England manager Don Revie made six changes from the previous qualifier, a 2-1 win against Finland a month earlier, but his new-look team, which included a starting place for maverick QPR striker Stan Bowles, were outplayed by a rampant Italy at the Stadio Olimpico in Rome. Midfielder Giancarlo Antognoni put the home side ahead in the first half with a deflected shot from outside the box before Roberto Bettega sealed victory for the Italians 13 minutes from time with a flying header after a flowing move. The defeat would eventually cost England a place in the finals in Argentina, the second World Cup in a row that the Three Lions would miss out on.

5) Holland 2 England 0, 13 October 1993

After an even first half, Holland should have been reduced to ten men when defender Ronald Koeman hauled back David Platt as he raced through on goal. Escaping with a yellow card – a decision which left England boss Graham Taylor fuming on the touchline – Koeman then added insult to injury by scoring with a twice-taken free kick just past the hour, his deft shot floating past a poorly positioned David Seaman. Six minutes later Dennis Bergkamp beat Seaman with a low drive at his near post to wrap up a win for the Dutch which almost entirely ended England's hopes of reaching the finals in the USA.

6) Switzerland 2 England 1, 30 May 1981

Having lost in Romania earlier in the qualifying campaign, England could ill-afford another poor result on their travels, but they were undone in Basel by two goals for the home side inside a minute after having had much the better of the opening half an hour. Substitute Terry McDermott pulled one back early in the second half with a fierce shot – England's first goal in almost eight hours of largely turgid football – but the Swiss held out for a surprise win. To add to England's woes, some of their supporters caused mayhem on the terraces leading FA secretary Ted Croker to call for a ban on England fans travelling abroad for future matches.

7) England 0 Germany 1, 7 October 2000
In the final match at the old Wembley before the bulldozers moved in, England got their World Cup qualifying campaign off to a disappointing start with a lacklustre defeat against old rivals Germany. The key moment came on 13 minutes when a 30-yard free kick by Liverpool midfielder Dietmar Hamann skidded across the wet surface and past David Seaman, who was slow to dive to his left and could only palm the ball into the net. England rarely threatened an equaliser, and signed off under the Twin Towers with the boos of the crowd ringing in their ears. Three Lions' boss Kevin Keegan announced his resignation after the defeat which, happily, proved to be only a hiccup on the road to the finals in Japan and South Korea under his successor, Sven-Göran Eriksson.

8) Northern Ireland 1 England 0, 7 September 2005
England manager Sven-Göran Eriksson suffered his first defeat in a qualifier, as the Three Lions surprisingly lost to local rivals Northern Ireland at Windsor Park in Belfast. A flat and disjointed performance by the visitors was eventually punished on 74 minutes when Leeds striker David Healy collected a dinked pass from Steven Davis before drilling in a firm shot past England goalkeeper Paul Robinson. However, the three points lost didn't prevent Eriksson's team from topping their group a point ahead of closest challengers Poland and qualifying for the 2006 finals in Germany.

9) England 0 Italy 1, 12 February 1997
The talking point before kick-off was the surprise inclusion by England manager Glenn Hoddle of Southampton's Matt Le Tissier, a hugely talented if inconsistent attacking player. However it was another Premier League striker, Chelsea's Gianfranco Zola, who grabbed the headlines with the only goal of a high-quality

match, shooting past England goalkeeper Ian Walker from a tight angle midway through the first half. Defeat left England with the unsettling prospect of having to qualify through the play-offs but, after Italy dropped points away to Poland and Georgia, the Three Lions were able to book an automatic slot in France with a gutsy 0-0 draw in Rome.

10) Romania 2 England 1, 15 October 1980
In front of a hostile crowd in Bucharest, England fell behind nine minutes before the break when Marcel Răducanu's low shot from the edge of the box beat Ray Clemence. The Three Lions hit back through Tony Woodcock, the Cologne striker calmly sliding the ball under the Romanian goalkeeper shortly after the hour. However, a controversial penalty, awarded for a foul by Kenny Sansom on Anghel Iordănescu and converted by the same player, condemned England to the first of three defeats of a nerve-wracking but ultimately successful qualifying campaign.

TOP 10 ENGLAND WOMEN GOALS

Over the years the Lionesses have scored some fabulous goals, many of their best strikes coming at major tournaments:

1) Georgia Stanway, England 2 Spain 1, European Championship quarter-final, 20 July 2022
In a tight quarter-final clash at the Amex Stadium, England and Spain were tied 1-1 in the first half of extra time when Georgia Stanway collected the ball some 45 yards from goal. Driving forward, the midfielder took the ball to the edge of the box before firing in a rocket-propelled piledriver which ripped into the net beyond the outstretched arm of the Spanish goalkeeper. The sensational strike proved to be the winner, taking England through to their fourth consecutive major tournament semi-final.

2) Ella Toone, England 2 Germany 1, European Championship Final, 31 July 2022
Just over an hour into a tense and feisty Euro 2022 Final at Wembley, Keira Walsh collected the ball in midfield, looked

up and then played a wonderful long pass to Ella Toone. The Manchester United star had only been on the pitch for six minutes after replacing Fran Kirby, but showed remarkable composure as she controlled the ball and then lifted it delightfully over German goalkeeper Merle Frohms to give England the lead in a match they would eventually win 2-1 in extra time.

3) Lucy Bronze, England 3 Norway 0, World Cup quarter-final, 27 June 2019

Four years earlier, Lucy Bronze had banged in a stunning winner for England against Norway at the World Cup in Canada. Now, at the 2019 tournament in France, she scored an even better goal against the same opponents to wrap up a convincing win for the Lionesses in Le Havre. Loitering on the edge of the box, the England right-back hit a blistering first-time shot from Beth Mead's rolled free kick that flew past the Norwegian goalkeeper and almost took off the roof of the net.

4) Eni Aluko, England 1 Netherlands 1, Cyprus Cup, 9 March 2015

A highly talented individualist, Eni Aluko scored many wonderful goals for England, but none better than this effort in Nicosia. Picking up the ball in midfield, the Lionesses' striker worked her way into the penalty area dribbling past four defenders, before curling a shot past the Dutch goalkeeper. 'Eni's goal was just fantastic,' said England boss Mark Sampson afterwards. 'You've got to be a great player to score a goal out of nothing and that's what she did.'

5) Alessia Russo, England 4 Sweden 0, European Championship semi-final, 26 July 2022

Alessia Russo was in superb form at the 2022 Euros, coming off the bench to score four goals for the Lionesses. The pick of the bunch came against Sweden in the semi-final at Bramall Lane when, soon after replacing Ellen White, she netted England's third in a comprehensive 4-0 defeat of the Scandinavians. Set up by Fran Kirby, Russo's initial shot was parried by Sweden goalkeeper Hedvig Lindahl, but the Manchester United striker quickly latched on to the rebound before sending an audacious back-heel into the net through the unfortunate Lindahl's legs.

6) Kelly Smith, England 3 Russia 2, European Championship group stage, 28 August 2009

Kelly Smith was a fantastic penalty box predator, but she could also score from long range as she proved with this glorious strike at the 2009 Euros in Finland. Standing just inside her opponents' half, Smith controlled a kick from hand by the Russian goalkeeper, let the ball bounce once, and then unleashed a powerful left-footer from fully 50 yards that sailed over the stranded keeper's head and into the net. The brilliant goal completed a superb comeback for the Lionesses, who won the match 3-2 after trailing 2-0 early on.

7) Beth Mead, England 8 Norway 0, European Championship group stage, 11 July 2022

In front of a rapturous crowd at the Amex Stadium, England dismantled a highly rated Norway side to record their biggest tournament win. Arsenal's Beth Mead chipped in with a hat-trick, with her second goal earning comparisons with John Barnes' legendary strike against Brazil in 1984. Receiving a pass from Fran Kirby, Mead drove into the penalty area, nonchalantly side-stepped a couple of Norwegian defenders before planting the ball firmly into the corner with a low, left-foot shot. A sensational goal on a truly memorable evening for the Lionesses.

8) Jill Scott, England 1 France 1, World Cup quarter-final, 9 July 2011

One of England's best ever players in the air, Jill Scott is also pretty decent with the ball at her feet, as she demonstrated with this terrific effort against France at the 2011 World Cup in Germany. Collecting the ball on the left wing, Scott burst between two defenders before sending a delicate chip from 20 yards over the French goalkeeper and into the net. The lovely goal put the Lionesses ahead in the quarter-final tie in Leverkusen, but they were pegged back to 1-1 and eventually lost on penalties.

9) Jodie Taylor, England 1 Italy 1, friendly, 7 April 2017

A powerful and hard-running striker, Jodie Taylor was also capable of scoring eye-catching goals which had a touch of Wayne

Rooney about them. This fine effort at Vale Park in 2017 was a case in point. Lionesses' midfielder Jordan Nobbs hit a long ball from the halfway line which Taylor watched as it bounced over her shoulder before smashing a powerful lob over the Italian goalkeeper and high into the net from just outside the box. Taylor would go on to take her scoring form into that summer's European Championship, winning the Golden Boot for her five goals in the tournament.

10) Fran Kirby, England 1 Brazil 0, friendly, 6 October 2018
Pint-sized Fran Kirby is not noted for her ability in the air, but the deep-lying striker scored with a beautifully deft header in this prestigious friendly against Brazil at Meadow Lane. Nikita Parris was the provider, receiving the ball on the right wing and then cutting inside her marker before sending over a cross which Kirby reached before the Brazilian defenders, sending a well-aimed header in off the bar from eight yards. 'Heading isn't something that comes naturally to me,' she said afterwards, 'so I think I was as surprised as anyone when I saw it hit the crossbar and go in.'

TOP 10 HOME VENUES

The stadiums where England have played the majority of their home fixtures:

1) Wembley
Opened in 1923, England played their first game at the original Wembley in April of the following year, a 1-1 draw with Scotland watched by a crowd of just 37,250. The Three Lions went on to play a total of 223 matches at the stadium, including all six of their games at the 1966 World Cup and all five at Euro '96. The curtain came down on the Twin Towers in 2000, England signing off with a tame 1-0 defeat to old enemies Germany in a World Cup qualifier. After years of delays, the new Wembley opened in 2007, England inaugurating the state-of-the-art £798m stadium with a 1-1 draw against Brazil in June of that year. The Three Lions have since played over 80 internationals at the new stadium, including the final of Euro 2020 which they lost on penalties to

Italy. The England Women's team have also played several games at Wembley, including the final of the 2022 Euros – a dramatic 2-1 win against old rivals Germany.

2) Old Trafford

Old Trafford has hosted a total of 17 England matches, coming into its own as an international stadium in the early 2000s when Wembley was being reconstructed. The most famous England match staged at the home of Manchester United was a World Cup qualifier against Greece in October 2001 when a last-minute free kick from Three Lions' skipper David Beckham, a United player at the time, earned Sven-Göran Eriksson's team a 2-2 draw and a guaranteed place at the 2002 World Cup finals in Japan and South Korea. In addition, the stadium hosted three games at the 1966 World Cup and four, all involving Germany, at Euro '96.

3) Goodison Park

England played 12 matches at Goodison Park between 1895 and 1973, the most significant coming in September 1949 when the Three Lions lost 2-0 to the Republic of Ireland – their first defeat on home soil by a non-British team. Everton's home since the Toffees moved from Anfield in 1892, Goodison Park also hosted five games at the 1966 World Cup, including the semi-final between West Germany and the Soviet Union.

4) Highbury

In 1913 the club then known as Woolwich Arsenal moved north of the river to Highbury, dropping 'Woolwich' from their name at the same time. The stadium continued to be the Gunners' home until 2006, when they moved to a larger new ground at Ashburton Grove, and it also hosted 12 England internationals between 1920 and 1961, the most famous in November 1934 when the Three Lions beat reigning world champions Italy 3-2 in a violent friendly dubbed 'The Battle of Highbury'.

5) Kennington Oval

On 8 March 1873 the Kennington Oval was the venue for the first international played on England's home soil, a 4-2 win against Scotland watched by an excited crowd of around 3,000. The previous year the ground hosted the first FA Cup Final, The

Wanderers beating Royal Engineers 1-0, and it was the venue for another nine England matches, the last a 3-2 defeat by Scotland in 1889.

6) Villa Park

Aston Villa's home ground since 1897, Villa Park hosted nine England games between 1899 and 2005 including Sven-Göran Eriksson's first match in charge of the Three Lions, a convincing 3-0 friendly win against Spain in February 2001. In addition, the ground staged three matches at the 1966 World Cup involving Argentina, Spain and West Germany, and four at Euro '96.

7) Anfield

Originally the home of Everton, Anfield has been the home ground of Liverpool since the club was formed in 1892. The stadium has hosted eight England internationals since then, the most significant in March 2001 when the Three Lions came from behind to beat Finland 2-1 in a vital World Cup qualifier. Anfield also staged four matches at Euro '96 and has hosted three Wales home games.

8) St James' Park

Newcastle United's home since 1892, St James' Park has hosted seven England games, the most significant being World Cup qualifiers against Albania (2001) and Azerbaijan (2005) while Wembley was being rebuilt. The ground was also used for three games involving France, Bulgaria and Romania at Euro '96 and six games at the 2012 Olympics.

9) White Hart Lane

Tottenham's home ground between 1899 and 2017, White Hart Lane has been the venue for five England matches between 1933 and 2001. The most famous was in December 1935 when England beat Germany 3-0 in a controversial friendly which attracted protests from Jewish groups and local trade unions because of the anti-semitic policies of the Nazi regime led by Adolf Hitler.

10) Bramall Lane

Opened in 1855, Bramall Lane is the oldest major stadium in the world still hosting professional matches. The home of Sheffield

United since the club's establishment in 1889, it was the venue for five England matches between 1883 and 1930. Along with the Kennington Oval, Bramall Lane is just one of two stadiums to have hosted England internationals, an England cricket Test match (v Australia in 1902) and the FA Cup Final (the 1912 replay between Barnsley and West Brom, which the Yorkshire side won 1-0).

TOP 10 PRE-FIRST WORLD WAR PLAYERS

With their knickerbockers and handlebar moustaches these Victorian and Edwardian-era England internationals may look slightly ridiculous to us, but in their day they were as famous as Harry Kane and Raheem Sterling today:

1) Steve Bloomer
Derby County's all-time leading goalscorer with an amazing 332 goals in all competitions, Steve Bloomer was also a top marksman for England, hitting a then-record 28 goals in just 23 appearances between 1895 and 1907. He was especially prolific at the start of his Three Lions career, finding the net in all of his first ten matches to set a record which still stands. Known for his ability to shoot hard and low with either foot, Bloomer scored a total of 317 league goals for Derby and Middlesbrough in the top flight – a total only bettered by Jimmy Greaves. After retiring in 1914, he moved to Germany to coach only for war to break out just weeks later and he spent most of the conflict in a civilian detention centre in Berlin.

2) Bob Crompton
A full back who was noted for his powerfully driven long passes, Bob Crompton spent the entirety of his career with Blackburn Rovers, playing 530 league games for the Lancashire outfit and helping them win the title in both 1912 and 1914. His England career was equally distinguished, starting with a debut against Wales at Wrexham in 1902. He went on to play 41 times for England – a record which stood until Billy Wright beat it in 1952 – and captained the side 22 times. Crompton later managed

both Bournemouth and Blackburn, dying of a heart attack after a Rovers match in 1941.

3) Vivian Woodward

An architect by profession, Vivian Woodward was also a talented footballer who captained Great Britain to victory at both the 1908 and 1912 Olympics. While playing for Tottenham and Chelsea, he appeared 23 times for England between 1903 and 1911, captaining the side on 14 occasions and scoring an impressive 28 goals – equalling Steve Bloomer's then-record. He also turned out 44 times for England Amateurs, scoring an incredible 57 goals. Woodward's football career ended during World War I when he was struck in the leg by a rifle grenade fragment while fighting in France.

4) Sam Hardy

Rated the best goalkeeper of his generation, Hardy was known as 'Safe and Steady Sam' and he certainly never let England down in his 21 appearances between 1907 and 1920, keeping a total of seven clean sheets. At club level, he won the league title with Liverpool in 1906 and the FA Cup with Aston Villa in both 1913 and 1920. After retiring shortly before his 40th birthday, he became the landlord of a pub in Chesterfield.

5) Jesse Pennington

Although his career was disrupted by World War I, left-back Jesse Pennington still made over 450 league appearances for West Brom, helping the Baggies win the title in 1920. Dubbed 'Peerless Pennington' for his consistent performances, he made his England debut against Wales in 1907 and went on to win 25 caps, making his last appearance for his country aged 36 against Scotland in 1920.

6) George Hilsdon

The first Chelsea player to score 100 goals, George Hilsdon was known as 'Gatling Gun' for the ferocity of his quickfire shooting. Surprisingly, he only played eight times for England but showed his international class by scoring 14 goals in total, including four in a 7-0 rout of Hungary in Budapest in June 1908. In World War I he served with the East Surrey Regiment and in June 1917 was badly gassed at Arras, the after-effects ending his football career.

7) Tinsley Lindley

He may have sounded like a celebrity London hairdresser, but Tinsley Lindley was England's finest forward of the 1880s, scoring 14 goals in just 13 appearances for the Three Lions. In February 1888, while with Nottingham Forest, he captained England against Wales at Crewe, scoring in a 5-1 win. Aged 22, Lindley was his country's youngest-ever captain – a record he held until surpassed by Bobby Moore in 1963. A barrister, he focused on his law practice after retiring from the game, eventually becoming a County Court judge.

8) Billy Wedlock

One of Bristol City's greatest players, Billy Wedlock made over 400 appearances for the club, helped City reach the FA Cup Final in 1909 and had a stand named after him at Ashton Gate. A short and stout half-back, he was known as 'Fatty' and the 'India Rubber Man', but his quality was evident in the fact that of his 26 appearances for England between 1907 and 1914 he only ever finished on the losing side once.

9) G.O. Smith

A schoolmaster by profession who eventually became the Headmaster of Ludgrove School, Gilbert Oswald Smith was a superb dribbler in the front line, known above all for his distinctive body swerve. While playing for amateur clubs Old Carthusians and Corinthians 'G.O.' represented England 20 times between 1893 and 1901, captaining the side on 13 occasions, and scoring 11 times while also creating numerous opportunities for his team-mates, especially the prolific Steve Bloomer who rated him as the best of his strike partners.

10) Billy Bassett

A moustachioed right-winger, Billy Bassett played over 260 times for West Brom, helping the Baggies win the FA Cup in both 1888 and 1892. He represented England 16 times, scoring eight goals and finishing on the losing side just twice. After he retired he became chairman of his former club, a role he held for almost 30 years until his death in 1937 when more than 100,000 people lined the streets of West Bromwich for his funeral procession.

TOP 10 PLAYER CHANTS

The best of the chants England fans have devised for their favourite stars:

1) 'Sterling's on fire, your defence is terrified! Sterling's on fire, your defence is terrified!'
Adapted from the dance classic 'Freed from Desire' by Italian singer Gala, this chant was originally sung about Will Grigg by Wigan Athletic fans. When the striker was selected by Northern Ireland for the 2016 European Championship in France the song really took off – despite Grigg not even making it on to the pitch at the tournament. Soon England fans had pinched the ditty, using it first in tribute to Jamie Vardy, and then to Raheem Sterling as the Manchester City forward scored some vital goals for the Three Lions at the 2020 Euros. Just make sure you're not holding your beer when it gets to the 'na na na' bit.

2) 'Harry Maguire, Harry Maguire, he drinks the vodka, he drinks the jäger, his head's f***ing massive!'
Sung to the tune of 'La Bamba', this chant is especially favoured by fans who've had a few pre-match drinks themselves and references Harry Maguire's reputation as a bit of a party animal. But does the England centre-back actually drink vodka and/or jäger bombs? Quite possibly. And is his head 'massive'? Well, it looks pretty big!

3) 'Harry, Harry Kane! Harry, Harry Kane!'
Inspired by the 1970s Boney M hit 'Daddy Cool', this chant pays tribute to England marksman Harry Kane and is usually heard after he has scored a goal – in other words, quite often!

4) 'Su-per su-per Jack, su-per su-per Jack, su-per su-per Jack, su-per Jackie Grealish'
A rousing chant that had been previously used for England legend Frank Lampard was revamped by the Wembley crowd

for twinkle-toed midfielder Jack Grealish when he finally broke into the England squad in 2020. 'When they are cheering my name like this and singing my song there's nothing more I want to do than pay them back with goals and assists so hopefully my goal will come soon,' he said the following year. Sure enough, he notched his first England goal in a 5-0 thrashing of Andorra in October 2021.

5) 'One David Beckham, there's only one David Beckham, one Daaaaavid Beckham, there's only one David Beckham'
Former England captain, ultimate dead-ball specialist, fashion icon, global marketing 'brand' and a man of many haircuts – you might be forgiven for thinking there was more than 'one' David Beckham. But, as this rather unoriginal chant pointed out, he was one of a kind.

6) 'Psycho! Psycho! Psycho!'
Cult hero Stuart 'Psycho' Pearce was regularly serenaded with this chant during Euro '96, usually after leaving an opponent crumpled on the Wembley turf following one of his trademark robust tackles.

7) 'England's, England's, number one, England's number one'
Peter Shilton was the first England goalkeeper to be hailed with this old football chant, hearing it for the last time at the 1990 World Cup, and since then the likes of David Seaman, Paul Robinson, Joe Hart and Jordan Pickford have all been accorded the honour of being deemed 'England's number one' by the fans.

8) 'Roo-ney! Roo-ney! Roo-ney!'
More complicated Wayne Rooney songs have been belted out at Old Trafford, but the Wembley crowd wisely decided to keep it simple and hailed England's star man for over a decade with a simple but heartfelt chant of appreciation.

9) 'Shear-er! Shear-er! Shear-er!'
Another no-nonsense chant in praise of a player who usually delivered the goods, never more so than at Euro '96 when Alan Shearer's five goals at Wembley won him the Golden Boot and powered England to the semi-finals and a painful shoot-out defeat at the hands of bitter rivals Germany.

10) 'Oh Tammy, Tammy! Tammy, Tammy, Tammy, Tammy Abraham!'

This chant in praise of the Roma striker has been around for a while, and is actually based on the Chicory Tip song 'Son of my Father', which topped the UK charts way back in February 1972.

TOP 10 THRASHINGS

The best of the games in which England really put their opponents to the sword:

1) Ireland 0 England 13, British Home Championship, 18 February 1882

In the first meeting between the two countries, England hammered Ireland 13-0 in Belfast to record their biggest ever victory. Aston Villa strikers Howard Vaughton and Arthur Brown made impressive debuts, grabbing five and four goals respectively – Vaughton becoming the first England player to 'go nap' and to this day his five-goal haul has never been beaten, only equalled by three others, most recently Malcolm Macdonald against Cyprus in 1975.

2) England 13 Ireland 2, British Home Championship, 18 February 1899

England equalled their best tally with 13 goals against Ireland at Sunderland's Roker Park, and would have had one more if Aston Villa's Jimmy Crabtree hadn't missed a penalty. Bury striker Jimmy Settle marked his debut with a hat-trick, but he was outdone by Corinthian's Gilbert Smith, the one amateur in the side and the team's skipper, who helped himself to four goals. Derby's Steve Bloomer also chipped in with a brace to take his England total to 17 – a then-record for the Three Lions – in just nine internationals.

3) Austria 1 England 11, friendly, 8 June 1908

Two days after trouncing Austria 6-1 in Vienna, England gave their hosts an even bigger hammering with Tottenham's

Vivian Woodward grabbing four goals in an emphatic 11-1 win. Frank Bradshaw of The Wednesday (later to become Sheffield Wednesday) also hit a hat-trick on his debut but, strangely, never appeared for the Three Lions again. After this match, England continued their goal-filled tour of central Europe with a 7-0 win against Hungary in Budapest and a relatively modest 4-0 defeat of Bohemia in Prague.

4) Portugal 0 England 10, friendly, 25 May 1947

In the first meeting between the two countries, England trounced Portugal 10-0 in Lisbon while putting on an outstanding display of attacking football. Chelsea striker Tommy Lawton opened the scoring after just 17 seconds – the fastest goal by the Three Lions – and Stan Matthews added a second a minute later. Lawton went on to fill his boots, scoring four goals – a tally matched by Blackpool's Stanley Mortensen on his debut. The goal of the game, though, came from Tom Finney, who beat three defenders before slotting past the Portuguese goalkeeper from a narrow angle.

5) San Marino 0 England 10, World Cup qualifier, 15 November 2021

England recorded their biggest win in a competitive match with a ten-goal annihilation of no-hopers San Marino, officially the worst team in the world. After Harry Maguire opened the scoring with a header from a corner and a San Marino defender diverted a Bukayo Saka shot into his own net, Harry Kane helped himself to four first-half goals, including two from the penalty spot. England didn't let up after the break, Emile Smith Rowe, Tyrone Mings, Tammy Abraham and Sako all getting on the scoresheet as the Three Lions hit double figures for the first time in 57 years.

6) USA 0 England 10, friendly, 27 May 1964

On an end-of-season tour which culminated in a four-team competition in Brazil, England hit double figures in New York in May 1964, with Roger Hunt (four) and Fred Pickering both grabbing hat-tricks. Southampton winger Terry Paine pitched in with a brace, while substitute Bobby Charlton also got on the scoresheet. As a member of the England side which surprisingly lost to the USA at the 1950 World Cup, Three Lions' boss Alf

Ramsey would have been pleased with a convincing win against outclassed opponents.

7) England 9 Luxembourg 0, European Championship qualifier, 15 December 1982

Watford striker Luther Blissett marked his full England debut with a hat-trick against minnows Luxembourg at Wembley – all his goals coming in and around the six-yard box. Glenn Hoddle scored the goal of the game with a left-footed volley from the edge of the box while full-back Phil Neal's was the strangest – a cross from the right which the Luxembourg goalkeeper somehow managed to fumble over the line.

8) Luxembourg 0 England 9, World Cup qualifier, 19 October 1960

England got their World Cup qualifying campaign off to an excellent start with a nine-goal thumping of part-timers Luxembourg. Jimmy Greaves and Bobby Charlton both scored hat-tricks while Tottenham centre-forward Bobby Smith nabbed two goals. However, it was Johnny Haynes in his fourth match as skipper who notched the goal of the game with a thunderous shot.

9) England 9 Ireland 0, British Home Championship, 9 March 1895

One of the greatest players in Derby County's history, Steve Bloomer marked his England debut with two goals in an easy win against an outclassed Ireland side at the County Ground, the home of Derbyshire County Cricket Club. There was a sad postscript to this game as one of the Ireland players, William 'Beg' Sherrard, died from influenza a few months later aged 23.

10) Belgium 1 England 9, friendly, 11 May 1927

England began playing regular friendlies against Belgium after World War I, and although the continentals had not won any of the four previous encounters they did manage a creditable 2-2 draw in Antwerp in 1923. So for England to cruise to a 9-1 victory in Brussels four years later was a notable result. Having scored two goals apiece in his first two matches for England, Everton striker Dixie Dean went one better, bagging a hat-trick in front of an appreciative crowd of 35,000.

TOP 10 BOSSES

The England managers who did their country proud:

1) Alf Ramsey

Former England international Alf Ramsey was appointed Three Lions' boss in 1963, a year after leading unfashionable Ipswich Town to the league title. He confidently predicted that England would win the World Cup in 1966, and was proven correct when his hardworking team of 'wingless wonders' defeated West Germany in the final at Wembley. Knighted the following year, Ramsey then led England to third place at the 1968 European Championship but his star began to dim after a shattering quarter-final exit at the 1970 World Cup in Mexico. When England then failed to qualify for the 1974 tournament the knives were truly out for the taciturn Ramsey, and he was soon sacked – a sad end to his 11-year reign as the Three Lions' most successful boss.

2) Gareth Southgate

Previously best-known as the player who missed the decisive penalty in England's shoot-out defeat to Germany at Euro '96, England under-21 manager Gareth Southgate took over as Three Lions' boss in September 2016 following the dismissal of Sam Allardyce. Initially appointed on an interim basis, Southgate was soon given a long-term contract and justified the faith in him by leading his country to the semi-finals of the 2018 World Cup in Russia. The thoughtful and articulate ex-Middlesbrough boss topped that feat three years later, taking his young squad to the final of the delayed Euro 2020 when only another penalty shoot-out loss against Italy at Wembley prevented him from becoming the first England manager since Sir Alf Ramsey to lift silverware.

3) Sarina Wiegman

A former Netherlands international with over 100 caps, Sarina Wiegman moved into management in the women's game in 2006, winning the Dutch championship with both Ter Leede and ADO Den Haag. Appointed Netherlands boss in January 2017, she led her country to glory at the Euros later that year. In August 2020 she replaced Phil Neville as manager of the England Women's team and two years later she guided the Lionesses to triumph in the Euros following a dramatic 2-1 win in the final against Germany at Wembley. Calm and composed throughout the tournament, she also earned praise for her tactical acumen and masterful use of substitutes.

4) Terry Venables

Formerly boss of Crystal Palace, QPR, Barcelona and Tottenham, chirpy cockney Terry Venables was a popular choice to succeed the hapless Graham Taylor as England manager in 1994. Tactically shrewd and an excellent man-manager, 'El Tel' led the Three Lions to the semi-finals of Euro '96 where they were unfortunate to lose a penalty shoot-out to Germany at Wembley. Despite only losing one of his 24 matches in charge during his two-year reign, Venables was not given a contract extension by the FA, elements of whom were uneasy about the negative publicity surrounding his business dealings.

5) Bobby Robson

Previously the long-serving manager of Ipswich Town, with whom he won both the FA Cup and UEFA Cup, Bobby Robson replaced Ron Greenwood as England manager in 1982. His eight-year reign was marked by some desperate lows – failure to qualify for the 1984 Euros and an abysmal showing at the 1988 finals – which had the tabloid newspapers screaming for his head. However, Robson's England side also recovered from a poor start at the 1986 World Cup to reach the quarter-finals and, four years later, were only denied a place in the final by a penalty shoot-out defeat to West Germany. He was knighted for services to football in 2002, while managing Newcastle United.

6) Sven-Göran Eriksson

After managing clubs in Sweden, Portugal and Italy, Sven-Göran Eriksson was appointed England's first foreign manager in 2001. The bespectacled Swede inherited a talented group of players including David Beckham, Steven Gerrard and Frank Lampard who the press dubbed 'The Golden Generation', but Eriksson's tenure proved to be ill-fated, his England team reaching the quarter-finals of three consecutive tournaments before being eliminated in agonising fashion. Newspaper reports linking Eriksson with other jobs and lurid headlines about his personal life contributed to the FA deciding not to renew his contract after the 2006 World Cup.

7) Walter Winterbottom

Having previously played for Manchester United and served in World War II in the Royal Air Force as a wing commander with overall responsibility for the training of PE instructors, Walter Winterbottom was appointed as the FA's first England manager in 1946. In his 16-year tenure the International Selection Committee continued to pick the England squad but Winterbottom had control of team affairs, and took his country to four consecutive World Cups, reaching the quarter-finals in both 1954 and 1962. He was knighted for services to sport in 1978 after working as the director of the Sports Council.

8) Ron Greenwood

After Don Revie's shock resignation as England manager in the summer of 1977, former West Ham boss Ron Greenwood was appointed as his successor, initially on a temporary basis. A steadying influence who was highly rated as a coach, Greenwood led England at both the 1980 Euros in Italy and the 1982 World Cup in Spain, losing just one of the eight tournament matches the Three Lions played in total. During his five-year reign, the first black players made their senior bows for England, Greenwood stating, 'Yellow, purple or black – if they're good enough, I'll pick them.'

9) Glenn Hoddle

After gaining plaudits for creating an attractive but trophyless Chelsea side, Glenn Hoddle was announced as the replacement for the departing Terry Venables after Euro '96. Hoddle's England did well to qualify automatically for the 1998 World Cup from a tough group which also included Italy, and at the finals in France were unfortunate to go out in the last 16 on penalties to Argentina. However, the following February his contract was terminated by the FA after he made comments in a newspaper interview about his belief in reincarnation which offended people with disabilities.

10) Joe Mercer

After Sir Alf Ramsey was sacked as England manager in May 1974, Coventry City boss Joe Mercer took over as caretaker for a couple of months. Mercer, who had previously enjoyed great success with Manchester City, only lost one of his seven matches in charge and impressed sufficiently for the FA to consider appointing him on a longer basis. However, eventually the job went to Leeds United manager Don Revie.

TOP 10 UNWANTED RED CARDS

The most memorable of the occasions when an England player has been sent off:

1) David Beckham, England 2 Argentina 2 (Argentina won 4-3 on penalties), World Cup last 16, 30 June 1998

A thrilling World Cup last 16 tie in Saint-Étienne was beautifully poised at 2-2 just after half-time when David Beckham was barged over by Diego Simeone. Stupidly, the prone Manchester United winger kicked out in petulant fashion at the Argentinian midfielder, who made the most of the light contact, falling over theatrically. Surrounded by players of both teams, Danish referee Kim Nielsen eventually showed a yellow card to Simeone and then a red one to Beckham. Forced to play most of the second half and all of extra time with ten men, Glenn Hoddle's team performed superbly to hold on to a draw but then lost on penalties.

2) Wayne Rooney, England 0 Portugal 0 (Portugal won 3-1 on penalties), World Cup quarter-final, 1 July 2006

After a frustrating hour in which he had seen little of the ball, Wayne Rooney became involved in a midfield tussle during which he appeared to stamp on Ricardo Carvalho's groin. While the Portuguese defender rolled around on the turf, his team-mates surrounded the Argentinian referee who soon showed Rooney the red card. England fought a brave rearguard action, taking the match in Gelsenkirchen into extra time, but the ten men were eventually beaten on penalties.

3) Alan Mullery, England 0 Yugoslavia 1, European Championship semi-final, 5 June 1968

Two minutes from the end of a tempestuous European Championship semi-final against Yugoslavia in Florence, Alan Mullery became the first England player to be sent off. After being hacked down by a Yugoslav player the Tottenham midfielder kicked out in retaliation and was promptly dismissed by the Spanish referee. 'Being the first is a bit of a bugbear,' Mullery told *The Guardian* in 2009, 'but I've got to accept it because I was.'

4) Ray Wilkins, England 0 Morocco 0, World Cup group stage, 6 June 1986

Annoyed at having been given offside, England midfielder Ray Wilkins picked up the ball and then hurled it in the direction of the Paraguayan referee. The peevish act was out of character for the normally mild-mannered AC Milan star, but it cost him dear as the ball struck the ref on the shins and resulted in him being shown the red card. Down to ten men for the whole of the second half and with the temperature on the pitch reaching 100 degrees in Monterrey, England did well to escape with a 0-0 draw.

5) Alan Ball, Poland 2 England 0, World Cup qualifier, 6 June 1973

A terrible day for England in Chorzów got worse 12 minutes from time when Alan Ball clashed with Lesław Ćmikiewicz, grabbing the Polish midfielder by the throat after a clash with Martin Peters on the halfway line. The Austrian referee immediately waved the red card at Ball, but he was reluctant to go, even making an aggressive move towards another Polish player. Eventually he made his way off to the touchline, only the second England player to be dismissed.

6) Trevor Cherry, Argentina 1 England 1, friendly, 12 June 1977

In front of a raucous crowd of 60,000 at La Boca in Buenos Aires, the Leeds defender Trevor Cherry was sent off eight minutes from the end for a tackle from behind on Daniel Bertoni. The Argentinian right-winger, who had equalised for his country with a curling free kick after Stuart Pearson's headed opener for

England, also got his marching orders after punching Cherry in the mouth in retaliation, knocking out two of his teeth.

7) Paul Scholes, England 0 Sweden 0, European Championship qualifier, 5 June 1999

The Manchester United midfielder became the first England player to be sent off on home soil when he received two yellow cards against Sweden in 1999. Living up to his reputation as a wild and reckless tackler, Scholes picked up a booking in the first half for a late challenge on Stefan Schwarz. Then, when he fouled the same player six minutes after the break, he was off for an early bath.

8) Harry Maguire and Reece James, England 0 Denmark 1, European Nations League group stage, 14 October 2020

Having been booked in the fifth minute for a late tackle, Harry Maguire was walking the tightrope against Denmark, and it wasn't long before he fell off. Just after the half hour the Manchester United centre-back miscontrolled the ball in midfield, lunged to retrieve it, but only succeeded in chopping down Kasper Dolberg to earn himself a second yellow card. A night which ended in defeat for Gareth Southgate's team got even worse after the final whistle, when young right-back Reece James was shown a straight red card for arguing with the Spanish referee – the first time that England have had two players sent off in the same match.

9) Rob Green, Ukraine 1 England 0, World Cup qualifier, 10 October 2009

West Ham's Rob Green became the first England goalkeeper to be sent off, after bringing down Ukrainian forward Artem Milevskiy in the box in the 14th minute. David James came on as substitute goalkeeper and was relieved to see Andriy Shevchenko put his penalty wide. England eventually lost the match in Dnepropetrovsk 1-0, their only dropped points in their qualifying campaign for the 2010 World Cup in South Africa.

10) Raheem Sterling, England 2 Ecuador 2, friendly, 4 June 2014

On just his fourth international appearance 19-year-old Raheem Sterling became the youngest England player to be sent off, seeing red for a foul on Ecuador midfielder Antonio Valencia in a World Cup warm-up match in Miami. Irritated by Sterling's slide tackle on him 12 minutes from the end, Valencia grabbed the youngster by the neck and was also dismissed by the American referee.

TOP 10 UNLIKELY TV APPEARANCES

We're used to seeing former England players on shows like *A Question of Sport* and *A League of Their Own*, but these appearances were altogether more surprising:

1) Teddy Sheringham, The Masked Singer
Were the producers of the ITV celebrities-in-disguise singing contest making a not so subtle point when they cast Teddy Sheringham as 'Tree' in the first series of The Masked Singer in 2020? The former England striker was not the most mobile of players, especially in the final years of his long career, but he still got around the pitch somewhat better than the average oak. Anyway, the one-time Tottenham and Manchester United star made it to the fourth episode before being voted out. The following year Glenn Hoddle (aka 'Grandfather Clock') was eliminated at the same stage of the competition while Michael Owen ('Doughnuts') made it through to the sixth episode in 2022.

2) John Fashanu, I'm a Celebrity... Get Me Out of Here!
Capped twice by England in 1989, the former Wimbledon striker went on to become a TV presenter in the 1990s and in 2003 appeared in the second series of ITV's Australia-based jungle challenge show, finishing as runner-up to former cricketer Phil Tufnell. Since then, five other England players – Neil Ruddock (2004), Rodney Marsh (2007), Wayne Bridge (2016), Dennis Wise (2017) and Ian Wright (2019) – have tried their hands at a variety of stomach-turning Bushtucker Trials but without quite matching the early success of 'Fash'.

3) Wayne Bridge, Celebrity SAS: Who Dares Wins
The former England left-back was a worthy winner of the first celebrity series of the Channel 4 military-training programme in 2019 after trekking across a Chilean glacier and surviving

a brutal interrogation. 'I knew it was going to be a real test,' he said afterwards. 'I wanted to push myself and test myself.' The following year John Fashanu dropped out of the show with three episodes remaining, while Kieron Dyer had to pull out for medical reasons in 2021.

4) Neil Ruddock, Celebrity Big Brother
Capped just once by England in 1994, former Tottenham and Liverpool defender Neil 'Razor' Ruddock had a much longer stint in the *Big Brother* house in 2013, eventually being evicted on the final day in fifth position. His stay was not without drama, and he was given a formal warning after clashing with American reality television personality Spencer Pratt. Five years later John Barnes also appeared on the show, but was the fourth housemate to be evicted after a 16-day stay.

5) David Seaman, Dancing on Ice
England's goalkeeping hero at Euro '96 appeared on the first series of the ITV show in 2006, coming a creditable fourth having previously won a similar BBC one-off special, *Strictly Ice Dancing at Christmas*. More importantly, he met his third wife, pro skater Frankie Poultney, on the stage version of the show. The following year Lee Sharpe also appeared on *Dancing on Ice*, coming fifth. In 2009 Graeme Le Saux fared less well, proving he was no Christopher Dean when he was the first celebrity to be eliminated.

6) Lee Sharpe, Celebrity Love Island
The former Manchester United and England winger proved quite a hit with the ladies when he spent 12 weeks on a stormy Fijian island in the first edition of the ITV reality programme in 2005. TV presenter Jayne Middlemiss confessed her love for the handsome ex-pro, but Sharpe had his eyes set on glamour model Abi Titmuss, who he dated for two years after the show.

7) Alex Scott, Strictly Come Dancing
The former England Women's right-back fared much better on the Beeb's popular dance contest show in 2019 than ex-Three Lions goalkeeper David James, eventually being eliminated in week 11 in a series won by actor Kevin Fletcher. Two other England

internationals have also appeared on the show: John Barnes (eliminated in week eight in 2007) and Peter Shilton (eliminated in week four in 2010).

8) Danny Mills, Celebrity Masterchef
England's right-back at the 2002 World Cup showed he is a dab hand in the kitchen when he came joint-second in the 2012 edition of the BBC cookery show, losing out to writer and actress Emma Kennedy in the Final. Four other England internationals have also appeared on the programme over the years: Graeme Le Saux (2006), Neil Ruddock (2019), John Barnes (2020) and Dion Dublin (2021).

9) Gary Lineker, Who Wants to Be a Millionaire?
The former England captain appeared on a Christmas special edition of the popular ITV quiz show with ex-rugby union star Austin Healey. The pair did pretty well, winning £50,000 for their chosen charity, the Nicholls Spinal Injury Foundation, but were eventually defeated by a question about Mary, Queen of Scots. Five years earlier David Seaman won £32,000 with Judith Keppel, the first contestant to win the £1m jackpot, but John Barnes had a disappointing experience on the show in 2020, winning just £1,000 for his charity after getting a poker question wrong.

10) Stan Collymore, The Farm
The three-cap England international striker appeared on the first series of Channel 5's rural reality show in 2004 but soon stormed off after a four-letter bust-up with rapper Vanilla Ice, who he accused of spending too much time on the toilet and not pulling his weight on the farm. Oh well, at least he didn't have to watch David Beckham's former personal assistant Rebecca Loos collecting a semen sample from a pig.

TOP 10 OVER-CAPPED PLAYERS

Amazingly, all of these players won over 20 international caps each – indeed, some accumulated considerably more. What on earth were the England managers of the time thinking?

1) Phil Jones

If they are aware of him at all, younger fans probably know of Phil Jones for the ridiculous facial expressions he pulls on his (very) rare appearances for Manchester United which have become memes on the internet. They may be surprised to hear that the much-mocked Jones also has 27 England caps to his name, most recently featuring in two defeats against Belgium at the 2018 World Cup in Russia. Former United manager Sir Alex Ferguson once said that Jones 'could be our best ever player' but, judging by the defender's thoroughly mediocre appearances in an England shirt, The Athletic was surely spot on when it described Fergie's comment as 'the biggest error of judgment he ever made in his career'.

2) Joe Hart

Incredibly, Joe Hart won two more caps than the legendary Gordon Banks – 75 compared to 73 for the fabled World Cup winner. Yet, for at least half of his international career Hart's form for both club and country was on the slide, culminating in some disastrous displays at Euro 2016. Eventually, after losing his place at Manchester City and beginning a dispiriting period as a goalkeeper-for-hire, Hart was dropped by Three Lions' manager Gareth Southgate to the relief of England fans everywhere.

3) Kieron Dyer

Kieron Dyer's playing career is best remembered for an on-pitch brawl with Newcastle team-mate Lee Bowyer during a match against Aston Villa in April 2005. Off the pitch the injury-prone midfielder was just as full of energy, indulging in an orgy in Ayia Napa in the summer of 2000 while his girlfriend was pregnant with their first child and then getting involved in a fight in an Ipswich nightclub which resulted in him being glassed in the face. In between all these hijinks, Dyer somehow managed to win 33 England caps without ever really contributing much of note to the team.

4) Chris Woods

After making his Three Lions debut in 1985, Chris Woods struggled to replace the veteran Peter Shilton in England's goal and was still only the backup to the 40-year-old at the 1990 World Cup. Following Shilts's retirement, Woods was installed as first choice by new England boss Graham Taylor but the Sheffield Wednesday man failed to shine at Euro 1992 and then endured a nightmare match as the Three Lions lost a vital World Cup qualifier against Norway in Oslo. Woods won the last of his 43 caps in a humiliating 2-0 defeat to the USA in the summer of 1993 – a fitting epilogue to a less-than-sparkling international career.

5) Stuart Downing

A decent but hardly outstanding left-winger with Middlesbrough, Aston Villa, Liverpool and West Ham, Stuart Downing enjoyed an England career which lasted almost a decade without ever winning over his critics. Yes, he set up a few goals against lesser opposition for the likes of Wayne Rooney and Peter Crouch, but never really looked genuine international quality. You ask if he managed to score himself in his 35 appearances between 2005 and 2014? Don't be silly.

6) Phil Neville

First capped by Terry Venables in 1996, Phil Neville went on to feature under another five England managers. A useful but somewhat limited defender who could also toil away in midfield if required, Neville won an impressive 59 caps – two more than Three Lions legend Jimmy Greaves – without ever really establishing himself in the team. That total is all the more astonishing given that the one memorable moment of his international career came at Euro 2000 when he was responsible for England being eliminated from the tournament after conceding a late penalty against Romania with a reckless tackle.

7) Jermaine Jenas

The boyish enthusiasm that so appeals to TV producers also served Jermaine Jenas well in his football career, with no fewer than three England managers selecting him for their squads between 2003 and 2009. His international career, though, got off to a bad start with a debut in the shock 3-1 defeat to Australia at Upton Park and never really took off after that. The so-called attacking midfielder managed just one goal for England, in a 2-1 defeat of Switzerland in 2008, and won the last of his 21 caps in a 1-0 defeat to Brazil in Qatar the following year.

8) David Batty

First capped during the calamitous Graham Taylor era, defensive midfielder David Batty was largely overlooked by Terry Venables before becoming a regular under Glenn Hoddle. He performed capably, if unspectacularly, in the qualifiers for the 1998 World Cup but at the tournament itself his most notable contribution was to have a poor penalty saved in the shoot-out defeat to Argentina. The following year he won the last of his 42 caps for England, but went out on another low as he was sent off against Poland in Warsaw.

9) Emile Heskey

Ask Michael Owen and he will tell you that Emile Heskey was the best strike partner he played with during his long England career. Powerful and pacy, Heskey certainly had the physique of a top-class centre-forward, but when it came to actually putting the ball in the back of the net he struggled. The stats tell a grim story: just seven goals for his country in 62 games – the sort of strike rate that would embarrass the average midfielder, let alone an international striker who has the occasional opportunity to really fill his boots against genuine minnows. Even worse, he went six years without scoring at all for England between 2003 and 2009. Surely, whatever Owen thinks, just about anybody else could have done better?

10) Dele Alli

Dele Alli, we often hear, is an attacking midfielder who loves getting into the box and scoring goals. Well, he's hardly fulfilled that brief for England, netting just three times in 37 games – although, to be fair, one of those goals was an important one in the 2018 World Cup quarter-final against Sweden. Since then, his form has declined so badly he has lost his place in the England squad and is only rarely spotted in Premier League action. Now stuck on the subs' bench at Everton, his chances of an international recall would appear to be extremely slim.

TOP 10 ENGLAND PLAYER QUOTES

A selection of comments from England players past and present:

1) 'My penalty was not good enough, it should have gone in, but I will never apologise for who I am and where I come from.'
Marcus Rashord, responding to online racist abuse after he missed a penalty in England's shoot-out defeat to Italy in the Final of Euro 2020

2) 'We were expecting Winston Churchill and instead we got Iain Duncan Smith.'
Gareth Southgate on Sven-Göran Eriksson's half-time team talk when England played Brazil in the World Cup quarter-final in 2002

3) 'The nice aspect of football captaincy is that the manager gets the blame if things go wrong.'
Gary Lineker, on becoming England captain in 1990

4) 'I remember the European Championship in 2004. Wayne Rooney was a special player in that tournament, and I definitely cried when we got knocked out.'
Harry Kane, 2015

5) 'I have to admit that I had a bit of sympathy for the Germans. They genuinely believed the ball had not crossed the line and they may be right.'
Geoff Hurst on his second goal in the 1966 World Cup Final

6) 'Whether you are white, brown, purple or blue, it's the same. When you are fortunate enough to make an England debut at Wembley, it's the greatest feeling in the world.'
Viv Anderson, who became England's first black full international in 1978

7) 'You look around and think, "I remember watching them on the telly – they're England." And you don't feel as if you should be here with them.'
England winger Chris Waddle, 1990

8) 'That man could talk and talk and talk until the cows came home and he'd continue talking until they were fast asleep. The problem was most of it didn't make any sense to me.'
England striker Ian Wright on Graham Taylor's team talks

9) 'After six weeks in the England camp, even Jack Charlton could look attractive.'
1966 World Cup winner George Cohen

10) 'Because of the booking I will miss the Holland game – if selected.'
Paul Gascoigne, 1993

TOP 10 EUROPEAN CHAMPIONSHIP WINS

The best of the games the Three Lions have won at the Euros:

1) England 2 Denmark 1, semi-final, 7 July 2021
On a nervy but ultimately joyous night at Wembley, England fell behind when Denmark's Mikkel Damsgaard powered in a free kick from fully 25 yards after half an hour. The Three Lions equalised ten minutes later with a rather scrappy goal, Bukayo Saka crossing from the right for Simon Kjær to bundle into his own net while under pressure from Raheem Sterling. With no further goals the match moved into extra time, England skipper Harry Kane scoring the winner in the 104th minute when he shot home from six yards after his penalty – awarded for a foul on Sterling – had been saved by Kasper Schmeichel.

2) England 2 Germany 0, last 16, 29 June 2021
Covid restrictions meant Wembley was half full for this much-anticipated knockout clash but the home fans nearly raised the roof when Raheem Sterling converted Luke Shaw's cross to break the deadlock with 15 minutes to play. Germany almost hit back with a quick equaliser, a rapid break ending with Thomas Müller's low shot going narrowly wide of Jordan Pickford's right-hand post. With four minutes to play Three Lions' skipper Harry Kane broke his tournament duck to seal victory, heading low into the net from sub Jack Grealish's left-wing cross.

3) England 4 Netherlands 1, group stage, 18 June 1996

Terry Venables' England had Wembley in raptures as they tore the Netherlands apart and booked their place in the quarter-finals of Euro '96. Alan Shearer started the rout midway through the first half, smashing home a penalty after Paul Ince had been fouled. Three goals in 11 breathless second-half minutes settled the contest: Teddy Sheringham headed in Paul Gascoigne's corner; then Gazza and Sheringham set up Shearer for a net-bursting shot; finally, Sheringham pounced on a rebound after Dutch goalkeeper Edwin van der Sar fumbled Darren Anderton's long-range drive. A late goal by Patrick Kluivert barely registered among the celebrating England fans, but allowed the Dutch to progress to the last eight on goal difference at the expense of Scotland.

4) England 2 USSR 0, third-place play-off, 8 June 1968

Three days after losing the semi-final to Yugoslavia in Florence, England faced the Soviet Union in the Stadio Olimpico in Rome with third place at the 1968 Euros up for grabs. Bobby Charlton drilled in Geoff Hurst's lay-off to put Sir Alf Ramsey's men ahead five minutes before half-time, and victory was sealed shortly after the hour when Hurst rounded Russian goalkeeper Yuri Pshenichnikov and then tapped in from two yards.

5) England 2 Scotland 0, group stage, 15 June 1996

In the first tournament meeting between the two neighbours, England overcame a stodgy start to claim all three points. Alan Shearer headed the Three Lions in front early in the second half from an excellent Gary Neville cross and, after Gary McAllister had seen his penalty saved by England goalkeeper David Seaman, Paul Gascoigne made the result safe for Terry Venables' side, flicking the ball over Colin Hendry's head before volleying in past Andy Goram.

6) England 1 Germany 0, group stage, 17 June 2000

Having thrown away a two-goal lead in their opening match against Portugal at Euro 2000, England desperately needed to win this clash with old rivals Germany in Charleroi. After Michael Owen saw his header pushed on to a post by German goalkeeper Oliver Kahn in the first half, England took the lead eight minutes after the break when Alan Shearer headed in David Beckham's wickedly spinning free kick. The Germans dominated the rest of the game, but a combination of alert goalkeeping by David Seaman and last-ditch defending preserved the Three Lions' narrow lead.

7) England 4 Ukraine 0, quarter-final, 3 July 2021

England made short shrift of Ukraine in Rome to reach the semi-finals of the European Championship for only the third time in their history. Skipper Harry Kane gave Gareth Southgate's team an early lead from Raheem Sterling's through pass, and Harry Maguire headed in a second from Luke Shaw's free kick straight after half-time. Less than five minutes later Shaw was the provider again, crossing from the left for Kane to head in, and sub Jordan Henderson then completed a comfortable victory, nodding in his first goal for England from Mason Mount's corner.

8) England 4 Croatia 2, group stage, 21 June 2004

After falling behind to an early Croatian goal in Lisbon, England hit back with two goals late in the first half to take the lead at the break, Paul Scholes heading in from close range before 18-year-old Wayne Rooney rifled in a piledriver from outside the box. Midway through the second half Rooney played a one-two with Michael Owen and then ran through to coolly slot home. Croatia hit back on 73 minutes with a header from Igor Tudor but Frank Lampard guaranteed the Three Lions' progress to the quarter-finals with a low left-footer 11 minutes from time.

9) England 2 Wales 1, group stage, 16 June 2016

Two substitutes came to England's rescue after Gareth Bale's long-range free kick gave Wales a half-time lead in Lens. First, Jamie Vardy shot on the turn inside the six-yard box on 56 minutes to equalise for Roy Hodgson's team; then, a minute into injury time, Daniel Sturridge squirted a shot between goalkeeper Wayne Hennessey and the near post to give England all three points in a closely fought British derby.

10) England 3 Sweden 2, group stage, 15 June 2012

After an encouraging 1-1 draw with France, England faced bogey side Sweden in Kiev and took the lead midway through the first half when Andy Carroll met Steven Gerrard's cross with a superb downward header. The Swedes responded with two quick goals early in the second half, before sub Theo Walcott levelled for the Three Lions with a long-range strike on 64 minutes. It was the Arsenal striker, too, who set up England's winner, crossing for Danny Welbeck to flick in with just 12 minutes to play.

TOP 10 WAGS

Some England players are married to women who are celebrities in their own right; indeed, some of them are arguably even more famous than their husbands!

1) Victoria Beckham

As 'Posh Spice' in the Spice Girls, Victoria Adams was part of the most successful female group of all time, selling over 100 million records worldwide. When the band split in 2001 she went solo, but soon concentrated on a career in fashion, creating her own high-end designer label. In July 1999 she married Manchester United and England star David Beckham at a castle in Ireland, the couple – by then known simply as 'Posh and Becks' – being pictured on their big day sitting on golden thrones. They now have four children, including model and photographer Brooklyn Beckham.

2) Cheryl

Cheryl first came to public attention in 2002 as a member of Girls Aloud, a group created through the ITV show *Popstars: The Rivals*. She began a solo career in 2009, enjoying five UK No 1 singles – at the time a record for a female singer. She has remained in the spotlight as a judge on both the UK and US versions of *The X Factor* and as the longstanding face of L'Oreal. In 2006 Cheryl married Chelsea and England left-back Ashley Cole but the union was short-lived, the couple divorcing four years later.

3) Perrie Edwards

Perrie rose to fame as a member of Little Mix, winners of the 2011 series of *The X Factor*. The band have since gone on to sell over 60 million records worldwide and have had five UK No 1 singles. In August 2013 she became engaged to One Direction singer Zayn

Malik, but the couple split up two years later. In 2016 she began dating England midfielder Alex Oxlade-Chamberlain, and five years later the pair announced the birth of their first child.

4) Louise Redknapp
Originally a member of Eternal, Louise quit the all-girl group in 1995 for a solo career, releasing three best-selling albums before becoming a TV presenter on shows including *The Farmer Wants a Wife* and *Something for the Weekend*. In 1998 she married England midfielder Jamie Redknapp in Bermuda, the couple having two children together before divorcing in 2019.

5) Frankie Bridge
Frankie broke into the music industry early, joining S Club Juniors (later S Club 8) in 2001 when she was aged 12. Since 2007 she has been a member of The Saturdays, enjoying more than a dozen Top 10 hits with the all-girl group. In 2011 she began a relationship with Manchester City and England left-back Wayne Bridge. The couple married three years later and now have two sons.

6) Christine Lampard
After cutting her teeth on TV in Northern Ireland, Christine Bleakley became co-host of BBC1's *The One Show* in 2007. Two years later she met Chelsea and England midfielder Frank Lampard at the Pride of Britain awards hosted by *The Mirror*. The couple married in 2015 and now have two children together. Christine has continued to work in TV, presenting shows such as *Dancing on Ice*, *This Morning* and *Loose Women*.

7) Joy Beverley
With younger twin sisters Babs and Teddie, Joy performed as The Beverley Sisters for over 60 years, the group having a string of hits in the 1950s including 'I Saw Mommy Kissing Santa Claus' and 'Little Drummer Boy'. In 1958 she married England captain Billy Wright, a year before he won the last of his then record 105 caps. The couple were together for 36 years until Wright died from lung cancer in 1994.

8) Abbey Clancy
Lanky striker Peter Crouch was once asked on *The Graham Norton Show* what he would be if he wasn't a footballer and

replied, rather wittily, 'A virgin.' So it was fortunate that when he first met Abbey Clancy in a bar in Liverpool in 2006, shortly after she had just been named runner-up on reality show *Britain's Next Top Model*, he was a famous face himself, banging in the goals for both the Reds and England. The couple married five years later and now have four children.

9) Joanna Taylor

Actress Joanna Taylor got her big break in the Channel 4 soap opera *Hollyoaks*, playing the role of Geri Hudson, the daughter of a wealthy biscuit factory owner, between 1999 and 2001. She later appeared in the BBC1 police drama *Merseybeat* and in the films *Post Impact* (2004) and *Back in Business* (2007). In 2004 she married Liverpool midfielder Danny Murphy, a year after he won the last of his nine caps for England. The couple had two children together before separating in 2017.

10) Frankie Poultney

Professional ice skater Frankie Poultney first appeared on the hit ITV show *Dancing on Ice* in 2007, when she was paired with former Manchester United and England winger Lee Sharpe. She has since appeared in six more series, most recently in 2014 when she teamed up with her fiancé, ex-England goalkeeper David Seaman, who she had first met on the stage version of the show. The couple married the following year, in a ceremony attended by a host of Seaman's former team-mates, including Ian Wright, Sol Campbell and Tony Adams.

TOP 10 SCOTTISH-BASED PLAYERS

The following players all represented England while plying their trade north of the border:

1) Terry Butcher

One of England's greatest defenders, Terry Butcher was an established international while with Ipswich Town before he joined Rangers in 1986. The brave and powerful centre-back was badly missed by England at the 1988 European Championship, which he watched from home after suffering a broken leg, but he returned to the fold to put in some imposing performances at the 1990 World Cup, captaining the side for most of the tournament after original skipper Bryan Robson was sidelined through injury. Butcher then retired from international football aged 31, having won 77 caps in total and 32 with Rangers – a record for an England player with a Scottish club.

2) Paul Gascoigne

The talismanic midfielder won 22 of his 57 caps during a three-year spell with Rangers, notably starring at Euro '96 when he scored a brilliant virtuoso goal against Scotland at Wembley. The following year Gazza helped England win Le Tournoi, a four-team competition which also featured Italy, France and Brazil, and qualify for the 1998 World Cup with a battling 0-0 draw against Italy in Rome. After moving to Middlesbrough he made just three more appearances for the Three Lions, before being controversially axed from Glenn Hoddle's squad ahead of the finals in France.

3) Gary Stevens

Twice a league title winner with Everton, reliable right-back Gary Stevens moved to Rangers in 1988 and won six consecutive Scottish Premier Division titles. He won 20 of his 46 caps while in Scotland, including appearances against the Republic of Ireland and hosts Italy at the 1990 World Cup. He was selected for Graham Taylor's Euro 1992 squad but had to drop out through injury and never featured for England again.

4) Joe Baker

The first player to represent England without having played in the English league system, Liverpool-born striker Joe Baker made his debut for the Three Lions while with Hibs in November 1959. He scored the opener and set up the winner for Ray Parry in a 2-1 defeat of Northern Ireland at Wembley and won another four caps while based in Edinburgh. After a five-year gap, and by now playing for Arsenal, he made three more appearances for England in the 1965/66 season, scoring two more goals, but failed to make the cut for Alf Ramsey's World Cup squad.

5) Trevor Steven

An energetic right-sided midfielder who started out at Burnley before winning two league titles with Everton, Trevor Steven won five of his 36 England caps while with Rangers. Three of those appearances came in the knockout stages of the 1990 World Cup, Steven coming on as a sub against both Cameroon and West Germany before starting the third-place play-off defeat against Italy in Bari. He would go on to finish his England career at Euro '92, by when he had moved on to Marseille.

6) Chris Woods

Goalkeeper Chris Woods won 20 of his 43 England caps while with Rangers between 1986 and 1991, with six of those appearances coming as a substitute. During this period he started just one match at a tournament, playing against the Soviet Union in England's final group game at Euro 1988. It was not a happy occasion for Woods, though, who conceded three times in a 3-1 defeat in Frankfurt – England's third loss of a desperately disappointing campaign.

7) Mark Hateley

A traditional centre-forward who was especially strong in the air, Mark Hateley was recalled to the England scene after a four-year gap during a prolific five-year stint with Rangers. However, he played just once for his country while with the Scottish giants, winning the last of his 32 caps in a 2-2 draw with Czechoslovakia in Strahov in March 1992.

8) Mark Walters

The first black player to appear for Rangers, left-winger Mark Walters won his only England cap on an end-of-season tour of Australia, New Zealand and Malaysia in 1991. He started the first of two matches against the Kiwis, but was subbed off before Gary Lineker scored the only goal of the game in Auckland in injury time.

9) Fraser Forster

Celtic goalkeeper Fraser Forster endured a difficult England debut against Chile at Wembley in November 2013, struggling with his distribution and at times looking shell-shocked in a dismal 2-0 defeat. The following year he came on for Joe Hart 15 minutes from the end of a 0-0 draw with Honduras in Bakersfield, California, a match that was suspended for 40 minutes in the first half due to a heavy thunderstorm. He subsequently won another four caps while with Southampton.

10) Alan Thompson
The first Celtic player to represent England, left-winger Alan Thompson was a surprise choice by Three Lions' boss Sven-Göran Eriksson for a friendly against Sweden in Gothenburg in March 2004. However, he failed to impress in a 1-0 defeat, was substituted after an hour and was not called up again.

TOP 10 ENGLAND WOMEN WORLD CUP WINS

The Lionesses have had some good showings at the World Cup in recent years, reaching the semi-finals in both 2015 and 2019 while recording some excellent victories along the way:

1) England 3 Norway 0, quarter-final, 27 June 2019
Watched by former England captain David Beckham, the Lionesses got off to a great start in their quarter-final against Norway in Le Havre, taking the lead after just three minutes when Lucy Bronze pulled the ball back for Jill Scott to shoot in off a post. Ellen White tapped in shortly before half-time and then Bronze made the game safe with a blistering shot into the roof of the net from the edge of the box on 57 minutes. Nikita Parris had a penalty saved late, but it mattered little. 'That was the best they have played under me,' said England boss Phil Neville afterwards, but it was a performance the Lionesses couldn't quite match in the semi-final which they lost 2-1 to eventual winners the USA.

2) England 2 Canada 1, quarter-final, 27 June 2015
In front of an excited crowd of 54,027 in Vancouver, England deservedly beat hosts Canada to reach the World Cup semi-finals for the first time in their history. Jodie Taylor gave the Lionesses the lead after 11 minutes, pouncing on a mistake by a Canadian

defender before driving forward to drill a low shot into the far corner. Three minutes later, Lucy Bronze doubled England's lead with a header which bounced off the crossbar before just crossing the line. Hotshot Canadian striker Christine Sinclair pulled one back just before the break after Karen Bardsley spilt a cross but England held on in a scrappy second half to march on to the last four.

3) England 1 Germany 0, third-place play-off, 4 July 2015

After losing in the semi-final to reigning champions Japan in agonising fashion – Lionesses defender Laura Bassett conceding an unfortunate last-minute own goal – England might have been forgiven for viewing the third-place play-off match in Edmonton as a bit of a chore. However, Mark Sampson's team showed a lot more drive, ambition and commitment than a lacklustre German outfit and fully deserved the bronze medals they received thanks to Fara Williams's perfectly executed penalty, awarded in extra time after substitute Lianne Sanderson was fouled.

4) England 6 Argentina 1, group stage, 17 September 2007

England recorded their biggest win at the World Cup with a 6-1 thrashing of Argentina in Chengdu, China. The Lionesses were two up inside the first ten minutes thanks to an own goal and a long-range shot by Jill Scott. However, England only really turned the screw in the second half after Argentina had a player sent off for a foul in the box, Fara Williams scoring from the resulting penalty. The South Americans did manage to reduce the arrears from a free kick but Kelly Smith added two poacher's goals for the Lionesses before sub Vicky Exley completed the rout with a last-minute penalty. The convincing win put England in the quarter-finals, where they lost 3-0 to the USA.

5) England 2 Norway 1, last 16, 22 June 2015

Norway had the better of the first half in Ottawa and might have taken the lead before Solveig Gulbrandsen headed in at the near post from a corner on 54 minutes. England, though, hit back quickly, skipper Steph Houghton rising above the Norwegian defence to power home a header from Fara Williams's corner. The Lionesses' winner was a beauty, Lucy Bronze smashing a rising shot high into the net from the edge of the area after subs Jill Scott and Karen Carney had combined well.

6) England 2 Scotland 1, group stage, 9 June 2019
England got their World Cup campaign off to a satisfactory start with a narrow victory over rivals Scotland in Nice. Nikita Parris gave the Lionesses the lead on 15 minutes with a well-struck penalty, an advantage that Ellen White doubled just before half-time when she clinically slotted home a half chance with a left-foot shot. What should have been a comfortable victory for the Lionesses became more nervy when the Scots pounced on a mistake by England skipper Steph Houghton, Claire Emslie scoring from close range.

7) England 3 Canada 2, group stage, 6 June 1995
After failing to qualify for the inaugural Women's World Cup in China in 1991, England recorded their first win at the finals in their opening fixture at the 1995 tournament in Sweden. A penalty apiece from Gillian Coultard and star striker Marieanne Spacey put the Lionesses in control in Helsingborg before Coultard appeared to wrap up the win with a third goal five minutes from time. However, the Canadians hit back with two late strikes of their own to leave England relieved to hear the final whistle.

8) England 2 Mexico 1, group stage, 13 June 2015
After losing their opening game against France, England bounced back with a hard-fought victory against Mexico in Moncton, Canada. However they had to wait until the 71st minute to take the lead, Fran Kirby dribbling past two defenders before poking her shot in off a post. Two subs then combined to make the points safe for England, Karen Carney heading in Alex Greenwood's excellent cross. Sloppy goalkeeping by Karen Bardsley gifted Mexico a late goal, but it was no more than a consolation.

9) England 2 Japan 0, group stage, 19 June 2019
Phil Neville's team topped their World Cup group with an excellent win against a slick-passing Japan side in Nice. Ellen White grabbed both goals for the Lionesses, the first after 14 minutes when she converted a defence-splitting pass by Georgia

Stanway. Sub Karen Carney set up White's second six minutes from time, the prolific striker bursting through to fire a low left-footer past the Japanese goalkeeper.

10) England 2 New Zealand 1, group stage, 1 July 2011

After a 1-1 draw with Mexico, England put themselves in a strong position in their group with a battling win over New Zealand in Dresden. However, the Lionesses had to come from behind after Sarah Gregorius's goal separated the teams at the break. Jill Scott levelled for Hope Powell's team just after the hour with a looping header from Alex Scott's cross, and it was Jill who set up sub Jess Clarke to ram in the winner with just nine minutes to play.

TOP 10 GOALKEEPING GAFFES

The worst of the mistakes made by England's last line of defence:

1) David Seaman, England 1 Brazil 2, World Cup quarter-final, 21 June 2002

A fine servant for England in the 1990s, David Seaman's powers were fading by the time of the 2002 World Cup and in the quarter-final against Brazil in Shizuoka he made a calamitous error which resulted in the Three Lions being knocked out of the tournament. There seemed little danger when Ronaldinho floated in a free kick from more than 40 yards out, but Seaman allowed the ball to sail over his head and into the top corner for the winning goal. A few months later Sven-Göran Eriksson called time on Seaman's international career after he let in a goal against Macedonia direct from a corner.

2) Rob Green, England 1 USA 1, World Cup group stage, 12 June 2010

England were leading through a Steven Gerrard goal in Rustenburg when USA striker Clint Dempsey fired in a low shot from 25 yards five minutes before half-time. Three Lions goalkeeper Rob Green appeared to have the rather weak effort covered but somehow contrived to let the ball slip through his hands and dribble agonisingly over the line. The dreadful mistake cost England two points and Green was promptly dropped by manager Fabio Capello, David James replacing him for the rest of the tournament.

3) Paul Robinson, Croatia 2 England 0, European Championship qualifier, 11 October 2006

Trailing 1-0 to Croatia in Zagreb, England's hopes of getting back into the match were dealt a mortal blow on 68 minutes when goalkeeper Paul Robinson attempted to kick clear a Gary Neville back-pass. Missing the ball completely after it hit a divot, Robinson could only watch in horror as it slowly bobbled over the line. Quite possibly the most comical goal England have ever conceded.

4) Ron Springett, France 5 England 2, European Championship preliminary round second leg, 27 February 1963

In arguably the worst display by any England goalkeeper, Sheffield Wednesday's Ron Springett was at fault for all five of France's goals in Paris in Alf Ramsey's first match in charge of the Three Lions. For the first two goals he was slow to come off his line to snuff out the danger, then for the third he flapped at a bouncing ball and only succeeded in presenting an unmissable chance to Lucien Cossou. After England fought back to 3-2 in the second half, Springett boobed twice more, letting a soft shot spill out of his hands to a waiting French striker and then allowing Cossou to flick the ball over him before volleying home. Little wonder he was promptly dropped by Ramsey, with Gordon Banks making his debut against Scotland a few weeks later.

5) Ray Clemence, Scotland 2 England 1, British Home Championship, 15 May 1976

A tight derby between Scotland and England at Hampden Park was level at 1-1 shortly after half-time when a howler by Ray Clemence settled the contest. A marauding run by Joe Jordan down the left ended with the Scottish striker crossing the ball to Kenny Dalglish. The Celtic man controlled the ball neatly, but his low shot from ten yards was straight at Clemence and lacked power. Somehow, though, the England goalkeeper allowed the ball to slip through his hands and legs and trickle over the line for the winning goal.

6) Peter Bonetti, England 2 West Germany 3, World Cup quarter-final, 14 June 1970

When Gordon Banks was ruled out of this quarter-final in León, Mexico, with food poisoning, his deputy Peter Bonetti was called upon to make just his seventh appearance for the Three Lions. 'The Cat', as he was known for his feline-like reflexes, watched on contentedly as England cruised into a two-goal lead, but on 68 minutes he was at fault when he dived over Franz Beckenbauer's low shot from the edge of the box. Bonetti was also left stranded for West Germany's equaliser, a looping header by striker Uwe Seeler, and remained rooted to his line as Gerd Müller volleyed in the winner from close range in extra time. The painful defeat ended England's reign as world champions and also brought down the curtain on Bonetti's international career.

7) Joe Hart, England 1 Iceland 2, European Championship last 16, 27 June 2016

Having been deservedly criticised for letting in Gareth Bale's 30-yard free kick in England's 2-1 win against Wales earlier in the tournament, Joe Hart's Euro 2016 hit rock bottom as the Three Lions were beaten by Iceland in Nice. He might have done more to prevent the minnows' equaliser from a long throw but he was certainly at fault for what proved to be the winning goal on 15 minutes, failing to stop a low shot from Kolbeinn Sigþórsson crossing the line despite getting his left hand to the ball. Surprisingly, the out-of-form Hart kept his England place for over a year until he was finally discarded by Gareth Southgate.

8) Peter Shilton, Italy 2 England 1, World Cup third-place play-off, 7 July 1990

England's most-capped player gave the Three Lions tremendous service for two decades, but Peter Shilton's final appearance for his country at the 1990 World Cup was one he would prefer to forget. Midway through the second half he failed to pick up a loose ball on the far edge of his penalty area, allowing Roberto Baggio to nick possession from him. The Italian striker exchanged passes with team-mate Salvatore 'Toto' Schillaci before netting from close range to set the hosts on course for an eventual 2-1 win in the third-place play-off in Bari. For Shilts, it was a sad way to hang up his gloves.

9) Scott Carson, England 2 Croatia 3, European Championship qualifier, 21 November 2007

Making just his second appearance for England, Scott Carson had a nightmare start at Wembley when he conceded an extremely soft goal against Croatia after seven minutes. When Niko Kranjčar tried a speculative shot from 35 yards Carson appeared to have the effort covered, but the ball struck the young goalkeeper on the chest and ricocheted into the goal. It proved to be a very costly mistake as England failed to qualify for the European Championship finals in Austria and Switzerland after losing the match 3-2.

10) David James, Austria 2 England 2, World Cup qualifier, 4 September 2004

The Manchester City goalkeeper lived up to his nickname, 'Calamity James', by conceding a poor second goal to Austria in this World Cup qualifier in Vienna. Andreas Ivanschitz's slightly deflected 25-yard shot was hopeful at best, but James allowed it to creep through his hands and over the line to the delight of the home fans. England boss Sven-Göran Eriksson was unimpressed, dropping James for Paul Robinson for the remaining qualifiers and the tournament proper in Germany.

TOP 10 LOWER-LEAGUE PLAYERS

The following England internationals won all their caps while playing for clubs outside the top flight:

1) Terry Paine

Right-winger Terry Paine's consistent performances for Southampton in the old Second Division earned him a first England call-up against Czechoslovakia in Bratislava in May 1963. He went on to win 19 caps over the next three years, scoring seven goals – including a hat-trick in an 8-3 rout of Northern Ireland at Wembley in November 1963 – before making his last appearance for his country at the 1966 World Cup against Mexico.

2) John Atyeo

Bristol City's all-time top scorer with an incredible 351 goals, John Atyeo was a part-time professional with the Second Division outfit while qualifying as a quantity surveyor when he won his first England cap against Spain in November 1955, scoring in a 4-1 win at Wembley. Over the next two years the tall and powerful striker featured five more times, scoring another four goals including a late equaliser in a 1-1 draw with the Republic of Ireland in Dublin that guaranteed England's place at the 1958 World Cup. Surprisingly, though, he did not make the squad for the finals in Sweden.

3) Peter Taylor

The star of Third Division Crystal Palace's run to the FA Cup semi-finals in 1976, left-winger Peter Taylor was rewarded with a first England cap in March that year and scored in a 2-1 victory against Wales in Wrexham. Six weeks later he hit the winner against the same opposition, this time in Cardiff, with a low 20-yarder. Taylor, who later admitted that some of the regular England players didn't have a clue who he was when he was first selected, won a further two caps before dropping out of Don Revie's squad.

4) Steve Bull

Wolves' all-time top goalscorer with 306 goals, bustling striker Steve Bull was the last player from the third tier to be capped by England when he made his debut against Scotland in May 1989, scoring in a 2-0 win at Hampden Park. Two goals against Czechoslovakia and another against Tunisia the following year earned him a place in Bobby Robson's squad for Italia '90, where he featured in four matches. In all he won 13 caps for England, before being discarded early in Graham Taylor's reign.

5) Bill Eckersley

A one-club man with Blackburn Rovers, left-back Bill Eckersley was chosen for England's 1950 World Cup squad despite plying his trade in the old Second Division. He made his debut for the Three Lions in their final group game, a 1-0 defeat against Spain in Rio de Janeiro which ensured they would be home before the postcards. His 17th and final appearance for his country was in the famous 6-3 defeat by Hungary at Wembley in November 1953.

6) Brian Clough

Although best known as a legendary manager with Derby County and Nottingham Forest, Brian Clough was also an exceptional striker in his playing days, scoring an impressive 251 goals in 274 games for Middlesbrough and Sunderland before injury cut short his career. While with Second Division Boro he played twice for England in October 1959 – in a rain-soaked draw with Wales in Cardiff and a 3-2 defeat by Sweden at Wembley – but his partnership with fellow poacher Jimmy Greaves failed to gel and it was Cloughie who paid the price.

7) Gill Merrick

England's first-choice goalkeeper in the early 1950s, Gill Merrick won 23 caps while playing for second-tier Birmingham City. His stats, though, make for fairly grim reading: he only kept five clean sheets and conceded 45 goals at an average of very nearly two per game. Merrick was in goal for the infamous 6-3 and 7-1 thrashings by Hungary in the 1953/54 season but, more significantly, performed poorly in the 4-2 defeat by Uruguay in the quarter-final of the 1954 World Cup in Basel – a match which turned out to be his last for his country.

8) Reg Matthews

Used to playing in front of crowds of under 10,000 for Coventry City in the Third Division South, goalkeeper Reg Matthews was a bag of nerves when he made his England debut in front of 132,817 fans against Scotland at Hampden Park in April 1956. However, he performed well in a 1-1 draw and kept his place for another four internationals that year before a mistake against Northern Ireland saw him dropped in favour of Tottenham veteran Ted Ditchburn.

9) Alan A'Court

Hard to believe now, but Liverpool spent eight consecutive seasons in the old Second Division between 1954 and 1962. However, the club's lowly status did not prevent left-winger Alan A'Court being called up for England duty, and he marked his international debut with a goal in a shock 3-2 defeat to Northern Ireland at Wembley in November 1957. The following year he deputised for the injured Tom Finney in three matches at the World Cup in Sweden before winning his final cap against Wales in November 1958.

10) Michael Gray
Best known as the Sunderland player who missed the decisive penalty in the play-off final shoot-out against Charlton which denied the Black Cats a chance to return to the Premier League in 1998, left-back Michael Gray was called up by England boss Kevin Keegan the following April, making his Three Lions debut as a sub against Hungary in Budapest. He made two further appearances that summer, once as a starter, before disappearing from the international scene.

TOP 10 DODGY REFEREEING DECISIONS

England fans were chanting 'Who's the whatsit in the black?' – or words to that effect – after these highly debatable decisions:

1) Diego Maradona's 'Hand of God' goal, England 1 Argentina 2, World Cup quarter-final, 22 June 1986
After a fairly uneventful first half, this quarter-final at the Estadio Azteca in Mexico City exploded into life when Argentina captain Diego Maradona jumped to challenge England goalkeeper Peter Shilton and punched the ball into the net with his outstretched left hand. Tunisian referee Ali Bennaceur gave the goal, and was promptly surrounded by furious England players who persuaded him to consult his linesman, but the two officials agreed that no foul had been committed. After Argentina's victory, Maradona described the goal as having been scored by the 'Hand of God', but England manager Bobby Robson was scathing in his response, 'It wasn't the hand of God. It was the hand of a rascal. God had nothing to do with it.'

2) Frank Lampard's 'ghost' goal, England 1 Germany 4, World Cup last 16, 27 June 2010
After falling two goals behind in this World Cup knockout match in Bloemfontein, England had halved the deficit through Matt

Upson's header and were hunting an equaliser. That moment seemed to have arrived on 38 minutes when Frank Lampard chipped Germany goalkeeper Manuel Neuer from the edge of the penalty area and saw his shot hit the crossbar before bouncing down a yard over the line. However, neither the Uruguayan referee nor his assistant signalled for a goal and Neuer was able to retrieve the ball and continue play. The officials' error seemed to knock the stuffing out of England, who went down to a heavy 4-1 defeat. On a more positive note, the notorious incident persuaded FIFA president Sepp Blatter to introduce goal-line technology at the next World Cup in Brazil ensuring similar mistakes would not occur again.

3) Ronald Koeman's yellow card, Netherlands 2 England 0, World Cup qualifier, 13 October 1993

The Three Lions desperately needed to win this World Cup qualifier in Rotterdam and looked to have a great chance of opening the scoring in the 56th minute when David Platt controlled Andy Sinton's long pass. Losing the foot race with Platt, Dutch defender Ronald Koeman hauled down the England midfielder, who fell inside the penalty area. German referee Karl-Josef Assenmacher, though, ruled that the offence took place outside the area and only awarded England a free kick. Then, to the disbelief of Graham Taylor's players, he deemed that the Dutchman's cynical foul was only worthy of a yellow card, not red. 'I was devastated,' recalled Platt. 'Koeman came over to me and said, "Sorry, I know I should have gone."' To add insult to injury, just five minutes later Koeman scored his side's first goal in their eventual 2-0 win.

4) Sol Campbell's disallowed goal, Portugal 2 England 2 (Portugal won 6-5 on penalties),, European Championship quarter-final, 24 June 2004

England and Portugal were locked at 1-1 in the last minute of normal time of this tense quarter-final in Lisbon when David Beckham whipped in a free kick from the left. Michael Owen met it with a header which struck the bar before Sol Campbell rose highest to nod the rebound over the line. However, Swiss ref

Urs Meier blew for a foul by John Terry on Portugal goalkeeper Ricardo, and the hosts went on to win the match on penalties. 'I still think if it was Portugal scoring, it would have been a goal,' reflected Campbell years later.

5) Penalty and 'goal' appeals turned down, England 0 USA 1, World Cup group stage, 29 June 1950

England were surprisingly trailing the USA by a first-half goal in Belo Horizonte when with just eight minutes to play centre-forward Stan Mortensen broke clear, only to be rugby tackled by American defender Charlie Colombo. The England players appealed for a penalty, but the Italian ref ruled that the foul took place outside the box. From Alf Ramsey's resulting free kick, Jimmy Mullen headed towards goal and, although his effort was saved by USA goalkeeper Frank Borgi, the England players again surrounded the ref, believing that the ball had crossed the line. Once again, though, their pleas were rejected and the Americans hung on for a famous win.

6) David Platt's disallowed goal, England 1 West Germany 1 (West Germany won 4-3 on penalties), World Cup semi-final, 4 July 1990

Ten minutes from the end of extra time in the World Cup semi-final in Turin, England were awarded a free kick in a dangerous position out on the right wing. Chris Waddle's dead ball was perfectly executed and met by a downward David Platt header which flashed past Bodo Illgner in the German goal. However, almost before the ball had crossed the line the Brazilian referee had blown for offside. Replays suggested that the call was marginal and that in today's game the VAR officials would have spent some minutes studying the lines on their screen before reaching a decision.

7) Phil Neal's handball, England 0 Denmark 1, European Championship qualifier, 21 September 1983

England's chances of reaching the 1984 European Championship finals in France were dealt a deadly blow when they lost this qualifier to Denmark at Wembley. The key moment came in the 35th minute when the Belgian referee ruled that Phil Neal handled the ball in the area when stumbling and, despite the Liverpool right-back's protests, awarded Denmark a penalty. Allan Simonsen beat Peter Shilton from the spot for what proved to be the only goal of the game, and at the final whistle England and Three Lions manager Bobby Robson were booed off by the home fans.

8) Sol Campbell's disallowed goal, England 2 Argentina 2 (Argentina won 4-3 on penalties), World Cup last 16, 30 June 1998

With nine minutes left of a thrilling World Cup knockout match in Saint-Étienne, England and Argentina were drawing 2-2 when Darren Anderton curled in a corner from the left. Challenged by Alan Shearer, Argentina goalkeeper Carlos Roa missed the ball allowing Sol Campbell to head into the unguarded goal. Campbell ran away in delight, but his celebrations were cut short when Danish referee Kim Nielsen disallowed the goal, ruling that Shearer had elbowed Roa.

9) Peter Brabrook's disallowed goal, England 0 USSR 1, World Cup group stage play-off, 17 June 1958

Making his debut for England in a vital play-off in Gothenburg with a World Cup quarter-final place at stake, Chelsea right-winger Peter Brabrook dribbled from the halfway line into the Russian penalty area before shooting. The ball rebounded to him off a defender, possibly striking Brabrook's arm, before he lashed a second shot past the legendary Lev Yashin in the Russian goal. If it was handball, it was clearly unintentional, but the German referee awarded the Russians a free kick and a few minutes later they scored what proved to be the winner.

10) Jack Charlton's foul, England 4 West Germany 2, World Cup Final, 30 July 1966

In the last minute of the 1966 World Cup Final England were leading West Germany 2-1 when Swiss referee Gottfried Dienst blew for a foul by Jack Charlton. 'I never took my eye off the ball, and as I jumped to head it I fell on top of somebody. I hadn't even known he was there!' recalled the big defender in his autobiography. The German free kick hit the England wall, pinballed around the six-yard box and was eventually stabbed in by Wolfgang Weber. Never mind, England went on to win the match 4-2 with a little help from the officials themselves.

TOP 10 WORLD CUP WINS

The best of the games the Three Lions have won on the biggest stage of all – no prizes for guessing which match tops the list.

1) England 4 West Germany 2, Final, 30 July 1966

In front of a packed Wembley and a worldwide TV audience of 500 million, England got off to a poor start in the 1966 World Cup Final when a weak headed clearance by left-back Ray Wilson was rifled in by Helmut Haller. Minutes later, however, the Three Lions were level, skipper Bobby Moore floating in a free kick for Geoff Hurst to head home. An exciting match seemed to be heading England's way when Martin Peters scored from close range with 12 minutes remaining, but a scrappy German equaliser just before full time cut short the home fans' celebrations. In the first half of extra time Hurst crashed a shot against the underside of the bar and, after consulting the Russian linesman, the referee ruled that the ball had just crossed the line when it bounced down. It was Hurst, too, who confirmed England as the new world champions when he clinched his hat-trick with a rasping drive into the roof of the net in the closing seconds.

2) England 2 Portugal 1, semi-final, 26 July 1966

England got the better of a talented Portuguese side at Wembley to reach the World Cup Final for the first – and, so far, only – time in their history. The Three Lions were indebted to Bobby Charlton who scored both their goals, the first coming on the half-hour mark when he calmly slotted a loose ball in from just outside the box. Then, on 80 minutes, Geoff Hurst laid the ball back for the Manchester United star, who smashed a typically powerful shot into the bottom corner. Portugal quickly responded with a penalty from the brilliant Eusébio, the top scorer at the finals, but it was not enough to prevent England marching on to a date with destiny.

3) England 3 Cameroon 2, quarter-final, 1 July 1990

On a dramatic and, at times, nerve-jangling night in Naples, Bobby Robson's England took the lead on 25 minutes when Stuart Pearce crossed for David Platt to head home at the far post. Inspired by 38-year-old sub Roger Milla, surprise package Cameroon scored twice in four minutes midway through the second half and the Three Lions were only saved from a humiliating defeat late on when Gary Lineker converted a penalty after he had been fouled. In the 14th minute of extra time the Tottenham striker raced on to a Paul Gascoigne through ball and was again brought down in the box as he attempted to round the Cameroon goalkeeper. Coolness personified, Lineker smashed in his second penalty of the game to book England a place in the World Cup semi-finals for the first time since 1966.

4) England 1 Argentina 0, quarter-final, 23 July 1966

In one of the most notorious matches in World Cup history, Argentina captain Antonio Rattín was sent off in the first half at Wembley for arguing with the referee but refused to leave the pitch. The match was held up for nine minutes until Rattín eventually trudged off, after which the South Americans' approach became even more physical. The tie was eventually settled on 78 minutes when Geoff Hurst headed in a left-wing cross by his West Ham team-mate, Martin Peters. At the final whistle England boss Alf Ramsey intervened to prevent his players swapping shirts with their opponents, and in his post-match press conference he condemned the Argentinians as 'animals' for their brutal tackling.

5) England 2 Sweden 0, quarter-final, 7 July 2018

England reached the World Cup semi-finals for the first time since 1990 with a deserved victory over Sweden in Samara, Russia. A threat from set pieces throughout the tournament, Gareth Southgate's team took the lead on the half-hour mark when Harry Maguire met Ashley Young's corner with a firm downward header. Dele Alli doubled England's lead on 58 minutes with a header from Jesse Lingard's cross and goalkeeper Jordan Pickford preserved the two-goal advantage with a couple of outstanding saves.

6) England 1 Belgium 0, last 16, 26 June 1990

England survived some scares in this last-16 tie in Bologna, Belgium twice striking Peter Shilton's right-hand post, before taking the match into extra time. With a penalty shoot-out looming, Paul Gascoigne ran at the Belgian defence from deep one last time and was fouled about 40 yards from goal. Gazza took the free kick himself, chipping the ball to the far post where substitute David Platt met it with a perfectly executed volley which flew into the net for a superb last-minute winner.

7) England 3 France 1, group stage, 16 June 1982

On a boiling hot afternoon in Bilbao, Ron Greenwood's men got their World Cup campaign off to a magnificent start when Bryan Robson scored after just 27 seconds – the fastest goal ever at the tournament by an England player. France equalised on 25 minutes with a well-taken goal by Gérard Soler, but Robson restored the Three Lions' lead midway through the second half with a powerful header, before Paul Mariner wrapped up an excellent victory late on when he pounced on a miscued defensive clearance.

8) England 1 Argentina 0, group stage, 7 June 2002

England gained some measure of revenge for their 1998 penalty shoot-out defeat by Argentina in France with a hard-fought win against the South Americans in Sapporo. The key moment arrived two minutes before half-time when Michael Owen, who had earlier seen a low shot hit a post, was brought down in the box by future Southampton and Tottenham boss Mauricio Pochettino. Three Lions skipper David Beckham, the villain of the piece when the two sides had met four years earlier, smashed in the resulting penalty for what proved to be the only goal of the game.

9) England 3 Paraguay 0, last 16, 18 June 1986

Bobby Robson's England set up a quarter-final clash with Argentina after an easy win against Paraguay in the Estadio Azteca in Mexico City. Gary Lineker tapped in from two yards to give the Three Lions the lead on the half hour, and his strike partner Peter Beardsley added a second on 56 minutes after Paraguay goalkeeper Roberto Fernandez failed to hold a low shot by Terry Butcher. The best goal of the game came 17 minutes from time, Glenn Hoddle and right-back Gary Stevens combining to set up Lineker for another poacher's finish.

10) England 3 Denmark 0, last 16, 15 June 2002
England strolled into the quarter-finals of the 2002 World Cup with a comfortable win over Denmark in Niigata, Japan. Leeds United defender Rio Ferdinand opened the scoring with a header from a David Beckham corner on five minutes that Danish goalkeeper Thomas Sørensen fumbled over the line. Midway through the first half Michael Owen made it two from eight yards, and the match was over as a contest shortly before half-time when Emile Heskey drilled in a shot from just outside the box.

TOP 10 OPPOSITION QUOTES

Players, managers and commentators from around the world have their say on England:

1) 'A little with the head of Maradona and a little with the hand of God.'
Diego Maradona, describing his first goal for Argentina against England in the 1986 World Cup quarter-final

2) 'Lord Nelson, Lord Beaverbrook, Sir Winston Churchill, Sir Anthony Eden, Clement Attlee, Henry Cooper, Lady Diana, Maggie Thatcher. Can you hear me? Your boys took a helluva beating. Norway has beaten England at football.'
Norwegian TV commentator Bjørge Lillelien, 1981

3) 'As we came round the corner from the 18th green, a crowd of members were at the clubhouse window, cheering and waiting to tell me that England had won the World Cup. It was the blackest day of my life.'
Scotland striker Denis Law, 1979

4) 'Live the way you want England! Iceland is going to play France. France-Iceland. You can go home. You can go out of Europe. You can go wherever the hell you want.'

Icelandic TV commentator Gudmundur Benediktsson, linking his country's victory over England at Euro 2016 with the Brexit referendum result

5) 'The 5-1 defeat by England was like the explosion of a nuclear bomb. The scars will last for life.'
Germany goalkeeper Oliver Kahn, reflecting on England's famous World Cup qualifying win in Munich in 2001

6) 'I read it in the papers every World Cup that this will be England's year. They won't win, just like Tim Henman never wins the Wimbledon title.'
Northern Ireland legend George Best, 2005

7) 'Maybe the England team underestimated us because our players aren't as famous as theirs.'
Germany captain Philipp Lahm after his team thrashed England 4-1 at the 2010 World Cup

8) 'At that moment I hated Gordon Banks more than any other man in soccer. But when I cooled down I had to applaud him with my heart for the greatest save I had ever seen.'
Pelé, reflecting on Gordon Banks's legendary save during the Brazil v England match at the 1970 World Cup in Mexico

9) 'It was not a goal, because the ball bounced down and hit the line. That's no goal, you know, the whole ball has to be behind the line. That's the rule.'
West Germany's Franz Beckenbauer, still unhappy that England's controversial third goal in the 1966 World Cup Final was given

10) 'We are just a little country of 30,000 people. For us, it is a dream just to be on the same field as England. To score such a famous goal is unthinkable – it is like winning the World Cup.'
Davide Gualtieri, on his first-minute goal for San Marino against England in 1993

TOP 10 FOOTBALLING FATHERS

The fathers of England internationals who had the best careers in the game themselves:

1) Ian Wright

After starting out with Crystal Palace, livewire striker Ian Wright moved to Arsenal in 1991 and over the next seven years went on to become the Gunners' all-time top goalscorer – although his total of 185 goals has since been passed by Thierry Henry. He was capped 33 times by England, but only started 17 of those games, and scored nine times. Wright later became a TV presenter and football pundit. His adopted son, Shaun Wright-Phillips, was a winger with Manchester City, Chelsea and QPR who had a very similar England career, starting just 15 of his 36 games for the Three Lions between 2004 and 2010 and scoring six goals.

2) Brian Clough

A prolific striker with Middlesbrough and Sunderland, Brian Clough played twice for England in 1959 without finding the net. As Derby County manager he led the Rams to their first league title in 1972 and repeated the trick with Nottingham Forest six years later, before guiding the Midlanders to back-to-back European Cup triumphs in 1979 and 1980. Witty, outspoken and charismatic, Clough was the people's choice to become England manager but his often controversial style was not to the FA's taste. His son, forward Nigel, won 14 caps for England between 1989 and 1993 while with Forest and Liverpool.

3) Mark Chamberlain

Speedy Stoke City winger Mark Chamberlain scored on his England debut in a 9-0 rout of minnows Luxembourg at Wembley in December 1982 and won another seven caps over the next two years. He later played for Sheffield Wednesday, Portsmouth, Brighton and Exeter. His son, Liverpool midfielder Alex Oxlade-Chamberlain, won 35 caps for England between 2012 and 2019, scoring seven goals.

4) Frank Lampard senior

A long-serving left-back with West Ham who helped the Hammers win the FA Cup in both 1975 and 1980, Frank Lampard senior was capped twice by England – oddly, his pair of appearances for the Three Lions came almost eight years apart. He was later assistant manager at Upton Park under his brother-in-law, Harry Redknapp. His son, midfielder Frank, won 106 caps for England and represented his country at the 2006, 2010 and 2014 World Cups.

5) George Eastham senior

While playing as an inside-forward for Bolton, George Eastham senior was capped just once by England, in a friendly against the Netherlands in Amsterdam in 1935. He later managed Accrington Stanley as well as clubs in Northern Ireland and South Africa. His son, also called George, won 19 caps for England and was a non-playing member of the victorious 1966 World Cup squad. A creative midfielder, he scored the winner for Stoke City in the 1972 League Cup Final against Chelsea at Wembley – the only major trophy won by the Potters.

6) Tony Hateley

Known for his ability in the air, Tony Hateley scored 249 goals in 499 league games in the 1960s and 1970s for a variety of clubs, including Notts County, Aston Villa, Chelsea and Liverpool. His son, Mark, was a similar type of centre-forward and was also much-travelled, having stints in Italy, France and Scotland along with spells at Coventry, Portsmouth and QPR. Between 1984 and 1992 he won 32 caps for England, scoring nine goals.

7) Harry Redknapp

As a young winger with West Ham, Harry Redknapp played in the England side that thrashed Spain 4-0 in the European Under-18 Championship Final in 1964, but he never went on to win a senior cap. He later managed the Hammers, Portsmouth and Tottenham, among others, guiding Pompey to FA Cup success in 2008. His son, Jamie, played 17 times for England between 1995 and 1999 while with Liverpool.

8) Ray Mabbutt

A solid and dependable midfielder, Ray Mabbutt played nearly 400 league games for Bristol Rovers between 1956 and 1969. He later turned out for Newport County before working in the insurance business. His son, Gary, was a defensive stalwart for Tottenham for many years and won 16 caps for England under Bobby Robson and Graham Taylor.

9) Terry Owen

After appearing just twice for Everton in the top flight, nippy striker Terry Owen dropped down the divisions to play for Bradford City, Chester and Rochdale, helping Chester win promotion from the fourth tier in 1975. His son, Michael, scored an impressive 40 goals for England in 89 appearances and represented his country at five major tournaments.

10) Mike Sutton

Mike Sutton started out as a midfielder for his hometown club Norwich City in 1962 and later played for Chester and Carlisle United before retraining as a teacher. His son, Chris, was a striker with Norwich, Blackburn Rovers – with whom he won the Premier League title in 1995 – Chelsea and Celtic and won a single England cap as a sub against Cameroon at Wembley in 1997.

TOP 10 NICKNAMES

The England players with the most impressive alter egos:

1) Stanley 'Wizard of the Dribble' Matthews

Stanley Matthews' superb dribbling skills allied to his sharp acceleration and bewildering body swerve earned him his nickname, which was coined early in his career by a journalist. An idol of fans at Stoke and Blackpool, his England career lasted an incredible 23 years, between 1934 and 1957, and he made his last appearance for the Three Lions at the age of 42 – a record which still stands. The first player to be voted Footballer of the Year (in 1948) and European Footballer of the Year (in 1956), Matthews was knighted in 1965 – the only footballer to be so honoured while still playing.

2) Martin 'The Ghost' Peters

The scorer of England's second goal in the 1966 World Cup Final against West Germany, midfielder Martin Peters was known as 'The Ghost' for his late runs into the opposition box which often gave the impression that he had appeared out of nowhere. The West Ham and Tottenham star was especially adept at haunting Scotland, scoring five goals in eight matches against England's most deadly rivals.

3) Bryan 'Captain Marvel' Robson

A complete midfielder who could pass accurately, shoot with power and tackle like a demon, Bryan Robson earned his 'Captain Marvel' tag for his irrepressible performances for Manchester United. The nickname stuck with England, who he skippered on 65 occasions including games at the 1986 and 1990 World Cups – although, sadly, both these tournaments ended early for Robson through injury.

4) Stuart 'Psycho' Pearce

An aggressive and combative left-back, Stuart Pearce was given his nickname by fans of Nottingham Forest, with whom he spent the majority of his career. Pearce's crunching tackles and ferocious free kicks quickly endeared him to England fans as well, leading to deafening chants of 'Psycho' reverberating around Wembley during the 12 years Pearce represented his country between 1987 and 1999.

5) Norman 'Bites Yer Legs' Hunter

An essential component of Don Revie's intimidating Leeds side of the 1960s and early 1970s, centre-back Norman Hunter earned his nickname for his uncompromising approach to the game. Sadly, his England career is mostly remembered for an uncharacteristically weak challenge which contributed to Poland's goal in a vital World Cup qualifier at Wembley in October 1973 – a spot of 'leg-biting' on that occasion would not have gone amiss!

6) Kevin 'Mighty Mouse' Keegan

Short in stature but big on work rate, desire and determination, England captain Kevin Keegan was given the nickname 'Mighty

Mouse' by Hamburg fans when he joined the German club from Liverpool in 1977. The following year he won the Ballon d'Or, an award he retained in 1979.

7) Nat 'The Lion of Vienna' Lofthouse

Nat Lofthouse had to wait until he was nearly 27 before earning his nickname, which was given to him after he scored a typically brave goal for England in a dramatic 3-2 win against Austria in Vienna in May 1952. Despite being elbowed in the face, tackled from behind and challenged by the Austrian goalkeeper, the Bolton striker still managed to squeeze the ball into the net for England's second goal.

8) Tom 'The Preston Plumber' Finney

One of England's greatest players, skilful winger Tom Finney won 76 caps and scored 30 goals for his country, as well as appearing at three World Cups in the 1950s. In an era where the maximum age applied it was not unusual for footballers, even established internationals, to have a second job which they concentrated on in the summer months. Finney was a qualified plumber who played all his career for his hometown club Preston North End, so his nickname was entirely appropriate.

9) Harry 'Slabhead' Maguire

Harry Maguire's outlandishly large head has been celebrated in song by England fans, and also explains his nickname. The Manchester United defender's outsized bonce has proven useful to the Three Lions on numerous occasions, of course, mainly for heading clear dangerous crosses but also for nodding in some vital goals, notably the opener in the 2-0 defeat of Sweden in the quarter-final of the 2018 World Cup in Russia.

10) Jack 'The Giraffe' Charlton

The tough-tackling Leeds defender was dubbed 'The Giraffe' for his long legs and neck, thin, rather pointed face and somewhat ungainly style on the pitch. Nonetheless, Charlton was an extremely effective performer for both club and country, helping the Yorkshiremen win a host of honours and playing in all six matches when England won the World Cup in 1966.

TOP 10 PENALTIES

The most important goals in England's history scored from precisely 12 yards:

1) David Beckham, England 1 Argentina 0, World Cup group stage, 7 June 2002
Four years after being foolishly sent off against Argentina at the 1998 World Cup in France and being vilified by the tabloid press as a result, England captain David Beckham enjoyed a redemptive moment when he scored the only goal of the game against the same opponents in Sapporo at the 2002 finals. The key moment of an absorbing match came just before half-time when Michael Owen was tripped while cutting past Argentina defender Mauricio Pochettino, Italian ref Pierluigi Collina pointing to the spot. Breathing heavily and looking a little nervous, Beckham drilled a hard low shot into the net just past the left leg of goalkeeper Pablo Cavallero to give England a crucial and emotionally charged victory.

2) Gary Lineker, England 3 Cameroon 2, World Cup quarter-final, 1 July 1990
England were trailing the African outfit 2-1 in Naples with only eight minutes to play and facing a shock exit from the 1990 World Cup when Gary Lineker was fouled in the box. The Tottenham striker stepped up to take the penalty himself, sending goalkeeper Thomas N'Kono the wrong way to level the scores. Then, just before the break in extra time, a superb defence-splitting pass from Paul Gascoigne put Lineker clear, only for N'Kono to bring him down. No matter; Lineker smashed the penalty down the middle for the winning goal to send England through to their first World Cup semi-final for 24 years.

3) Harry Kane, England 1 Colombia 1 (England won 4-3 on penalties), World Cup last 16, 3 July 2018
In an earlier match at the 2018 World Cup in Russia, England skipper Harry Kane had scored twice from the spot in a 6-1 rout of Panama in Nizhny Novgorod. In the last 16-tie against Colombia in Moscow he was again called upon to test his nerves in a one-on-one duel with the goalkeeper after he was wrestled to the floor at

a corner on 56 minutes. Once more, Kane rose to the challenge to give his side the lead, firing down the middle as Colombia keeper David Ospina dived to his right. The match eventually finished in a 1-1 draw, but in the shoot-out that decided the tie Kane was one of four England scorers from the spot in a nerve-jangling triumph.

4) Alan Shearer, England 2 Argentina 2 (Argentina won 4-3 on penalties), World Cup last 16, 30 June 1998

In one of the most exciting matches in England's history, Glenn Hoddle's men were trailing to an early Argentina penalty when they were given a chance to equalise after Danish ref Kim Nielsen ruled Michael Owen had been fouled in the box after an enterprising forward run. A hugely experienced penalty taker, Three Lions skipper Alan Shearer thumped home his kick above the dive of Argentina keeper Carlos Roa to level the scores. The Newcastle striker also netted in the shoot-out that followed the nail-biting 2-2 draw with a near-identical penalty, but England were knocked out when Roa saved David Batty's weak spot-kick.

5) Tom Finney, England 2 Soviet Union 2, World Cup group stage, 8 June 1958

In their opening World Cup match in Gothenburg, England were trailing the Soviet Union 2-0 midway through the second half when West Brom striker Derek Kevan reduced the arrears with a close-range header. Six minutes from time the Three Lions were awarded a penalty for a trip on Blackburn winger Bryan Douglas, although legendary Russian goalkeeper Lev Yashin believed the offence took place outside the area and manhandled the Hungarian referee while making his case. Once order was restored, Preston star Tom Finney drilled a low penalty past Yashin into the corner to give England a valuable point.

6) Ron Flowers, England 3 Argentina 1, World Cup group stage, 2 June 1962

Veteran Wolves half-back Ron Flowers was on target from the spot in England's opening match at the 1962 World Cup in Chile, a disappointing 2-1 defeat to Hungary. Two days later he had the opportunity to grab another goal against Argentina in Rancagua when Middlesbrough striker Alan Peacock had a shot handled on the line in the 17th minute. Not one to mess around, Flowers smashed his shot high down the middle to put England ahead in an eventual 3-1 victory which helped the Three Lions qualify for the quarter-finals on goal average at the expense of the South Americans.

7) Allan Clarke, England 1 Poland 1, World Cup qualifier, 17 October 1973

On his England debut, at the 1970 World Cup in Mexico, Leeds striker Allan Clarke showed remarkable composure to score the only goal of a group game against Czechoslovakia from the spot. Three years later he took an even more important penalty against Poland in a must-win World Cup qualifier at Wembley. After laying siege to the Polish goal, England were trailing 1-0 just past the hour when the Belgian ref awarded a penalty for a foul on Martin Peters. Clarke calmly side-footed his shot high into the net to give Sir Alf Ramsey's team hope, but despite continuing to batter away at the Polish defence England could not find a way through and were held to a 1-1 draw which saw them eliminated from the competition.

8) Kevin Keegan, Hungary 1 England 3, World Cup qualifier, 6 June 1981

England's stuttering World Cup qualification campaign was given a timely boost with a vital win in Budapest against Hungary. Ron Greenwood's men were leading 2-1 with just under 20 minutes to play when they were given a golden opportunity to make the game safe, captain Kevin Keegan being brought down in the box as he bore down on goal. Keegan brushed himself down to roll in the spot-kick and secure the first leg of a double over the Hungarians which enabled England to nab one of two qualification spots in a tightly contested group.

9) Frank Lampard, England 1 Austria 0, World Cup qualifier, 8 October 2005

With David Beckham having missed his last three penalties for England, the Three Lions' captain handed over spot-kick duties to Frank Lampard, a regular scorer from 12 yards for Chelsea. It proved to be a wise decision as Lampard calmly slotted home a 25th-minute penalty – awarded after Michael Owen had been pulled back by Austrian defender Paul Scharner – to score what proved to be the only goal of the game at Old Trafford. The narrow victory all but ensured England would be going to the 2006 World Cup finals in Germany, with qualification being guaranteed later that evening after results elsewhere.

10) Alf Ramsey, England 4 Rest of the World XI 4, friendly, 21 October 1953
In a prestigious friendly at Wembley celebrating the 90th anniversary of the Football Association, England were trailing the Rest of the World XI 4-3 in the final minute and facing their first defeat on home soil by opposition from outside the British Isles. However, in a final twist on a dramatic afternoon, the Three Lions were awarded a penalty when centre-forward Stan Mortensen was fouled in the box. Tottenham right-back Alf Ramsey stepped up to take the spot-kick and slammed a powerful shot high past Yugoslav goalkeeper Vladimir Beara.

TOP 10 TATTOOED LIONS

The most impressive inkings among past and present England players:

1) David Beckham
From quite early in his career the former England captain was a tattoo trailblazer, inspiring hundreds of other players and millions of fans to get inked. At the last count, Beckham has around 65 different tattoos, including some on his head, neck and hands – often no-go areas for the more timid enthusiast. The most striking tattoo is on his back – a large, bald, winged figure described by Becks as his 'guardian angel' and created by Manchester-based artist Louis Molloy in 1999. Other tattoos have religious significance or pay tribute to Beckham's four children, and his wife Victoria.

2) Raheem Sterling
The Manchester City forward caused a stir in the build-up to the 2018 World Cup in Russia when he was spotted training

for England with a new tattoo of a machine gun on his right calf. Criticised by anti-gun campaigners, Sterling defended his choice of tattoo, saying it had a 'deeper meaning' and referred to his father, who was shot dead in Jamaica when he was a boy. The England star also has a load of other less-controversial inkings, including a portrait of daughter Melody on his left shoulder, a palm tree on his right forearm and a cross with stars on his chest.

3) Kieran Trippier
Possibly the most tattooed player in England's current squad, the Newcastle right-back has numerous inkings on his arms, including a portrait of his wife Charlotte, two children surrounded by flowers, and an angel. Trippier also has a large tattoo across his chest of a huge diamond ringed by roses.

4) Kyle Walker
The Manchester City defender's heavily inked arms include tattoos of a human eye (a tribute to Walker's late grandfather who introduced him to football) and an angel (commemorating the loss of his sister's baby). On his midriff, meanwhile, large Roman numerals celebrate the birthday of one of his sons.

5) John Stones
The England centre-back has numerous tattoos, including one of Norman Rimmington, his former kit man at his first club, Barnsley, surrounded by roses. Popularly known as 'Mr Barnsley' for his services to the local community, Rimmington died in 2016 aged 93. Stones also has a tattoo on his leg of a favourite school teacher, Bob Runt.

6) Fabian Delph
The veteran utility player has the words 'Family Forever' inscribed across his chest, surrounded by a pair of large wings. Lower down on his torso he has a tattoo of Jesus carrying a cross.

7) Jamie Vardy
In May 2016 the Leicester and England striker underwent a gruelling seven-hour session in a tattoo parlour owned by Foxes captain Wes Morgan, the final design on his torso featuring a

hand holding a stopwatch. He also has a couple of tattoos on his back, one reading 'Carpe Diem' and the other 'Vardy'.

8) Beth England

The England and Chelsea striker is one of the most heavily inked players in the women's game, her tattoos including a trio elephants in tribute to her three sisters and an angel representing a beloved aunt who died of leukaemia. On her lower forearm she has the word 'twin' inscribed in Chinese, a tattoo replicated by her twin sister.

9) Dele Alli

Dele Alli's first name is Bamidele so, obviously, the former England midfielder decided it would be a good idea to get a tattoo of cartoon character Bamm-Bamm Rubble – the adopted son of Barney and Betty in *The Flintstones* – on his left forearm.

10) Ben Chilwell

In a nod to his New Zealand roots – his father Wayne is a Kiwi – the Chelsea and England left-back has a tattoo of the map of the country on his left foreman. Fans, though, were unimpressed when they spotted it during the delayed Euro 2020 finals, with one commenting on social media, 'Trying to work out if that is a simple tattoo on Ben Chilwell's forearm, or someone scribbled on it.'

TOP 10 ONE-CAP WONDERS

The England players who impressed on their debuts but never played for the Three Lions again:

1) Albert Allen

A lightly built inside-forward with Aston Villa, 21-year-old Albert Allen enjoyed a tremendous debut with England, scoring three goals in a 5-1 win against Ireland in Belfast in April 1888. Quite why he was never given a second chance is something of a mystery, especially as he was Villa's top scorer in the inaugural 1888/89 Football League season with 18 goals in 21 matches. Sadly, his career ended prematurely when he contracted tuberculosis and he died from the disease aged 32.

2) Jack Yates

The first Burnley player to be capped by England, 28-year-old Jack Yates made his debut against Ireland at Anfield in March 1889, the fixture clashing with the quarter-finals of the FA Cup which ruled out several established internationals. Yates, though, made the most of his opportunity, scoring a hat-trick in a 6-1 victory, including a spectacular overhead kick for his first goal. He then returned to relative obscurity with the Clarets before later working as a cotton weaver and as the landlord of a pub near to Turf Moor.

3) John Veitch

For England's match against Wales at Wrexham in March 1894 the selectors chose a team made up entirely of players with connections to the amateur Corinthian club. Forward John Veitch was one of three debutants and made a good impression, scoring a hat-trick in a 5-1 win, with his first goal being described by one reporter as 'a shot which no goalkeeper would have stopped'. He later joined the family horticulture business.

4) Walter Gilliat

Called up the day before England played Ireland in Birmingham in February 1893 following an injury to another player, Walter Gilliat took his chance with both hands, scoring a hat-trick inside the opening 30 minutes as the Three Lions romped to a 6-1 win. A forward with the Old Carthusians – the team made up of former pupils of Charterhouse School in Godalming – Gilliat might have won more caps had he not devoted himself to the Church of England, becoming an ordained minister in 1895 and later the vicar of Iver.

5) Joe Payne

Famously, Luton Town half-back Joe Payne was moved to centre-forward for a game against Bristol Rovers in April 1936 and scored an incredible ten goals in a 12-0 rout. Playing as a striker the following season he banged in 55 goals in 39 games as the Hatters won the Third Division South title. Payne's scoring feats alerted the England selectors, and he was picked for a friendly against Finland against Helsinki in May 1937. He scored two goals in an 8-0 win but was not picked again, despite continuing to find the net regularly in the top flight with Chelsea, who he joined in March 1938.

6) Frank Bradshaw

An FA Cup winner with Sheffield Wednesday in 1907, inside-left Frank Bradshaw was picked to play against Austria on a tour match in Vienna the following year. He couldn't have chosen an easier game in which to make his debut as England won 11-1, with Bradshaw contributing three goals. He remains the last of the five players to have scored a hat-trick for the Three Lions in their solitary appearance.

7) William Kenyon-Slaney

Selected to play for England against Scotland in March 1873 in just the second international match, Wanderers forward William Kenyon-Slaney opened the scoring in the second minute after a mistake by the Scottish goalkeeper. As the first meeting between the two sides had ended goalless the previous year, this was the first goal in international football. Kenyon-Slaney added a second on the hour, helping England win the match 4-2. He later became a Conservative MP.

8) Danny Wallace

After scoring five goals in his last five games for Southampton, lively winger Danny Wallace was called up by Bobby Robson for England's friendly against Egypt in Cairo in January 1986. The in-form Wallace scored the Three Lions' third in a rather flattering 4-0 win, neatly volleying in a right-wing cross by Trevor Steven. However, he was competing for a wide spot with the likes of Steven, John Barnes and Chris Waddle and failed to make the cut for the 1986 World Cup squad. Sadly, his later career was cut short by a diagnosis of multiple sclerosis.

9) Phil Parkes

Giant QPR goalkeeper Phil Parkes was one of six new caps in England's team to face Portugal in a friendly in Lisbon in April 1974, Sir Alf Ramsey's last match in charge of the Three Lions. The 23-year-old performed capably enough in a 0-0 draw, but with Peter Shilton and Ray Clemence ahead of him in the pecking order was always going to find his opportunities limited. Parkes was recalled to the England squad by Don Revie for a match against Wales in March 1976, but after not making the substitute appearance he felt he had been promised he decided not to make himself available for international selection again.

10) Tony Kay
When he moved from Sheffield Wednesday to Everton in December 1962 for £60,000, wing-half Tony Kay became Britain's most expensive footballer. By the end of that season he had been installed as the Toffees' skipper and helped them win the league title for the first time since 1939. An England call-up duly followed, and in June 1963 he played and scored in a stunning 8-1 friendly win against Switzerland in Basel. More caps seemed likely to follow but the next year he was implicated in a match-fixing scandal, and in 1965 he was sent to prison for four months and banned from football for life.

TOP 10 EUROPEAN CHAMPIONSHIP GOALS

The best goals scored by England players at the finals of the Euros:

1) Paul Gascoigne, England 2 Scotland 0, group stage, 15 June 1996
Just one minute after England goalkeeper David Seaman had saved a Gary McAllister penalty to preserve England's one-goal lead, Paul Gascoigne received a pass from Darren Anderton, flicked the ball over Scottish defender Colin Hendry's head with his left foot and then smashed in an unstoppable volley from 12 yards with his right. 'It's the best goal I ever scored in an England shirt and the greatest goal ever scored in 100 years at Wembley,' Gazza later recalled. Well, he's certainly right about the first part, and many would agree with him on the second part too.

2) Ray Wilkins, England 1 Belgium 1, group stage, 12 June 1980
In 84 appearances for England Ray Wilkins scored just three goals. However, this one against Belgium in Turin in 1980 was

a real beauty: chesting down a clearance, the midfielder then chipped the ball over an advancing line of Belgian defenders before calmly lobbing over goalkeeper Jean-Marie Pfaff into the top corner. Wilkins' moment of inspiration gave England the lead but Belgium hit back to draw a match which was marred by hooliganism.

3) Wayne Rooney, England 4 Croatia 2, group stage, 21 June 2004

Having announced his arrival on the international scene four days earlier with two goals against Switzerland, 18-year-old Wayne Rooney continued his red-hot form with another brace against Croatia in Lisbon. His first goal just before half-time was a scorcher, a ferocious drive from nearly 25 yards which goalkeeper Tomislav Butina got a hand to but was unable to prevent ripping into the net.

4) Alan Shearer, England 4 Netherlands 1, group stage, 18 June 1996

England's best performance of the Euro '96 finals was adorned by a delightful goal by Alan Shearer to put the Three Lions three up after 57 minutes. Paul Gascoigne was the creator, driving past a Dutch defender before laying the ball back to Teddy Sheringham. The Tottenham striker feinted to shoot, but unselfishly passed the ball to Shearer, who lashed home from 12 yards with a shot which almost burst through the Wembley netting.

5) Luke Shaw, England 1 Italy 1 (Italy won 3-2 on penalties), Final, 11 July 2021

Luke Shaw chose the biggest stage of all to open his account for England, putting the Three Lions ahead in the second minute of the Final of Euro 2020 at Wembley. A sweeping move from one end of the pitch to the other saw skipper Harry Kane play the ball out wide to right wing-back Kieran Trippier. His deep cross to the far post was met on the half-volley by Shaw, who managed to beat Italian Gianluigi Donnarumma with a crisp shot from seven yards.

6) Eric Dier, England 1 Russia 1, group stage, 11 June 2016

In their opening match at the 2016 Euros in Marseille, England had to wait until 17 minutes from the end to break through a stubborn Russian defence. Dele Alli was fouled on the edge of the box and Eric Dier stepped up to curl a delightful shot over the Russian wall and past goalkeeper Igor Akinfeev. However, the Russians hit back with a late equaliser to prevent Roy Hodgson's men claiming all three points.

7) Andy Carroll, England 3 Sweden 2, group stage, 15 June 2012

Lacking subtlety and somewhat immobile, Andy Carroll didn't really look up to international class during his nine England appearances. However, he scored a beautiful goal in this match against Sweden in Kiev, getting on the end of a deep Steven Gerrard cross to head powerfully into the bottom corner from 14 yards. His brilliant effort gave England a 1-0 lead midway through the first half, setting Roy Hodgson's team up for an eventual 3-2 win against their bogey side.

8) Raheem Sterling, England 2 Germany 0, last 16, 29 June 2021

In a tense last-16 encounter at Wembley Raheem Sterling started and finished a superb move to give England a hard-fought lead after 75 minutes. Collecting the ball in midfield, the Manchester City winger darted past two German players before passing to Harry Kane. The England skipper moved the ball on to Jack Grealish, who in turn laid it off to overlapping wing-back Luke Shaw. His firm, low cross was right on the money enabling the onrushing Sterling to side-foot in past Manuel Neuer from six yards.

9) Danny Welbeck, England 3 Sweden 2, group stage, 15 June 2012

An exciting game with Sweden in Kiev was tied at 2-2 with just over ten minutes to play when Theo Walcott burst into the box past two defenders. His cross was just behind Danny Welbeck but somehow the Manchester United striker managed to flick the ball in on the volley with his heel while facing away from goal. The Three Lions held on to win 3-2, their first competitive victory over the Scandinavians in eight attempts.

10) Steven Gerrard, England 3 Switzerland 0, group stage, 17 June 2004

Sven-Göran Eriksson's England wrapped up a comfortable victory against Switzerland in Coimbra, Portugal, with a well-worked goal eight minutes from time. David Beckham fed the overlapping Gary Neville and the Manchester United right-back drilled a low cross across the six-yard box for Steven Gerrard to side-foot home at the far post.

TOP 10 SCANDALS

The times when the Three Lions were front page news for all the wrong reasons:

1) Wembley stormed

On the morning of the Euro 2020 final between England and Italy, thousands of home fans began grouping together outside Wembley in anticipation of one of the most important matches in the Three Lions' history. The majority were ticketless, and many were drunk or under the influence of drugs, creating a threatening atmosphere for fans turning up to attend the match. Around two hours before kick-off hundreds of fans without tickets forced their way into the stadium, despite the efforts of police and stewards to stop them. The unsavoury scenes marred what should have been a showpiece occasion and resulted in the police making over 50 arrests, while UEFA later hit the FA with a fine of €100,000 and ordered England to play one future home match behind closed doors.

2) The Bogotá bracelet

In May 1970, England captain Bobby Moore was accused of stealing a valuable emerald bracelet from the Fuego Verde jewellery store in the lobby of the Hotel Tequendama in Bogotá, Colombia, where the Three Lions were playing a warm-up match ahead of the World Cup in Mexico. When the England squad returned to Bogotá from another friendly in Ecuador, Moore was arrested and detained at the house of a Colombian FA official while the rest of the party flew on to Mexico. After three days he was released and the charges against him were eventually dropped.

3) Nazi salute controversy

Before the start of a friendly match against Germany in Berlin on 14 May 1938, the England team gave the Nazi salute while the German anthem was played, having received a message from the British ambassador that it was vital the players adhered to protocol at a time of delicate relations between the two countries. Many leading Nazi figures were present in the swastika-waving 110,000 crowd, including Hermann Goering, Joseph Goebbels and Rudolf Hess, but they wouldn't have enjoyed what followed – a stunning 6-3 victory for the visitors. Nonetheless, the fact that Stanley Matthews and Co raised their arms in salute of Adolf Hitler's murderous regime remains a dark blot on England's football history.

4) Dublin riot

On 15 February 1995, England travelled to Dublin to play a friendly against the Republic of Ireland. Terry Venables' side were trailing 1-0 midway through the first half when, after a David Platt goal had been ruled out for offside, England fans in the upper tier of a stand began throwing debris on to Irish supporters in the lower tier. The Dutch referee took the players off the pitch and, 12 minutes later, the game was abandoned as missiles continued to rain down. Around 20 people were injured and more than 40 arrests were made in the riot, which was blamed on far-right elements among England's support.

5) Glenn Hoddle's reincarnation comments

In January 1999, England manager Glenn Hoddle gave an interview to *The Times* in which, among other things, he spoke about his belief in reincarnation. He was quoted as saying, 'You and I have been physically given two hands and two legs and half-decent brains. Some people have not been born like that for a reason. The karma is working from another lifetime.' Disability rights groups were outraged by the comments and, a few days after the interview was published, Hoddle and the FA agreed to terminate his contract with the ex-England boss apologising for 'a serious error of judgment'.

6) The dentist's chair

After playing a warm-up match in Hong Kong ahead of Euro '96, several England players celebrated Paul Gascoigne's 29th birthday at the trendy China Jump club. The unique feature of the bar was a dentist's chair which customers would recline in while staff poured a mixture of intoxicating spirits into their gaping mouths. Some of the players found the gimmick irresistible, with results that were completely predictable. The English media was appalled by the players' boozy antics on the eve of a home tournament and the incident was the subject of negative headlines for a few days.

7) Kevin Keegan arrested

Arriving at Belgrade Airport ahead of a match against Yugoslavia in June 1974, some England players were fooling around on the baggage conveyor belt while waiting for their luggage to appear. Although he had only sat down on the belt, Three Lions' striker Kevin Keegan was hauled off by security guards to a back room where he was punched, clubbed and kicked and then charged with sexually assaulting a stewardess, disturbing the peace and causing an obstruction. FA officials soon intervened to secure Keegan's release, and the Liverpool star had the last laugh the following day when he scored a late equaliser in an exciting 2-2 draw.

8) Sent home from Iceland

After making their England debuts in a Nations League victory against Iceland in Reykjavík in September 2020, Phil Foden and Mason Greenwood were sent home in disgrace after meeting up with two local women in breach of coronavirus regulations at the team hotel. The pair were both fined £1,360 by Reykjavík Metropolitan Police and were castigated in the media. 'I made a poor decision and my behaviour didn't meet the standards expected of me,' Foden later admitted in a social media post.

9) Cathay Pacific flight

Flying back from a short tour of the Far East ahead of Euro '96, members of the England squad were accused of damaging some state-of-the-art TV sets and an overhead locker in the upper business class section of a Cathay Pacific plane. At the time, the players adopted a policy of 'collective responsibility' for the incident and they were each docked £5,000 to pay for the repairs. Some years later, however, maverick midfielder Paul Gascoigne admitted he had punched and kicked two of the TV sets.

10) Gazza's tantrum

After being left out of Glenn Hoddle's England squad for the 1998 World Cup in France, Middlesbrough midfielder Paul Gascoigne reacted violently to the bad news at the Three Lions' training camp at the La Manga sports complex in southern Spain. According to Hoddle, Gazza smashed his fist into a large lamp and swore 'like a man possessed' before David Seaman and Paul Ince ran into the room in a bid to calm him down. The talented but temperamental star never played for England again.

TOP 10 INTERNATIONAL BOSSES

The England players who later managed other countries:

1) Jack Charlton

After stints with Middlesbrough, Sheffield Wednesday and Newcastle, the 1966 World Cup winner took over as manager of the Republic of Ireland in 1986. Two years later 'Big Jack' led his adopted country to their first international finals, the European Championship in West Germany where they beat England 1-0 in their opening match in Stuttgart. In 1990 Charlton guided the Republic to the quarter-finals of the World Cup in Italy after they again kicked off their campaign against England, this time with a 1-1 draw in Sardinia. Four years later, his team's direct style of play was not really suited to the roasting conditions in the USA, although the Republic still managed to reach the last 16 before losing to the Netherlands. He retired the following year, after Ireland just missed out on qualification for Euro '96.

2) Tony Waiters

The Blackpool goalkeeper won five caps for England in 1964, but wasn't selected for the World Cup squad two years later. After managing Plymouth between 1972 and 1977, he tried his luck in Canada with Vancouver Whitecaps and in 1981 became the boss of the national side. He led Canada to the quarter-finals of the 1984 Olympics, where they were unlucky to lose to eventual finalists Brazil on penalties. Waiters then guided Canada to victory at the 1985 CONCACAF Championship, ensuring their qualification for the following year's World Cup – their first appearance at the finals. Waiters quit after the tournament, although he briefly managed the side again in 1990.

3) Terry Venables

Five months after leading England to within a whisker of the final of Euro '96, Terry Venables was appointed manager of Australia. The following year he led the Socceroos to the Final of the inaugural Confederations Cup in Saudi Arabia, which they lost 6-0 to reigning world champions Brazil. In November 1997 Venables' side met Iran in a two-legged play-off with a World Cup place in France at stake, but missed out in agonising fashion when they conceded two late goals in the return in Melbourne to be eliminated on the away goals rule. The crushing disappointment led Venables to quit the Socceroos and return to English football with Crystal Palace.

4) Peter Withe

An aggressive striker with Nottingham Forest, Newcastle and Aston Villa, for whom he scored the winning goal in the 1982 European Cup Final, Peter Withe won 11 caps for England in the early 1980s. After a brief spell in charge of Wimbledon he became manager of Thailand in 1998, leading the South-East Asian country to victory in the ASEAN Football Championship in 2000 with a 4-1 win over Indonesia in the Final. Two years later he repeated the feat, following a penalty shoot-out triumph over the same opposition. In 2004 Withe almost made it a hat-trick after becoming Indonesia manager, but his side lost a two-legged Final 5-2 on aggregate to Singapore.

5) John Barnes

After representing England at the 1986 and 1990 World Cups, John Barnes moved into management with Celtic in 1999 but was sacked after just eight months. In September 2008 Barnes became manager of his birth country, Jamaica, leading the Reggae Boyz to first place in their Caribbean Championship group. However, he was keen to return to British football and, after being linked with Port Vale, accepted an offer to become Tranmere boss in June 2009. He might, though, have been better off staying in Jamaica as he was sacked after just 11 league games in charge.

6) Don Revie

After failing to bring England anything like the success he had previously enjoyed as manager of Leeds United, Don Revie jumped ship in the summer of 1977 to become the manager of the United Arab Emirates on an eye-watering £340,000 four-year contract. Despite his massive wage packet, Revie failed to improve the UAE's fortunes, and in 1979 they came sixth out of seven nations at the Arabian Gulf Cup. However, in his three years in charge he did help to improve football facilities in the country, laying the foundations for the Gulf nation's surprise qualification for the 1990 World Cup in Italy.

7) Bill McGarry

A tough-tackling midfielder with Huddersfield, Bill McGarry was capped four times by England in the mid-1950s. A strong disciplinarian, he then managed Bournemouth, Watford, Ipswich and Wolves, guiding Wanderers to a League Cup triumph in 1974. Two years later he took the job as manager of Saudi Arabia, replacing legendary Hungarian Ferenc Puskás. However, he only stayed in the Middle East for 15 months before returning to England with Newcastle. In 1983 McGarry had another short stint in international football, taking charge of Zambia for a year.

8) Ken Armstrong

Wing-half Ken Armstrong was capped once by England in a 7-2 rout of Scotland in 1955 – the same year he helped Chelsea win the league title for the first time in the club's history. He emigrated to New Zealand two years later and shortly afterwards became player-manager of the Kiwis' national team, playing in a further 13 internationals. In six years in charge, he oversaw 11 victories in 32 matches – a significant improvement on previous results. In 1980 Armstrong briefly returned to the international limelight, taking the helm of the New Zealand women's team.

9) Ray Wilkins

The creative midfielder won 84 caps for England between 1976 and 1986 and later tried his hand in management with QPR and Fulham, before assisting Chelsea and the England under-21 side. In September 2014 Wilkins was appointed head coach of Jordan, leading the country at the 2015 Asian Cup, where they failed to qualify from a group also featuring Japan, Iraq and Palestine. Later that year he returned to England to become assistant manager at Aston Villa.

10) Harold Hassall

A striker with Huddersfield and Bolton, Harold Hassall won five caps for England in the early 1950s, scoring a total of four goals. After his career was ended by a knee injury aged 26, he became a lecturer in physical training and an FA coach at Lilleshall. In 1968 he was appointed manager of the Malaysia national side, at a time when the country didn't even enter the World Cup. He held the role for two years, planting the seeds that enabled Malaysia to qualify for the 1972 Olympic football tournament, before returning to England, working as a scout for Preston.

TOP 10 FILM APPEARANCES

1) Bobby Moore, *Escape to Victory*

England's 1966 World Cup-winning captain appeared alongside Michael Caine, Sylvester Stallone, Pelé and Ossie Ardiles in this 1981 World War II prison escape drama which is still a staple of the Christmas television schedules. Moore plays Terry Brady, one of the Allied prisoners who manage to evade their Nazi captors after playing in an exhibition football match against a crack German team, and delivers his occasional lines competently enough while also scoring a lovely volley in the tense 4-4 draw that dominates the latter part of the film.

2) Ian Wright, *Gun of the Black Sun*

The former Arsenal and England striker made an impressive acting debut as Duke in this 2011 action film, whose rather convoluted plot revolves around a World War II Nazi gun with magical powers which resurfaces in modern-day Bucharest. One online review – possibly from a Gunners fan, it has to be said – claimed Wright 'is clearly leagues ahead of Vinnie Jones in the acting stakes'. High praise, indeed!

3) David Beckham, *King Arthur: Legend of the Sword*

The former England captain had a cameo in this big-budget fantasy action adventure film in 2017, playing Trigger – a scarred guard who oversees the prisoners attempting to pull the sword Excalibur from the stone. Reviews of Beckham's performance were not great, however, with *The Telegraph's* critic suggesting he 'showed just enough dramatic range to have played the stone the sword gets stuck in'. Ouch!

4) Stan Collymore, *Basic Instinct 2*

Collymore plays a footballer called Kevin Francis in the 2006 erotic thriller, but is given little time to develop his character as the car he is riding in with star Sharon Stone crashes into the Thames and, before the opening credits are even over, the former Liverpool and England striker is sinking into a watery grave. Perhaps, though, Stan's early exit was all for the best as the film received very negative reviews and flopped at the box office.

5) Tony Currie and Mel Sterland, *When Saturday Comes*

Former England midfielder Tony Currie plays the role of a Sheffield United coach in this sporting drama from 1996, which stars Sean Bean as a hard-drinking non-league footballer who makes the jump into the big time and, somewhat implausibly, scores the winner for the Blades in the FA Cup semi-final against Manchester United. Ironically, Mel Sterland, who spent most of his career with Sheffield Wednesday and won a single England cap in 1988, plays the Sheffield United captain, his half-decent portrayal of a fiery old pro gaining him the acting garlands ahead of the largely mute Currie.

6) Barry Venison, *Mike Bassett: England Manager*

The twice-capped ex-Newcastle defender appears as himself in the 2001 mockumentary, as a studio pundit chatting to England boss Mike Bassett ahead of the start of the World Cup in Brazil. Unfortunately, there is a delay on the line to South America and the conversation between the pair is a rather confused affair. The film, which starred Ricky Tomlinson in the title role, was well-received by fans and was followed by a TV series in 2005.

7) Gary Lineker and John Barnes, *Bend It Like Beckham*
The former England internationals appear as themselves in the 2002 football comedy, in a fantasy sequence set in the *Match of the Day* studio where the duo discuss the skills of young female player Jess Bhamra with fellow pundit Alan Hansen. The film, which starred Parminder Nagra as Jess and Keira Knightley as her Hounslow Harriers team-mate, was a surprise hit, becoming the biggest-grossing 'soccer'-themed film in the USA at the time.

8) Steven Gerrard and Jamie Carragher, *Will*
The 2011 comedy drama film starring Damian Lewis and Bob Hoskins centres around an 11-year-old boy whose dream is to see Liverpool play in the Champions League Final in Istanbul. Setting off to Turkey on his own, he teams up with a former Bosnian footballer before finally reaching his destination, where the Liverpool and England duo kindly sort him out with tickets for the big match.

9) Tommy Lawton, *The Great Game*
One of England's finest centre-forwards, Tommy Lawton was still playing for Arsenal when he had a cameo role as himself in this 1953 film starring James Hayter, Diana Dors and Thora Hird. Based on a play by Basil Thomas, the plot revolves around an illegal approach by a club chairman to buy a star player from a rival team, with many of the scenes being filmed at Brentford's old ground, Griffin Park.

10) Alan Hudson and Peter Osgood, *The Football Factory*
In the cult 2004 film starring Danny Dyer, the two former Chelsea and England stars of the early 1970s appear as themselves on a TV screen in a rowdy pub, making the draw for the FA Cup third round. When they pull out a cracking tie between Millwall and Chelsea, the hooligan firms of the two London rivals can barely contain their glee and are soon planning a violent confrontation which forms the film's pulsating climax.

TOP 10 NIGHTMARE DEBUTS

These players dreamed about pulling on the England shirt for the first time but, sadly, it all went wrong on their big day:

1) Ryan Shawcross and Carl Jenkinson

In the first match at Sweden's new stadium in Stockholm in November 2012, England manager Roy Hodgson gave debuts to six players. With England leading 2-1 and just over a quarter of an hour to play, Hodgson brought on Stoke central defender Ryan Shawcross and Arsenal right-back Carl Jenkinson for their international bows – two of six substitutions he made on the night. Neither player was really up to England standard even at their best, but in their 15 minutes on the pitch they both performed like rabbits in the headlights as Swedish striker Zlatan Ibrahimović battered the Three Lions' defence and added three more goals to the one he had scored in the first half. Given their hellish introduction to international football, both Shawcross and Jenkinson were probably relieved not to be called up again.

2) Tom Wilson

A member of the great Huddersfield Town side which won three consecutive league titles between 1924 and 1926, centre-half Tom Wilson certainly deserved to be capped by England. However, when he was selected for a home fixture against Scotland in March 1928 he was 31 and some way past his best. On one of the most famous days in Scottish football history, Wilson endured a torrid debut as the 'Wembley Wizards' toyed with the English defence and strolled to a superb 5-1 victory. Unsurprisingly, Wilson never appeared for England again and, indeed, he only played a handful more league games before retiring the following year.

3) Hugh Turner

The Huddersfield goalkeeper was given a first England cap on a tour match against France in Paris in May 1931. On six previous trips to France dating back to 1923 England had beaten the home side every time, racking up 25 goals and conceding just six, so the team would have had every reason to feel confident. However, on this occasion, the Three Lions slumped to a 5-2 defeat partly due to a poor goalkeeping display by Turner. He kept his place for a 4-1 win against Belgium in Brussels two days later, but that proved to be his last appearance for England.

4) Ron Henry

New boss Alf Ramsey's first England side for a European Championship preliminary round match against France in Paris in February 1963 featured a debut for Tottenham left-back Ron Henry. A member of the 1961 Spurs Double-winning side, the 28-year-old was given the runaround by French right-winger Maryan Wisniewski, who scored two of his side's goals in a crushing 5-2 win. Although goalkeeper Ron Springett also had a poor night, it was Henry who paid the bigger price as he was never selected by Ramsey again.

5) David Seaman and Mel Sterland

In November 1988 England played a friendly against Saudi Arabia in Riyadh, a match arranged as part of a military trade deal with the oil-rich nation. Prince Charles and Princess Diana were in the crowd to watch Bobby Robson's team stumble to a poorly received 1-1 draw, which saw five players make their England debuts. Among the quintet, QPR goalkeeper David Seaman and Sheffield Wednesday right-back Mel Sterland were both at fault for the home side's goal on 15 minutes scored by local hero Majed Abdullah. Seaman was forgiven, going on to enjoy a long England career; Sterland, on the other hand, never pulled on the Three Lions jersey again.

6) Bedford Jezzard

While playing for Fulham, a mid-table team in the old Second Division, Bedford Jezzard was a surprise selection for England's friendly in Budapest against Hungary in May 1954. The fleet-footed striker could hardly be blamed for the 7-1 defeat – the Three Lions' worst ever reverse – but, all the same, it was a debut best forgotten. He did play once more for England in a 3-0 win against Northern Ireland at Wembley the following year, but enjoyed greater success with the B team, scoring a record six goals in just three games.

7) Jay Rodriguez

With places on the plane to the World Cup in Brazil up for grabs, Southampton forward Jay Rodriguez was given an opportunity to stake his claim by Roy Hodgson when he made his England debut against Chile at Wembley in November 2013. Sadly, he failed to take the chance, a fairly anonymous display in a disappointing 2-0 defeat coming to a premature end when he was replaced by Andros Townsend on 57 minutes. It turned out to be his one and only cap.

8) Brian Stein

Originally from South Africa, Brian Stein became the first African-born player to win a senior England cap when he lined up against France in Paris in February 1984. Playing up front with his Luton strike partner Paul Walsh, Stein should have felt at home but he had a very quiet game and was subbed off 12 minutes from the end of a 2-0 defeat against the soon-to-be European champions. Having failed to impress manager Bobby Robson, he never played for England again.

9) George Robb and Ernie Taylor

Tottenham winger George Robb and Blackpool inside-forward Ernie Taylor both made their debuts for England against Hungary at Wembley in November 1953, a match which the Three Lions lost 6-3 – their first defeat on home soil against continental opposition. With the 'Magical Magyars' dominating possession neither player had much chance to show what he could do with the ball, although of the two Robb was slightly more involved in his team's rare attacking moves. The calamitous defeat led to the selectors calling time on six players' international careers, with both debutants among the casualties.

10) James Beattie

While enjoying a free-scoring season with Southampton, burly striker James Beattie was picked by Sven-Göran Eriksson to play in a friendly against Australia at Upton Park in February 2003. In a poor England performance which ended in a shock 3-1 defeat he barely had a sniff of goal, and was subbed off at half-time – along with the rest of the starting 11. Beattie won another four caps later in the same year, but failed to get on the scoresheet at international level.

TOP 10 HAT-TRICKS

The most memorable of the occasions when an England player claimed the match ball:

1) Geoff Hurst, England 4 West Germany 2, World Cup Final, 30 July 1966

West Ham striker Geoff Hurst became the first – and so far, only – player to score a hat-trick in a World Cup Final, enabling England to win the Jules Rimet Trophy on home soil against West Germany in 1966. His first on 19 minutes was a classic downward header from Hammers team-mate Bobby Moore's flighted free kick to level the scores at 1-1. Eleven minutes into extra time, Hurst put England 3-2 up with one of the most controversial goals in football history, his shot on the turn from Alan Ball's centre bouncing down off the crossbar and either on or just over the line, requiring the Swiss ref to consult with his Russian linesman before pointing to the centre-spot. Then, with just seconds remaining, Hurst controlled Moore's long pass, raced forwards and – ignoring the people on the pitch, who thought it was all over – smashed a powerful left-footer high into the net to seal England's historic triumph.

2) Michael Owen, Germany 1 England 5, World Cup qualifier, 1 September 2001

Germany sweeper Jens Nowotny's pre-match prediction – 'You can't keep Michael Owen quiet for 90 minutes, he will get chances' – proved spot-on as the Liverpool striker scored three fine goals in a wonderful England win in Munich. His first, a firm shot after Nick Barmby had intelligently headed the ball down to him, put England level after the Germans had gone ahead after just six minutes. Another headed knock-down, this time by Emile Heskey from David Beckham's cross, allowed Owen to drill a shot past German goalkeeper Oliver Kahn for his second on 48 minutes, and midway though the second half the livewire striker grabbed his third, collecting Steven Gerrard's incisive pass before knocking in England's fourth goal on the night.

3) Gary Lineker, England 3 Poland 0, World Cup group stage, 11 June 1986

Gary Lineker scored five hat-tricks for England, but this one in a must-win World Cup match against Poland in Monterrey, Mexico, was by far the most important. His first goal, on seven minutes, followed a good England move which ended with right-back Gary Stevens crossing low for Lineker to side-foot home from six yards. Steve Hodge's excellent left-wing cross set up the Everton striker for a half-volleyed finish just six minutes later and Lineker's third goal was gift-wrapped by the Polish goalkeeper when he dropped a corner, allowing the England marksman to lash the ball into the roof of the net to complete a first-half treble.

4) Theo Walcott, Croatia 1 England 4, World Cup qualifier, 10 September 2008

In only his second start for England, 19-year-old Arsenal striker Theo Walcott scored a brilliant hat-trick in Zagreb against a Croatia side which had beaten the Three Lions twice in Euro 2008 qualifiers. Walcott put England ahead on 26 minutes with a hard, low shot from a narrow angle, and doubled his side's lead on the hour with a similar finish from Wayne Rooney's pass. It was Rooney, England's other scorer on the night, who also put Walcott through for his third goal, a low left-footed shot after he had raced clear of the Croatian defence. It was a fabulous start to the youngster's international career, but sadly it was not a performance Walcott would ever come close to matching in an England shirt.

5) Malcolm Macdonald, England 5 Cyprus 0, European Championship qualifier, 16 April 1975

Newcastle United striker Malcolm Macdonald filled his boots against minnows Cyprus at Wembley, becoming only the fourth England player to score five goals in a match and the first to do so under the Twin Towers. Strangely, all but one of his goals were headers – the best coming from a cross by sub Dave Thomas which 'Supermac' powered into the net – the one exception coming in the first half when he jabbed in Kevin Keegan's pull-back with his trusty left foot.

6) Paul Scholes, England 3 Poland 1, European Championship qualifier, 27 March 1999

Paul Scholes got Kevin Keegan's reign as England manager off to a bright start with the only hat-trick of his international career. The ginger-haired midfielder opened the scoring at Wembley after 11 minutes, racing on to Alan Shearer's pass before dinking the ball over the advancing Polish goalkeeper. Ten minutes later, Scholes scored again, heading in David Beckham's superb right-wing cross. The Poles soon pulled a goal back, but Scholes made the game safe for England on 71 minutes with a powerful header into the corner after Gary Neville's long throw was flicked on by Shearer.

7) Bobby Charlton, England 8 Mexico 0, friendly, 10 May 1961

Bobby Charlton was to the fore as England inflicted Mexico's worst defeat in their history, just two years after the central Americans had beaten the Three Lions 2-1 in Mexico City. The Manchester United winger opened his account on 12 minutes, blasting home left-footed from near the penalty spot. His second was a similar effort just after the hour, and on 73 minutes he clinched the third of his four England hat-tricks with a smart shot on the turn from eight yards.

8) Harry Kane, England 5 Albania 0, World Cup qualifier, 12 November 2021

England captain Harry Kane grabbed three goals inside 29 minutes as the Three Lions put Albania to the sword at Wembley, going into the break 5-0 up. After Harry Maguire had headed Gareth Southgate's men in front, Kane nodded in Jordan Henderson's cross to open his account. He then smashed in a left-footer from an angle before completing his hat-trick with the best goal of the lot, an acrobatic scissor-kick volley from Phil Foden's corner. Three days later he went one better, hitting four goals against San Marino.

9) Jimmy Greaves, England 9 Scotland 3, British Home Championship, 15 April 1961

Goal poacher supreme Jimmy Greaves scored a record six hat-tricks for England, with this one against bitter rivals Scotland probably giving him most pleasure. His first on 20 minutes was a typically ruthless finish from a Bobby Smith pass and Smith was involved in Greaves's second, his shot being fumbled by hapless Scottish goalkeeper Frank Haffey straight into the young Chelsea striker's path for a tap-in. As England piled on the goals, Greavsie surprisingly had to wait until the 82nd minute to complete his hat-trick, rounding a couple of Scottish defenders before nonchalantly stroking the ball past Haffey.

10) Jermain Defoe, England 4 Bulgaria 0, European Championship qualifier, 3 September 2010

A reliable scorer off the bench for England, Tottenham striker Jermain Defoe made the most of a rare start for the Three Lions to score his only hat-trick for his country. Ashley Cole set up Defoe for an easy opener in the third minute, after the full-back's shot had rebounded off the Bulgarian goalkeeper. An England break led to Defoe's second just after the hour, Wayne Rooney providing the final pass. Then, with just four minutes left on the clock, Rooney again fed the Spurs man, who finished with aplomb to claim the match ball.

TOP 10 WITTY FAN CHANTS

The chants that have brought a smile to England fans' faces – and sometimes even to supporters of the opposition:

1) 'One Mike Bassett, there's only one Mike Bassett'

After England drew 0-0 with Costa Rica in their final group game at the 2014 World Cup in Brazil, fans of the Three Lions celebrated their team's only point of an abject campaign with this chant in tribute to the hero of the 2001 satirical comedy *Mike Bassett: England Manager*. Were they, by any chance, suggesting that the bumbling Bassett could have done a better job than England's manager at the time, the under-fire Roy Hodgson? Surely not.

2) 'Does your mummy know you're here?'

When England played Egypt at Wembley in a friendly just before the 2010 World Cup in South Africa the home fans expressed their concern for their North African counterparts with this amusing chant, set to the tune of 'Bread of Heaven'. England had the last laugh, too, winning 3-1 on the night.

3) 'You're shit, but your birds are fit!'

Sung to the tune of 'Go West', the disco classic originally by Village People but later memorably covered by the Pet Shop Boys, this chant is invariably rolled out when England play one of the Scandinavian nations. At the 2012 European Championships, Swedish fans responded in kind by chanting, 'Go home to your ugly wives.' Touche!

4) 'Woah, England are in Russia; woah, drinking all your vodka; woah, England's going all the way'

Sung to the tune of the old Earth, Wind and Fire hit 'September', this was a popular chant during England's 2018 World Cup campaign in Russia. In the end, Gareth Southgate's team didn't quite go 'all the way' but they gave it a good go, reaching the semi-finals before losing to Croatia.

5) 'Five-one, even Heskey scored!'

England fans rubbed German noses in the ground by pointing out that not only had their team thrashed their hosts 5-1 in a World Cup qualifier in Munich in September 2001 but that Emile Heskey, a striker with a pitiful goal record at international level, had managed to find the net for once. Another chant set to the ever-popular 'Go West'.

6) 'Are you Scotland in disguise?'

During England's 10-0 win in San Marino in November 2021 the away fans couldn't help pointing out that the mountain-top minnows reminded them a bit of another footballing nation. However, the chant – set to the tune of 'Bread of Heaven' – was rather unfair on Scotland, who have improved greatly in recent years and held England to a 0-0 draw at Wembley in the delayed Euro 2020 finals.

7) 'We didn't start the fire … it was ITV, it was ITV!'

The day before England played away in Andorra in a 2022 World Cup qualifier a fire broke out in the television gantry, destroying the equipment there and even burning a patch of the artificial pitch. During England's comfortable 5-0 victory the next day the visiting fans adapted the old Billy Joel hit 'We Didn't Start the Fire' to point out that they were not to blame for the conflagration, instead trying to pin responsibility on match broadcaster ITV.

8) 'Cheer up, Gordon Strachan'

In a four-year spell as Scotland manager between January 2013 and October 2017 Gordon Strachan led his nation against England four times, without managing a single win (three defeats and a draw). The England fans were remarkably sympathetic to the pint-sized Scot's troubles, urging him on numerous occasions to 'cheer up' in a chant set to the 1967 Monkees hit 'Daydream Believer'.

9) 'Shit Andy Carroll, you're just a shit Andy Carroll'

England fans directed this chant, sung to the tune of 'Guantanamera', at star Swedish striker Zlatan Ibrahimović during a 3-2 win for the Three Lions in Kyiv at Euro 2012. Presumably, the great Zlatan wasn't too pleased at being compared unfavourably to the lumbering English centre-forward as the next time the two sides met, in a friendly in Stockholm a few months later, he scored all four goals in a stunning 4-2 victory for the Swedes.

10) 'Two world wars and one World Cup, doo-dah, doo-dah!'

A chant referencing England's historical encounters with Germany, sung to the tune of 'The Camptown Races', has been a popular one among fans for decades but is rather frowned upon by the authorities. Before the 2006 World Cup in Germany, the Foreign Office attempted (without much success) to dissuade fans from singing the song on German soil for fear of provoking the locals. In Leicester, meanwhile, market traders were banned from selling T-shirts featuring the phrase 'Two world wars and one World Cup' by the local council amid concerns that they 'could cause offence'.

TOP 10 UNLIKELY HELPERS

The people and things that have come to England's aid in their hour of need:

1) Tofiq Bahramov

Tofiq Bahramov was the linesman who raised his flag to signal a goal in the 1966 World Cup Final when Geoff Hurst's shot in extra time struck the underside of the German crossbar and bounced down either on, or just over, the line. After consulting with his silver-haired assistant, Swiss referee Gottfried Dienst pointed to the centre circle, and England took what proved to be a decisive lead in the match. Although often described as 'the Russian linesman', Bahramov was actually from Azerbaijan, and after his death in 1993 the national stadium in Baku was renamed in honour of the eagle-eyed official.

2) Pickles

On 20 March 1966 the World Cup trophy was stolen from Central Hall, Westminster, where it was on public show ahead of that year's finals in England. The police launched a huge operation to recover the prize and eventually arrested 47-year-old Edward Betchley in connection with the theft. The cup was still missing, however, and wasn't found until a black and white mongrel dog called Pickles discovered it under a bush in Beulah Hill, south London. The inquisitive mutt became an instant national hero and was rewarded with a load of his fave nibbles by a dog food company. Sadly, later that same year, Pickles was strangled by his lead while chasing after a cat.

3) Uri Geller

The famous spoon-bender and hypnotist claims to have helped England beat Scotland in the group stage at Euro '96. Terry Venables' team were leading 1-0 when the Scots were awarded a penalty with less than 15 minutes to play. Geller, who was circling Wembley in a helicopter at the time, says he used his mind-over-matter powers to make the ball move slightly just as Gary McAllister ran up to take his kick. Whether it was some form of telepathy or just a gust of wind, the ball did seem to move a fraction, but most of the credit must go to England goalkeeper David Seaman who made a superb save from McAllister's fiercely struck shot.

4) Danny Makkelie

Dutch referee Danny Makkelie became something of a hero to

England fans when he awarded the Three Lions a controversial penalty in extra time of their Euro 2020 semi-final against Denmark. There didn't seem to be a great deal of contact when Raheem Sterling went down in the box when challenged by Joakim Mæhle, but Makkelie pointed to the spot and his decision was confirmed by the VAR officials. Although his spot-kick was saved by Kasper Schmeichel, Harry Kane scored from the rebound to send England through to the final and leave Denmark fuming. 'It was a penalty which was not a penalty,' said furious Danish boss Kasper Hjulmand afterwards.

5) Sean Connery

The day after England began their 1966 World Cup campaign with a frustrating 0-0 draw with Uruguay at Wembley, boss Alf Ramsey decided to lighten the mood by taking his squad to Pinewood Studios to meet the cast of the James Bond film *Thunderball*. Among the famous names the players encountered on the set were Yul Brynner, Britt Ekland, Cliff Richard and, of course, 007 himself, Sean Connery. After a fun day out, Bobby Moore and Co. returned to their hotel in Hendon in much better spirits and four days later beat Mexico 2-0 in their second match of the tournament.

6) Eileen Drewery

The Essex pub landlady turned faith healer was an important member of England's inner sanctum during Glenn Hoddle's time as manager between 1996 and 1999. A room was made available for her at the team's hotel in Burnham Beeches, near Maidenhead, and players were told they could visit her if they had an injury or wanted to discuss a personal problem. Some England players, including winger Darren Anderton, felt they were helped by their sessions with Drewery but others treated her as a joke figure. Famously, when she put her hands on midfielder Ray Parlour's head and asked him what he wanted, he quipped back, 'A short back and sides, please!'

7) Findus

Concerned that the local spicy cuisine would not agree with his players, Sir Alf Ramsey arranged with frozen food specialists

Findus for a refrigerated container packed with beefburgers, sausages and fish fingers to be flown out to Mexico ahead of the 1970 World Cup. Unfortunately, the Mexican authorities deemed that England was a foot and mouth disease-afflicted country and ordered that the meat products be destroyed on their arrival. The result was that the players' diet consisted mainly of fish fingers and chips for the duration of the tournament. 'I've never eaten a fish finger since,' recalled midfielder Alan Mullery. 'We ate so many, it's put me off for life.'

8) Debbie Jackson

Although England beat France 3-1 in their opening match in Bilbao at the 1982 World Cup the players complained afterwards that their thick polyester shirts were extremely uncomfortable to wear in the scorching conditions. So, a request was sent to England's kit supplier Admiral to provide a lighter kit as a matter of urgency. Five new kits in a more breathable material were quickly produced at the Admiral HQ in Leicester and then driven by design manager Debbie Jackson to Manchester Airport, where she spent the night at a hotel sewing on all the badges and logos by hand. Inevitably, tiredness took its toll and not all the badges were in exactly the right place – but nobody could question her commitment to the England cause!

9) Japanese fans

Around 8,000 England fans travelled to Japan to support their team at the 2002 World Cup, which was also co-hosted by South Korea, but their numbers were boosted by thousands of Japanese supporters who adopted the Three Lions as their favourite team – a phenomenon partly explained by the huge popularity of then-Three Lions' skipper David Beckham in the Land of the Rising Sun. 'I like him more than all the others put together,' was one young female fan's verdict. Roared on by a combination of English and Japanese fans, Sven-Göran Eriksson's team reached the quarter-finals before losing to eventual winners Brazil.

10) Olga Stringfellow

In a last-ditch attempt to heal his Achilles tendon injury, England skipper Bryan Robson requested to see a faith healer at the 1990

World Cup in Italy. Olga Stringfellow was duly flown out by the FA and tried to work her magic on the stricken midfielder, but without success: Robson played no further part in the tournament and could only watch from the sidelines as his team-mates reached the semi-final.

TOP 10 TEENAGE TYROS

Barely out of school, these players still managed to make a big splash for England:

1) Wayne Rooney
Everton striker Wayne Rooney was just 17 years and 111 days when he played his first game for England, coming on as a half-time sub in a 3-1 friendly defeat to Australia at Upton Park in February 2003 – at the time he was his country's youngest ever player, although he has since ceded that title to Theo Walcott. Rooney was still only 18 when he was the Three Lions' outstanding player at Euro 2004, scoring four goals in total and earning comparisons with the legendary Pelé from his manager, Sven-Göran Eriksson. It was just the start of a wonderful England career for the boy from Croxteth, who went on to score a record 53 goals in 120 internationals.

2) Michael Owen
A teenage phenomenon with Liverpool, Michael Owen was aged 18 years and 59 days when he made his England debut in a 2-0 friendly defeat against Chile at Wembley in February 1998. The speedy striker went on to star at that summer's World Cup in France, scoring a sensational solo goal against Argentina that made him one of the game's hottest properties. Unfortunately, a series of hamstring injuries robbed him of some of his pace but he still had an excellent England career, scoring 41 goals in 89 appearances.

3) Theo Walcott
Lightning-quick Arsenal winger Theo Walcott became England's youngest ever player when he came on as a 65th-minute sub in a

3-1 friendly win against Hungary at Old Trafford in May 2006. He was a surprise choice in Sven-Göran Eriksson's squad for that summer's World Cup, having yet to appear in the Premier League for the Gunners after joining from Championship side Southampton, but failed to come off the bench in Germany. He went on to win 47 caps, scoring eight goals.

4) Duncan Edwards

Powerful midfielder Duncan Edwards was aged 18 years and 183 days when he made an impressive debut for England in a 7-2 rout of Scotland at Wembley in April 1955. Twice a league title-winner with Manchester United, Edwards had already accumulated 18 caps and had a glittering future ahead of him when he tragically died, aged just 21, from injuries he sustained in the Munich air crash in February 1958.

5) Raheem Sterling

Liverpool winger Raheem Sterling had played just 20 senior games when he was chosen by Roy Hodgson to make his England debut in a 4-2 friendly defeat against Sweden in Stockholm in November 2012. Although he had to wait another 16 months for a second cap, the fleet-footed Sterling was still only 19 when he played in all three games at the 2014 World Cup in Brazil. He has gone on to win over 70 caps, starring for England at the delayed Euro 2020 finals.

6) Micah Richards

Energetic Manchester City right-back Micah Richards was aged 18 years and 144 days when he made his England debut in a 1-1 draw against the Netherlands in Amsterdam in November 2006. Strangely, he won 11 of his 13 caps while still a teenager as injuries disrupted his later career and robbed him of his searing pace. However, he enjoyed success with City, winning the FA Cup in 2011 and the Premier League the following year.

7) James Prinsep

Clapham Rovers half-back James Prinsep became England's youngest ever player when he featured in an exciting 5-4 win against Scotland at Kennington Oval in April 1879. Aged just 17 years and 252 days, it was a record Prinsep would hold until Wayne

Rooney beat it in 2003. Although he never again played for the Three Lions, Prinsep won the FA Cup with the Old Carthusians in 1881. A captain in the Essex Regiment, he served in Egypt before dying from pneumonia aged 34 while on holiday in Scotland.

8) Jude Bellingham
Borussia Dortmund midfielder Jude Bellingham became England's third-youngest player when he made his debut as a substitute in a 3-0 win against the Republic of Ireland at Wembley in November 2020, aged 17 years and 136 days. The following year he became his country's youngest ever player at the European Championship when he came on against Croatia in England's opening match. Incredibly, in his first ten international matches (three starts and seven appearances as a sub) England won all the games without conceding a single goal.

9) Callum Hudson-Odoi
Chelsea winger Callum Hudson-Odoi had a good first experience with England, coming on as a sub in a European Championship qualifier against the Czech Republic at Wembley in March 2019, when aged 18 years and 135 days, and forcing an own goal in a convincing 5-0 win. However, he has only played twice more for his country, his progress slowed by injury and the stiff competition for attacking slots at Stamford Bridge.

10) Tot Rostron
Darwen winger Tot Rostron was aged just 17 years and 311 days when he made his England debut in a 1-0 defeat against Wales in February 1881 – at the time his country's second-youngest player, although he has since dropped to fifth in the rankings. He played in the Three Lions' next match – a humiliating 6-1 home loss to Scotland – before disappearing from the international scene. He died aged just 28, following a short illness.

TOP 10 ENGLAND WOMEN EUROPEAN CHAMPIONSHIP WINS

After several near misses, including defeats in the Final in 1984 and 2009, the Lionesses finally won the European Championship on home soil in 2022. Unsurprisingly, matches from that fantastic tournament dominate this list:

1) England 2 Germany 1, Final, 31 July 2022

After a tense first half in front of a record 87,192 crowd at Wembley, England took the lead against eight-time winners Germany just after the hour when sub Ella Toone raced on to Keira Walsh's defence-splitting pass and calmly lobbed the ball over goalkeeper Merle Frohms. The Germans, though, hit back with a close-range strike from Lina Magull to take the match into extra time. Ten minutes from the end another England sub, Chloe Kelly, poked the ball over the line from a couple of yards out for the winning goal, sparking ecstatic celebrations in the stadium and all over the country.

2) England 4 Sweden 0, semi-final, 26 July 2022

The Lionesses might have fallen behind at a packed Bramall Lane in the first minute but for a good save by goalkeeper Mary Earps and they endured a sticky start before Beth Mead fired them ahead with a smart turn and shot from Lucy Bronze's cross on 34 minutes. Early in the second half, Bronze headed in Mead's deep corner although England's celebrations were delayed until after a VAR check had been completed. Supersub Alessia Russo then made the game safe with an outrageous back-heel and the tireless Fran Kirby wrapped up a magnificent victory when she chipped the ball over the head of Swedish goalkeeper Hedvig Lindahl.

3) England 2 Netherlands 1, semi-final, 6 September 2009

England reached the final of the European Championship for just the second time in their history thanks to a narrow victory over an extremely defensive Netherlands side. The Lionesses had to wait until the hour mark to take the lead when Eni Aluko squared for Kelly Smith to score from six yards. The Dutch, though, equalised three minutes later through Marlous Pieëte and held on to the end of normal time. In the first minute of extra time Lianne Sanderson smashed a shot against the bar but England were not to be denied, and eventually won the match when Jill Scott headed in Karen Carney's corner. However, the final proved to be a forgettable occasion for Hope Powell's team, who were thrashed 6-2 by Germany in Helsinki.

4) England 2 Spain 1, quarter-final, 20 July 2022
England struggled to gain control against a technically gifted Spanish side at the Amex Stadium, and had to dig deep after falling behind to Esther González's composed finish on 54 minutes. Only six minutes were left on the clock when two subs combined to bring Sarina Wiegman's side level, Ella Toone volleying in Alessia Russo's headed knockdown. Spain vainly appealed for a foul by Russo, but they could have no complaints about Georgia Stanway's magnificent winner five minutes into extra time, the midfielder powering forward before unleashing an unstoppable blockbuster from the edge of the box.

5) Denmark 0 England 1, semi-final second leg, 28 April 1984
The Lionesses secured their place in the final of the 1984 European Championship after a goal by midfielder Debbie Bampton just before half-time in Hjørring secured a 3-1 aggregate victory over Denmark. England drew 1-1 with Sweden over the two-legged final, but lost 4-3 in the shoot-out at Kenilworth Road after both Linda Curl and Lorraine Hanson had their spot-kicks saved.

6) England 1 France 0, quarter-final, 30 July 2017
England made it through to the semi-finals of the 2017 European Championship after a tense win against France in the Dutch city of Deventer. The crucial moment of a tight encounter came just before the hour when Lucy Bronze surged forward with the ball, and then slipped in Jodie Taylor to shoot in from a narrow angle – her fifth goal of the tournament.

7) England 2 Denmark 1, semi-final first leg, 8 April 1984
After easily qualifying with two wins apiece against Scotland, Northern Ireland and the Republic of Ireland, England met Denmark over two legs in the semi-final. In the first match at Gresty Road, Linda Curl gave England a first-half lead before they were pegged back just after half-time by Inge Hindkjær's penalty. Two minutes later, though, Liz Deighan popped up with the winner to give the Lionesses an advantage to take with them to Denmark.

8) England 8 Norway 0, group stage, 11 July 2022

Norway were expected to provide England with stiff opposition at the Amex Stadium, but the side rated the 11th-best in the world were torn apart by the rampant Lionesses. Arsenal's Beth Mead grabbed the headlines with a hat-trick, which included a brilliant individual goal as England roared into a 6-0 half-time lead. England's all-time top scorer Ellen White nabbed two, while Georgia Stanway with a penalty, Lauren Hemp and sub Alessia Russo were also on target as the Lionesses recorded the biggest ever win at the tournament.

9) England 3 Finland 2, quarter-final, 3 September 2009

After qualifying from their group as one of the best third-placed teams, England got the better of hosts Finland in a five-goal thriller in Turku. Striker Eni Aluko slotted home after 15 minutes to give England the lead, with Fara Williams doubling the Lionesses' advantage shortly after the break. The Finns pulled one back from a corner midway through the second half, but just a minute later Aluko smashed the ball into the net after dribbling past three defenders. The home side cut the deficit late on from another corner but it was not enough to prevent England progressing further in the competition.

10) England 3 Russia 2, group stage, 28 August 2009

After losing their opening match to Italy, England needed to get their campaign going against Russia, supposedly the weakest team in the group. However, in Helsinki the Russians soon showed they were no makeweights, roaring into a two-goal lead after 22 minutes. The Lionesses, though, pulled a goal back through a low left-footer from Karen Carney before Eni Aluko equalised with a firm shot from close range. Three minutes from the break, striker Kelly Smith grabbed what proved to be an extraordinary winner, controlling the ball just inside her opponents' half and then lobbing the Russian goalkeeper from fully 50 yards.

TOP 10 BASED-ABROAD PLAYERS

The England internationals who represented their country while plying their trade in largely sunnier climes:

1) David Beckham

After winning a host of silverware with Manchester United, including the Champions League and domestic Double in 1999, David Beckham joined Real Madrid for £25m in July 2003. In a four-year stay with the Spanish giants he won La Liga in 2007, while captaining England at the 2004 Euros and the 2006 World Cup. Famed the world over for his pinpoint crosses and accurate delivery from dead balls, Beckham moved on to MLS outfit LA Galaxy in 2007 and in 2009 had a loan spell with AC Milan. In all he won a record 55 of his 115 England caps while with foreign clubs, although the majority of his latter appearances under then Three Lions manager Fabio Capello were as a substitute.

2) David Platt

A year after impressing in the England team that reached the World Cup semi-finals in 1990, attacking midfielder David Platt joined Bari from Aston Villa in a £5.5m deal. He would spend the next four seasons in Italian football, helping Juventus win the UEFA Cup in 1993 before moving on to Sampdoria. Meanwhile, Platt was the star man in an underperforming England team, captaining the side and scoring an impressive 19 goals in 33 games while he was based in Italy, including seven in the Three Lions' failed qualification bid for the finals of the 1994 World Cup in the USA.

3) Gary Lineker

After scoring six goals for England at the 1986 World Cup to win the Golden Boot, Gary Lineker joined Barcelona from Everton for £2.75m. While with the Catalan giants, the prolific striker won the Copa del Rey and the European Cup Winners' Cup. He also collected 24 caps while based in Spain and scored 17 goals, including all four in England's 4-2 friendly win against his adopted nation in Madrid in February 1986. In the summer of 1989 he returned to England, rejecting interest from Manchester United to team up again with his old Barça boss, Terry Venables, at Tottenham.

4) Kevin Keegan

After helping Liverpool win the European Cup for the first time in 1977, England captain Kevin Keegan joined Hamburg for

£500,000. In a brilliant three-year stint in German football, the diminutive striker helped Hamburg win the Bundesliga title in 1979 and was twice voted European Footballer of the Year. His time away from English football, though, coincided with a decline in the fortunes of the national team, which failed to qualify for the 1978 World Cup and made little impression at the 1980 Euros in Italy. However, Keegan's standards never dropped and he scored 12 goals in the 25 games he played for England while based on the continent.

5) Owen Hargreaves

Born and raised in Canada by British parents, Owen Hargreaves moved to Germany to join Bayern Munich aged 16 in 1997. The hardworking defensive midfielder went on to win four Bundesliga titles with the German giants as well as the Champions League in 2001. In the same year he made his Three Lions debut against the Netherlands at White Hart Lane, becoming the first England player who had never lived in the country to win senior honours. Hargreaves won 39 of his 42 caps while with Bayern and was voted England Player of the Year in 2006.

6) Trevor Francis

A mobile striker who could play in a central position or out wide, Trevor Francis became Britain's first £1m player when he joined Nottingham Forest from Birmingham City in February 1979, repaying much of that fee when he scored the winner for his new club in the European Cup Final against Malmö. In 1982, following a short spell with Manchester City, he joined Sampdoria for £700,000. In a four-year stint in Italy he won the Coppa Italia in 1985 and gained another 20 England caps, taking his total to 52 by the time he appeared on the international stage for the last time in a 2-1 defeat of Scotland at Wembley in April 1986.

7) Mark Hateley

Shortly after scoring for England with a header in a famous 2-0 win away to Brazil in June 1984, Mark Hateley joined AC Milan from second-tier Portsmouth in a £1m deal. Nicknamed 'Attila' for his battling performances up front with the *Rossoneri*, he won 20 caps while based in Italy, including three at the 1986 World

Cup in Mexico, and a further seven after moving to Monaco the following year. The last of his 32 caps came in 1992, by when he had returned to the UK with Rangers.

8) Ray Wilkins

First capped as a teenager with Chelsea, Ray Wilkins moved on to Manchester United before joining Italian giants AC Milan in 1984. The smooth-passing midfielder won 22 caps for the Three Lions while enjoying *la dolce vita*, but blotted his copybook by being sent off against Morocco at the 1986 World Cup after throwing the ball at the referee. Wilkins only played twice more for England after that notorious incident, taking his total number of caps to an impressive 84.

9) Chris Waddle

Having previously played for Newcastle and Tottenham, talented winger Chris Waddle joined Marseille for £4.5m in July 1989. Over the next three seasons he won a trio of league titles with the French club, was a runner-up in the European Cup and won the last 17 of his 62 England caps. Waddle had some of his best games for his country at the 1990 World Cup in Italy but, sadly, his tournament ended in disaster when he skied his penalty over the bar in the semi-final shoot-out against West Germany in Turin.

10) Tony Woodcock

After helping Nottingham Forest win the league title and European Cup in consecutive seasons, nippy striker Tony Woodcock joined German side Cologne in 1979. In a three-year stint with the Bundesliga outfit he played for England 16 times, representing his country at the 1980 Euros in Italy, where he scored in a 2-1 win against Spain. Just before the 1982 World Cup he returned to England, signing for Arsenal with whom he won the last of his 42 caps in February 1986.

TOP 10 PENALTY SAVES

The England goalkeepers who thwarted the opposition from the penalty spot:

1) David Seaman, England 2 Scotland 0, European Championship group stage, 15 June 1996

In an eagerly anticipated derby at Euro '96, England were leading Scotland at Wembley through Alan Shearer's header when the visitors were awarded a 78th-minute penalty for Tony Adams' foul on Gordon Durie. Gary McAllister hit his spot-kick hard and high but, diving to his right, Arsenal goalkeeper David Seaman pulled off a fantastic save, diverting the ball over the bar with his left elbow. It proved to be the pivotal moment in the match, made all the more significant as Terry Venables' men wrapped up victory just a minute later with a marvellous individual goal from midfield maverick Paul Gascoigne.

2) Ray Clemence, England 2 Spain 1, European Championship group stage, 18 June 1980

Having picked up just one point from their first two games, England still had an outside chance of making the third-fourth place play-off against Czechoslovakia at the 1980 Euros when they faced Spain in Naples. With the scores tied at 1-1 on 54 minutes, Southampton defender Dave Watson was penalised and Spain were awarded a second spot-kick. Dani scored again from 12 yards but was ordered to retake his kick, and this time Liverpool goalkeeper Ray Clemence dived to his right to make a vitally important save. Tony Woodcock grabbed the winner for the Three Lions on the hour, but it wasn't enough to prolong England's interest in the tournament.

3) Joe Hart, England 2 Brazil 1, friendly, 6 February 2013

England and Brazil were drawing 0-0 in a friendly at Wembley in February 2013 when the visitors were awarded a rather soft penalty, given for handball against Jack Wilshere as he turned away from Ronaldinho's cross into the box and the ball struck his arm. Ronaldinho took the spot-kick himself, but Joe Hart dived to his left to save and then blocked the Brazilian's attempted tap-in from the rebound with his right hand. The extremely close shave seemed to inspire England who went on to record a memorable 2-1 win against the five-time world champions.

4) Bill Rowley, Ireland 0 England 2, British Home Championship, 5 March 1892

Nine months after penalty kicks were approved by the International Football Association Board, England conceded their first one late in the second half while leading Ireland 2-0 in Belfast. Stoke goalkeeper Bill Rowley rose to the historic occasion, diving to save from Sam Torres and then blocking Bill Dalton's follow up. Despite his heroics, Rowley was not selected for England again, his international career amounting to just two caps.

5) Paul Robinson, Spain 1 England 0, friendly, 17 November 2004

In a friendly in Madrid tarnished by racist chants from the home fans, England were trailing to an early headed goal by Asier del Horno when Three Lions' goalkeeper Paul Robinson was harshly judged to have brought down Spain striker Raúl. However, the Tottenham goalkeeper ensured justice was done, diving to his left to make an excellent save from Raul's well-struck spot-kick and then punching the air with delight as the loose ball was whacked downfield.

6) Peter Shilton, England 3 West Germany 0, friendly, 12 June 1985

Sadly, Peter Shilton was unable to stop any of West Germany's spot-kicks in the 1990 World Cup semi-final shoot-out in Turin, but five years earlier he made a good penalty save against the same opposition in a friendly in Mexico City. England were leading through Bryan Robson's well-placed shot when, just before half-time, the Germans were given a golden chance to equalise after Southampton defender Mark Wright chopped down Uwe Rahn. Shilton, also with the Saints at the time, crouched low on his line before springing to his left to turn Andreas Brehme's kick around the post for a corner.

7) Nigel Martyn, England 3 Spain 0, friendly, 28 February 2001

On a rainy night at Villa Park, new England boss Sven-Göran Eriksson took charge of the Three Lions for the first time and was delighted to see his side roar into a three-goal lead. The only blemish on an otherwise near-perfect occasion came on 78 minutes when Middlesbrough defender Ugo Ehiogu, scorer of England's third goal with a powerful header from a corner, was judged to have tripped Spanish sub Javi Moreno in the box. Moreno stepped up to take the penalty himself, but his effort was palmed away by Leeds goalkeeper Nigel Martyn who dived to his left to make a fairly comfortable save.

8) Gordon Banks, Brazil 2 England 1, friendly, 12 June 1969

Gordon Banks produced arguably the greatest save in the history of the game at the 1970 World Cup against Brazil, when he somehow managed to divert Pelé's bullet header for a corner. By comparison, this penalty save against the same opposition in the Maracanã Stadium in Rio was no more than routine, the Stoke keeper diving to his right to snaffle up Carlos Alberto's tame spot-kick. At the time England were leading through Colin Bell's close-range opener, but the home side hit back with two late goals from Tostão and Jairzinho to delight the massive crowd of around 135,000.

9) Ron Springett, England 2 Northern Ireland 1, British Home Championship, 18 November 1959

England were leading 1-0 in this British Home Championship fixture at Wembley when a jinking run by Northern Ireland midfielder Jimmy McIlroy was ended after he was sandwiched by two England defenders as he bore down on goal. The Burnley maestro took the penalty himself, but his weak side-footed shot was pounced on by Sheffield Wednesday's Ron Springett on his Three Lions debut. Northern Ireland did manage to equalise late on through Billy Bingham, but an even later goal by Bolton's Ray Parry gave England a hard-fought victory.

10) Harry Hibbs, Wales 0 England 4, British Home Championship, 22 November 1930

A minute after taking a commanding 3-0 lead against Wales in Wrexham, England gave the home side a glimmer of hope after conceding a penalty for handball. However, Wales skipper

Fred Keenor struck his shot pretty much straight at Harry Hibbs and the Three Lions' goalkeeper saved easily. Just a minute later Hibbs's Birmingham City team-mate Joe Bradford rounded off a comfortable victory with England's fourth goal.

TOP 10 BIZARRE MOMENTS

The incidents which had England players and fans scratching their heads:

1) Matches without fans

The Covid-19 pandemic created death and misery around the globe and also had a huge impact on sport, causing many events to be postponed or cancelled entirely. In England the 2019/20 season was brought to a shuddering halt in the spring, with the result that the Three Lions did not play a match of any description for almost ten months. When fixtures resumed they were played behind closed doors with no fans allowed anywhere near the stadiums, let alone inside. Starting with a 1-0 win in Iceland in the Nations League in September 2020, England played a total of 11 matches in empty grounds before a crowd limited to under 9,000 was permitted into the Riverside Stadium in Middlesbrough to see the Three Lions beat Austria 1-0 in a friendly in June 2021. Larger crowds then attended that month's matches at the Euro 2020 finals, which had been put back a year due to the pandemic.

2) Goalkeeping confusion

Rather like a ragtag Sunday league team, England struggled to find a regular goalkeeper in the early days of the national team, with no fewer than 14 players filling the position in the Three Lions' first 12 games. In two of these matches England fielded two different keepers: Robert Barker and William Maynard both playing a half in goal and a half as outfielders in the first international against Scotland in 1872; then, three years later, striker Alex Bonsar played the opening ten minutes between the sticks before the nominated goalkeeper, Bill Carr of Owlerton FC, arrived. The first goalkeeper to turn out more than once for

England was John Hawtrey of London-based Remnants FC and the Old Etonians who played against Wales and Scotland in 1881 – a full nine years after the Three Lions' first match!

3) Kit chaos

England's opening match of the 1982 World Cup against France took place on a scorchingly hot day in Bilbao, with the thermometer touching 33° Celsius at pitch level. To make matters worse, the team had been issued with thick polyester shirts, more suited to a cold winter's evening in Stoke than a summer afternoon in Spain. Adding to England's kit woes, the red numbers ironed on to the shorts to satisfy a new FIFA protocol began to peel off under the burning sun. 'None of them seemed to stick on,' recalled centre-half Terry Butcher. 'The pitch was littered with our numbers by the end. It was embarrassing.' However, England played brilliantly on the day and won the match 3-1 with two goals from midfielder Bryan Robson and one from striker Paul Mariner.

4) Bobby Moore plays for the opposition

In May 1976 England played in the USA Bicentennial Cup, a four-team tournament to celebrate the 200th anniversary of the American Declaration of Independence. The three other teams involved were Brazil, Italy and Team America, whose multinational squad was made up of players performing in the North American Soccer League. After a 1-0 defeat to Brazil and a 3-2 win against Italy, the Three Lions lined up in Philadelphia against a Team America side captained by Bobby Moore, England's legendary 1966 World Cup-winning skipper. Moore, who was playing a summer season for San Antonio Thunder on loan from Fulham, ended up on the losing side as England won 3-1 in a match which was not recognised as a full international by the FA.

5) Two matches on the same day

On three occasions in the early 1890s England played two matches on the same day. Fortunately, perhaps, none of the players involved appeared in both games, the selectors deciding to use entirely different teams for the matches against Wales and Ireland which were viewed essentially as trials for the much more important fixture against Scotland later in the season. The unusual policy worked well, with England winning all three of the double-headers while banging in a total of 26 goals and conceding just four.

6) The 'scorpion kick'

A dreary 0-0 draw with Colombia at Wembley in September 1995 would have been erased from England fans' collective memory bank but for one amazing incident midway through the first half. Playing in his first match for England, Liverpool midfielder Jamie Redknapp received the ball 25 yards out and chipped it into the penalty area. However, his cross was mishit and looked to be drifting into the hands of Colombia goalkeeper René Higuita. Rather than catching the ball, though, Higuita lived up to his nickname – 'El Loco' ('the crazy man') – and let it sail over his head before diving forwards and clearing from the goal line with his heels, a totally unconventional save later dubbed the 'scorpion kick'.

7) Matthews' bare-faced cheek

In September 1947 England crossed the Channel to play in a friendly in Brussels to mark the Golden Jubilee of the Belgian FA. Wing wizard Stanley Matthews was the star of the show, setting up all of England's goals in a 5-2 win and earning a standing ovation from the 62,500 crowd. However, it was Matthews' involvement in England's final goal which really got tongues wagging, as boss Walter Winterbottom later recalled, 'He took off on one of his dribbles from the halfway line and the centre-half, who was wearing gloves, dived at him to try to rugby tackle him to the ground. Instead, he pulled Stan's shorts down. Stan never flinched, went on with his mazy dribble even with his shorts around his knees. He ended the breathtaking run with a delicate chip for Tom Finney to score.' A 'cheeky' goal, indeed.

8) All change v Oz

Ahead of England's friendly with Australia at Upton Park in February 2003 Three Lions' boss Sven-Göran-Eriksson announced that he would use the occasion to play one team in the first half and a totally different XI after the break. He was good to his word, so the likes of David Beckham, Rio Ferdinand and Michael Owen were withdrawn at half-time, with the home side surprisingly trailing 2-0. For the first time in an England international, a completely different set of players came on for the second half, including debutants Jermaine Jenas, Paul Robinson and Wayne Rooney. The youngsters actually performed better than the senior pros, drawing their 45-minute 'match' 1-1 thanks to a goal from another player making his debut, Arsenal striker Francis Jeffers. However, with England going down to a 3-1 defeat, it was not an experiment Eriksson tried again.

9) Fan fury

After a disappointing 1-1 draw with the USA in their opening match at the 2010 World Cup in South Africa, England produced an even more disjointed display in their next game, drawing 0-0 with minnows Algeria in Cape Town. The thousands of Three Lions fans in the stadium let their feelings be known, booing the England team off the pitch. However, one fan, 32-year-old Pavlos Joseph from London, took his protest a stage further, somehow finding his way into the England dressing room while looking for a toilet and telling former captain David Beckham, a member of Fabio Capello's coaching team, that the performance was 'a disgrace'. Rather unfairly, Joseph was arrested, charged with trespassing and 12 days later fined around £35.

10) Jimmy's canine pal

Soon after the start of England's 1962 World Cup quarter-final against Brazil in Viña del Mar, Chile, a small black dog wandered on to the pitch, halting play. Crouching down on his haunches, Three Lions' striker Jimmy Greaves beckoned the little pooch over and was able to grab him before handing him over to a steward. Unfortunately, the mutt didn't care for being manhandled and responded by urinating all over Greaves's pristine white England shirt. With nobody laying claim to the dog, it was raffled off to the Brazilian squad with winger Garrincha, scorer of two goals in his side's 3-1 victory, collecting the prize.

TOP 10 WORLD CUP GOALS

The best goals England players have scored on the biggest stage of all:

1) Michael Owen, England 2 Argentina 2 (Argentina won 4-3 on penalties), last 16, 30 June 1998

Eighteen-year-old Michael Owen became an overnight sensation after scoring a wonderful individual goal against Argentina in Lens. Paul Ince began the move by winning back possession just outside the England penalty area, before passing to David Beckham. The Manchester United midfielder quickly fed Owen, who held off a challenge from José Chamot while racing towards goal. He then skipped past Robert Ayala before letting rip with an unstoppable shot from 12 yards which sped past goalkeeper Carlos Roa and into the roof of the net for one of the greatest goals in the history of the tournament.

2) Bobby Charlton, England 2 Mexico 0, group stage, 16 July 1966

After a disappointing 0-0 draw with Uruguay in England's opening match at the 1966 World Cup, Bobby Charlton got the Three Lions' campaign up and running with a brilliant trademark long-range strike at Wembley. Collecting the ball in the centre circle, the Manchester United star ran forward, swerving to his right to create space before unleashing a thunderous shot into the top corner from fully 25 yards which left the Mexican goalkeeper rooted to the spot.

3) Geoff Hurst, England 4 West Germany 2, Final, 30 July 1966

With just seconds remaining in the final at Wembley, England skipper Bobby Moore played a long ball out of defence to Geoff Hurst. The West Ham striker ran forward, ignoring the handful of people who ran on to the pitch believing the game was all over, and then smashed a left-footed drive high into the net from just inside the penalty area to complete a unique hat-trick and, more importantly, clinch an historic victory for Alf Ramsey's team.

4) David Platt, England 1 Belgium 0, last 16, 26 June 1990

A last-16 tie in Bologna looked to be heading for penalties when, in the last minute of extra time, England midfielder Paul Gascoigne was fouled after a surging run forward. Taking the free kick from 40 yards out, Gazza floated it towards the far post where David Platt watched the ball all the way before connecting with a magnificent swivel-volley which flew past Belgian goalkeeper Michel Preud'homme to send England into the quarter-finals.

5) Gary Lineker, England 3 Poland 0, group stage, 11 June 1986

In a must-win game for England in Monterrey, Mexico, Gary Lineker had already opened the scoring when he doubled his tally on 14 minutes following a superb team move. Left-back Kenny Sansom played the ball down the line to Peter Beardsley, who spun sharply while setting Steve Hodge free down the wing with a magnificent first-time pass. Hodge's pinpoint cross was sweetly met by Lineker on the half-volley, his high shot from just outside the six-yard box giving the Polish goalkeeper no chance.

6) Dennis Wilshaw, Switzerland 0 England 2, group stage, 20 June 1954

In only his second match for England, Dennis Wilshaw secured the Three Lions' progress to the quarter-finals with a wonderful individual goal to wrap up victory against hosts Switzerland in Bern. Collecting a pass from Bill McGarry, the Wolves inside-forward skipped past three defenders before picking his spot with a low shot into the corner from 12 yards.

7) Jesse Lingard, England 6 Panama 1, group stage, 24 June 2018

England made light work of Panama in Nizhny Novgorod, Russia, storming into a five-goal half-time lead before eventually winning 6-1. Harry Kane hit a hat-trick – only the third by an Englishman at the World Cup – but the best goal of the afternoon came from Jesse Lingard. The nippy Manchester United midfielder played a quick one-two with Raheem Sterling just outside the Panama box before curling a delicious right-foot 20-yarder into the far corner which left veteran goalkeeper Jaime Penedo for dead.

**8) David Beckham, England 2 Colombia 0, group stage,
26 June 1998**

David Beckham's World Cup ended in misery when he was sent off against Argentina, but in the previous match against Colombia he scored a top-class goal in Lens to help England qualify for the knockout stages. After Paul Ince was fouled 30 yards from goal, Beckham lined up a free kick before curling a powerful shot over the wall and into the corner of the net past the dive of goalkeeper Faryd Mondragón.

**9) Bryan Robson, England 3 France 1, group stage,
16 June 1982**

On a scorching hot day in Bilbao, England began their World Cup campaign with an excellent win over eventual semi-finalists France. The goal of the game came from Bryan Robson in the 67th minute, the dynamic Manchester United midfielder leaping to meet a Trevor Francis cross with a bullet header from eight yards which flew over France goalkeeper Jean-Luc Ettori and high into the net.

**10) Steven Gerrard, England 2 Trinidad and Tobago 0,
group stage, 15 June 2006**

England made heavy weather of beating minnows Trinidad and Tobago in Nurnberg, having to wait until the 83rd minute before Peter Crouch's header put them ahead. In the first minute of injury time Steven Gerrard wrapped up a rather laboured victory with a stunning goal, cutting inside a defender on the edge of the penalty area before powering a left-footed thunderbolt into the far corner past goalkeeper Shaka Hislop.

TOP 10 OFFICIAL SONGS

The England songs which fans loved to belt out on the terraces or, in some cases, had them covering their ears:

1) 'World in Motion', New Order and the England national team

After rather dismal offerings from the England squad in 1986 and 1988, the FA decided on a change of tack and commissioned cult band New Order to provide the team's official song for the 1990 World Cup in Italy. The highly danceable tune was matched with non-cheesy lyrics co-written by actor Keith Allen, topped off by an iconic rap by John Barnes, one of just half a dozen England players to turn up for the recording session at Led Zeppelin legend Jimmy Page's studio in Berkshire. Embraced by New Order and England fans alike, 'World in Motion' spent three weeks at number one in May 1990 and is widely considered to be the best football song ever.

2) 'Three Lions', David Baddiel, Frank Skinner and the Lightning Seeds

Released to celebrate England's participation as hosts in Euro '96, 'Three Lions' was written by comedians David Baddiel and Frank Skinner, presenters of the then-popular TV show *Fantasy Football League*, with music by Ian Broudie of the Lightning Seeds. Although the song was far from the usual tub-thumper, its rather melancholic and downbeat opening morphed into a catchy chorus which helped propel it to the top of the charts. More significantly, the song was adopted by England fans as their tournament anthem as Terry Venables' exciting team just missed out on a place in the final, and has remained a favourite with match-going supporters ever since.

3) 'Back Home', England 1970 World Cup squad

England's first official song was released ahead of the 1970 World Cup, Sir Alf Ramsey's squad travelling to Mexico as holders following their victory on home soil four years earlier. The rousing track was sung entirely by the players and penned by Phil Coulter and Bill Martin, the latter having previously had major hits with Sandie Shaw (Eurovision winner 'Puppet on a String') and Cliff Richard ('Congratulations'). 'Back Home' proved to be equally popular with the record-buying public, spending three weeks at number one in May 1970 after knocking 'Spirit in the Sky' by Norman Greenbaum off the top spot.

4) 'This Time (We'll Get It Right)', England 1982 World Cup squad

After a depressing 12-year gap, England returned to World Cup action in Spain and celebrated by releasing an up-tempo song written by Smokie band members Chris Norman and Pete Spencer, who had previously penned a minor hit for Three Lions' skipper Kevin Keegan, 'Head Over Heels in Love'. Backed by a promotional video showing the squad recording the brass-heavy song at Abbey Road studios in London, Keegan and Co enjoyed a major hit, only being kept off the top spot by 'Ebony and Ivory' by Paul McCartney and Stevie Wonder.

5) 'Jerusalem', Fat Les

England's official song for the 2000 Euros in Belgium and the Netherlands was an adaptation of William Blake's hymn 'Jerusalem' by Fat Les, a band formed by Blur bassist Alex James, actor Keith Allen and artist Damien Hirst. The stirring song, which featured a 60-piece orchestra and four different choirs, just made it into the Top 10 but failed to inspire Kevin Keegan's England team, who were knocked out of the tournament at the group stage.

6) 'World at Your Feet', Embrace

Asked to write England's official song for the 2006 World Cup in Germany, Yorkshire rock band Embrace came up with 'World at Your Feet'. The rather pedestrian track didn't really stir the passions of the thousands of England fans who followed the team at the tournament, but it was a hit with the wider public and reached number three in the charts.

7) '(How Does It Feel to Be) On Top of the World', England United

Written by Echo and the Bunnymen frontman Ian McCulloch, along with Johnny Marr, formerly the guitarist in indie band The Smiths, this official England song for the 1998 World Cup in France also featured members of the Spice Girls, Ocean Colour Scene and Space. All the ingredients were there for a massive hit, but the rather forgettable song lacked punch and only made number nine in the charts, being outperformed by rivals 'Three Lions '98' and 'Vindaloo' by Fat Les.

8) 'We're on the Ball', Ant & Dec

TV presenters Ant & Dec revived their musical careers with this number three chart hit, England's official song for the 2002 World

Cup in Japan and South Korea. The lyrics weren't up to much – 'Over the wall, and into the net! David Beckham has done it!' was a particularly groan-worthy couplet – and the song never really caught on with England fans, but the video was jolly enough, featuring the Geordie duo disguising themselves as boss Sven-Göran Eriksson and his assistant Tord Grip so that they could penetrate the Three Lions' camp.

9) 'We've Got the Whole World at Our Feet', England 1986 World Cup squad

Sung to the tune of the traditional African-American spiritual 'He's Got the Whole World in His Hands', this ditty was a modified version of the Nottingham Forest anthem released in 1980 for the European Cup Final. England's effort, which peaked at a disappointing number 66 in the charts, was for the 1986 World Cup in Mexico and optimistically predicted, 'We've got the whole world at our feet, there's not a single team we can't beat.' Sadly, that didn't apply to Argentina, who knocked out Bobby Robson's team in the quarter-finals.

10) 'All The Way', England Football Team

Released ahead of the 1988 Euros in Germany, this jaunty Stock, Aitken and Waterman number was very much of its time but flopped badly, only reaching number 64 in the charts. Bobby Robson's England fared just as poorly on the pitch, crashing out at the group stage after losing all three of their matches.

TOP 10 WORST BOSSES

1) Steve McClaren

An assistant under Sven-Göran Eriksson, Steve McClaren replaced the Swede as England manager in 2006 after Portugal boss Luiz Felipe Scolari had turned down the role. Despite inheriting a talented squad nicknamed 'The Golden Generation', McClaren struggled to create a coherent team and results in the Three Lions' qualifying campaign for Euro 2008 were patchy. Nevertheless, they only needed a draw in their final match against group winners Croatia at Wembley to reach the finals, but on a wet night in London McClaren's side slumped to a desperate 3-2 defeat, the 'Wally with the Brolly' watching on from the sidelines under a giant FA umbrella. Only 16 months into a four-year contract, McClaren was unceremoniously removed from his position the following day.

2) Don Revie

After winning numerous trophies with his uncompromising Leeds side in the 1960s and early 1970s, Don Revie became England manager in 1974. He soon came under pressure after the Three Lions failed to qualify for the finals of the 1976 European Championship, being especially criticised for his inability to pick a settled team. Then, with qualification for the 1978 World Cup finals in Argentina also looking remote, Revie resigned from the England job after negotiating a secret and lucrative deal to manage the United Arab Emirates – an act of treachery which, for a while, made him one of the most unpopular men in the country.

3) Graham Taylor

Having enjoyed relative success with Watford and Aston Villa, Graham Taylor stepped up to take charge of England after the 1990 World Cup. An advocate of direct football, Taylor oversaw some promising results initially, his Three Lions team losing only once in his first 23 matches. However, after a dismal 2-1 defeat by hosts Sweden at Euro 1992, he was dubbed 'Turnip Taylor' by *The Sun* and was unable to shake off the tag during a disastrous World Cup qualification campaign which included defeats against Norway and the Netherlands. When England's failure to reach the finals in the USA was confirmed he resigned, later returning to club football with Wolves.

4) Howard Wilkinson

The last English manager to win the English top flight – with Leeds United in 1992, the final season of the old First Division before it became the Premier League – Howard Wilkinson became the technical director of the FA five years later. On two occasions while performing this role he stepped into the breach as England caretaker manager, first for a 2-0 friendly defeat against reigning world champions France at Wembley in February 1999, following

Glenn Hoddle's resignation. Just 18 months later Wilkinson was called upon again after Kevin Keegan quit as England boss, but the dour northerner again failed to inspire his players as the Three Lions could only manage a 0-0 draw with Finland in a World Cup qualifier in Helsinki.

5) Kevin Keegan

Former England captain Kevin Keegan was a popular choice as Three Lions' manager in February 1999, taking over the side after Glenn Hoddle had been forced to resign. The ex-Newcastle and Fulham boss led his country to the Euro 2000 finals after a play-off victory against Scotland, but at the tournament his tactical naivety was shown up in defeats against Portugal and Romania. A few months later England lost poorly at home to Germany in a World Cup qualifier and Keegan resigned straight after the match, admitting that he was out of his depth in international management.

6) Roy Hodgson

Aged 64 when he was appointed in May 2012, Roy Hodgson was the oldest man ever to take charge of the England team and the only one to have had previous international experience (with Switzerland, United Arab Emirates and Finland). A safe but uninspiring choice, he led the Three Lions to the quarter-finals of Euro 2012 but fared less well at the 2014 World Cup in Brazil, his side only managing a single point from their three matches. Worse was to come at Euro 2016 in France when England suffered one of the most humiliating defeats in their history, losing 2-1 to minnows Iceland in the last 16 in the final match of his reign.

7) Stuart Pearce

After spells in charge of Nottingham Forest, Manchester City, England's under-21s and the Great Britain side which competed at the London Olympics, Stuart Pearce acted as caretaker manager for the Three Lions' friendly against the Netherlands at Wembley in February 2012. His inexperienced side showed the fighting qualities associated with 'Psycho' the player, battling back from two goals down to level 2-2 in injury time, only to fall to a late winner by Dutch winger Arjen Robben.

8) Sam Allardyce

An experienced Premier League manager with Bolton, Newcastle, Blackburn, West Ham and Sunderland, Sam Allardyce was appointed Three Lions' boss on a two-year contract in July 2016. However, he was only in charge for one match, a 1-0 win in Slovakia in a World Cup qualifier, before he left the job by mutual consent following an investigation into corruption in English football by *The Telegraph*. He had only been in charge for 67 days, the shortest reign of any permanent England manager.

9) Peter Taylor

While boss of Premier League outfit Leicester City, Peter Taylor was appointed England caretaker manager for one match, a friendly against Italy in Turin in November 2000. The former England under-21 supremo chose a youthful side and made David Beckham captain for the first time, but his big night ended in defeat after AC Milan midfielder Gennaro Gattuso struck the only goal of the game from long range in the second half.

10) Fabio Capello

A serial trophy winner in Italian and Spanish football, Fabio Capello arrived in England with a massive reputation when he succeeded the hapless Steve McClaren as Three Lions' boss in December 2007. The former AC Milan, Real Madrid, Roma and Juventus manager oversaw a highly satisfactory World Cup qualifying campaign but cracks began to appear at the finals in South Africa, his strict disciplinary regime and struggles with the English language helping to create an unhappy camp. Despite the Three Lions' disappointing showing at the tournament, Capello stayed on to secure qualification for Euro 2012 before resigning when the FA removed the captaincy from John Terry.

TOP 10 TV ADVERTS

The England players who popped up on our screens trying to sell us something during the commercial break:

1) Gary Lineker and Paul Gascoigne, Walkers Crisps

Gary Lineker has been the face of Walkers Crisps since 1994, recently signing a new three-year deal worth a cool £1.2m. Of all the ads he has appeared in, this one from 1995 is possibly the best-loved. Gary is eating a packet of 'Salt & Lineker' crisps while watching a match from the stands. Paul Gascoigne, sitting just behind him, tries to steal a handful of crisps but is foiled by Gary and starts crying while 'Nessun Dorma' plays in the background – a reference, of course, to Gazza's famous tears during the World Cup semi-final at Italia '90.

2) Peter Crouch, T-Mobile

Getting dressed in the changing room after a match, Peter Crouch tells his young team-mates, 'Football's a simple game, lads. It's not about tactics or formations, it's how you celebrate goals.' The other players are clearly expecting Crouchy to launch into his much-loved 'robot' dance, but he shows them a new routine as 'The Only Way Is Up' by Yazz plays in the background. It's all moderately amusing and Crouch plays the role of the seen-it-all senior pro expertly, but what's it got to do with mobile phones?

3) David Beckham, Haig Club

In this 2014 ad for the scotch whisky, David Beckham joins a group of good-looking friends at a remote Highland estate. After dressing up for dinner the chums gather outside and stare moodily at the beautiful scenery while David pours them all a shot from his bottle of Haig, which he has brought along especially for the occasion. Filmed by Guy Ritchie, the ad hit the headlines when Alcohol Concern complained to the Advertising Standards Authority that it was likely to appeal to children and associated drinking with success and social acceptance, but the complaint was rejected.

4) Ian Wright, Chicken Tonight Sizzle & Stir

Dressed in a purple jacket and sporting a cravat round his neck, Ian Wright puts on a ridiculously plummy voice in this late 1990s ad as he tells us, 'Now for something more sophisticated than your everyday cooking sauce.' As Wrighty explains the USP of Sizzle & Stir – you get two pots to mix in with your fried poultry instead of just one – we see him dancing across the screen and singing 'One feels like chicken tonight!' There has to be a football reference, of course, and it comes at the end with the England striker quipping, 'You could say it's a game of two halves.'

5) Bobby Moore and Martin Peters, pubs
A suited and booted Bobby Moore and Martin Peters join their wives in their local boozer for a post-match drink and a game of darts in this 1966 ad for the pub industry. Bobby is a bit disparaging about his wife's abilities at the oche – 'Tina's not the best darts player in the world' he intones – but the key message comes at the end when a voice over says, 'Like Mr and Mrs Bobby Moore, look in at the local.'

6) Alan Shearer, McDonald's
It's 1998 and England captain Alan Shearer is the most popular man on Tyneside – everywhere he goes he's surrounded by kids wanting to get his autograph. It's hungry work so Al pops into a drive-thru McDonald's for some grub, where he pays for his takeaway with a cheque for £4.87 and makes the day of the young man behind the till by signing his name on a piece of paper after his original signature is cheekily queried.

7) Kevin Keegan, Brut
After working up a sweat in the gym in this ad from 1980, England captain Kevin Keegan and boxer Henry Cooper enjoy a bit of post-shower laddish joshing in the changing room. 'Nothing beats the great smell of Brut,' the pair tell us as Henry throws a towel over Kev's face. It's a blokey, old-fashioned ad, but the chemistry between the pair feels natural, almost as though they are good mates in real life.

8) Raheem Sterling, Gillette ProGlide
In this 2021 ad for Gillette ProGlide razor blades, Raheem Sterling shaves while looking in the mirror, 'Human' by Rag'n'Bone Man playing in the background. The England winger's acting skills are barely tested, but at least he ends up with a clean-looking face, not a nick in sight.

9) Wayne Rooney, Casillero del Diablo
In a 2011 ad for Manchester United's Chilean wine sponsor, England star Wayne Rooney warns Ryan Giggs and Patrice Evra

that a 'new Devil' is arriving at Old Trafford. Sadly, his chin-stroking performance is so wooden he makes his United team-mates look like Robert De Niro and Al Pacino by comparison.

10) Stuart Pearce, Gareth Southgate and Chris Waddle, Pizza Hut

Having just missed a penalty in the semi-final shoot-out against Germany at Euro '96, it seems poor Gareth Southgate can only appear in public in disguise. So, when he joins Pearce and Waddle – who also know the pain of failing from the spot for the Three Lions – for a meal at his local Pizza Hut he, naturally enough, wears a brown paper bag over his head. Some excruciating puns on the word 'miss' follow, before Southgate heads to the toilet only to run into a pillar. 'This time he's hit the post!' laughs 'Psycho'. Although not the worst ad ever, it didn't go down well with England fans who felt that the players shouldn't have been cashing in on agonising defeats which scarred the nation.

TOP 10 MANAGERS' QUOTES

The great Sir Alf Ramsey had an extended say earlier; now let's hear from England's other, rather less successful, managers:

1) 'Do I not like that!'
Graham Taylor, launches a catchphrase after a mistake by John Barnes led to a Poland goal in a World Cup qualifier in 1993

2) 'We didn't underestimate Cameroon. They were a lot better than we thought.'
Bobby Robson, after England scraped past the African side in the 1990 World Cup

3) 'I never heard a minute's silence like that.'
Glenn Hoddle, after the Wembley crowd paid tribute to the late Princess Diana in 1997

4) 'We have to reduce our expectations of England and we have the players to do it.'
Steve McClaren, who followed his own advice by failing to lead England to the 2008 European Championship

5) 'I always thought I did a good job with England. But people at the time didn't think so. They had had enough of the Swedish guy only making the quarter-finals.'
Sven-Göran Eriksson, reflecting on his time as England boss

6) 'As soon as it dawned on me that we were short of players who combined skill and commitment, I should have forgotten all about trying to play more controlled, attractive football and settled for a real bastard of a team.'
Don Revie after resigning as England manager in 1977

7) 'Being an ex-England manager, one that failed to qualify for the World Cup, is like being a dead politician.'
Graham Taylor

8) 'I want more from David Beckham. I want him to improve on perfection.'
Kevin Keegan, setting a tricky challenge for his star midfielder

9) 'I'm slightly concerned, because as a centre-half who took a lot of knocks to the head I'm not usually synonymous with being a fashion icon.'
Gareth Southgate, reacting to news that sales of waistcoats boomed after he wore one at the 2018 World Cup in Russia

10) 'I am still a little bit unsure what I'm doing here.'
Roy Hodgson, speaking at a press conference after resigning as England manager in 2016

TOP 10 WORLD CUP DEFEATS

The most disappointing of England's losses at the finals:

1) England 0 USA 1, group stage, 29 June 1950

After a comfortable 2-0 win against Chile in their first World Cup match, having not taken part in the pre-World War II tournaments, an England side containing household names like Billy Wright, Tom Finney and Stan Mortensen were expected to make mincemeat of an unheralded American side in Belo Horizonte, Brazil. However, in one of the biggest shocks in the history of the tournament the USA won 1-0, thanks to a first-

David Beckham, England's most-capped player with foreign clubs.

Harry Kane scores the winner in England's best victory at the Euros, the semi-final against Denmark at Wembley in 2021.

England's greatest ever boss, 1966 World Cup winner Sir Alf Ramsey.

Georgia Stanway belts in the Lionesses' best ever goal, the winner against Spain in the quarter-final of Euro 2022.

England's oldest ever player, Stanley Matthews, also has the best nickname, 'The Wizard of the Dribble'

David Seaman lets in Ronaldinho's free kick in the World Cup quarter-final in 2002. The worst ever mistake by an England goalie?

Kevin Keegan models England's best ever home kit in 1980.

Is Lucy Bronze, pictured here in action at Euro 2022, England's greatest ever female player?

Jimmy Greaves scores in England's biggest ever win against arch-rivals Scotland, a 9-3 rout at Wembley in 1961.

Hailing originally from Jamaica, Raheem Sterling is England's best 'born abroad' player.

Bobby Moore, England's greatest ever captain, holds aloft the World Cup trophy in 1966.

Victoria Beckham, pictured here at the 2004 Euros in Portugal, is the queen of England's WAGS.

Michael Owen celebrates one of his three goals against Germany in 2001, England's best ever win in a World Cup qualifier.

With 28 goals in just 23 appearances, Steve Bloomer was England's greatest player in the pre-World War I era.

Steve McClaren, arguably England's worst ever manager, looks suitably miserable during a dismal 3-2 defeat to Croatia in 2007.

Chloe Kelly celebrates scoring the winner against Germany in the final of Euro 2022, the Lionesses' greatest ever victory!

half header by Haitian-born Larry Gaetjens. 'In the game we must have hit the woodwork half a dozen times,' centre-forward Roy Bentley later ruefully recalled. The embarrassing defeat was followed by another 1-0 loss to Spain three days later, ending England's involvement in the tournament at the group stage.

2) England 2 West Germany 3, quarter-final, 14 June 1970
For over an hour, reigning world champions England were in control of this quarter-final in Léon, Mexico, and looked set to repeat their victory against West Germany in the 1966 final. However, a two-goal lead established by Alan Mullery and Martin Peters was halved on 69 minutes when a 20-yard shot from Franz Beckenbauer slipped under Three Lions goalkeeper Peter Bonetti. Eight minutes from time a freakish back header by Uwe Seeler somehow sailed over Bonetti and into the net, and in extra time England's grip on the Jules Rimet Trophy was ended when the Germans' ace marksman Gerd Müller volleyed home from six yards.

3) England 1 Croatia 2, semi-final, 11 July 2018
After safely negotiating their way through the easier half of the draw, England faced a decent but not outstanding Croatia side in Moscow with a place in the World Cup Final at stake. Gareth Southgate's men got off to the best possible start when right-wing-back Kieran Trippier curled in a fifth-minute free kick, but good chances to increase their lead before half-time were spurned. After the break, Croatia began to dominate in midfield and equalised through Ivan Perišić midway through the half. The match went into extra time and was settled in favour of the Croats when Mario Mandžukić drilled in from close range.

4) England 1 Argentina 2, quarter-final, 22 June 1986
Following a cagey first half on a bumpy pitch in Mexico City, England fell behind in controversial circumstances when Argentina's captain and star player Diego Maradona clearly used his hand to flick the ball into the net. Minutes later, Maradona scored one of the greatest goals of all time, dribbling past the entire Three Lions defence before planting the ball past goalkeeper Peter Shilton. A late headed goal by Golden Boot winner Gary Lineker

from John Barnes's cross was not enough to save England from a disappointing exit.

5) England 1 Germany 4, last 16, 27 June 2010
After failing to impress in the group stage, England met old rivals Germany in Bloemfontein, South Africa, and found themselves two goals down within half an hour thanks to some poor defending. Central defender Matthew Upson restored hope with a header, and when a Frank Lampard shot crashed against the crossbar and over the line it seemed the Three Lions would go into the break on level terms – except, bewilderingly, the clear goal was not awarded. In the second half the unlucky Lampard hit the bar again with a long-range free kick before the Germans wrapped up a comprehensive win with two goals from Thomas Müller on the counter attack.

6) England 2 Uruguay 4, quarter-final, 26 June 1954
World Cup winners in 1950 and fresh from a 7-0 rout of Scotland, Uruguay represented a formidable barrier to England's prospects of reaching the semi-finals. The Three Lions, though, put up a good fight in Basel and might have had more to show for their efforts than goals from Nat Lofthouse and Tom Finney if it had not been for a poor goalkeeping display by Birmingham City's Gil Merrick. 'On his day Merrick was as good as any, but he was prone to errors we could not afford,' was the damning verdict of Three Lions' boss Walter Winterbottom.

7) England 1 Brazil 2, quarter-final, 21 June 2002
England's hopes of a first World Cup victory over Brazil were boosted in Shizuoka when, midway through the first half, Michael Owen put the Three Lions ahead. Just before half-time, though, Brazil's star man Ronaldinho set up Rivaldo for the equaliser and the initiative swung towards the South Americans. Brazil's winning goal, a floated Ronaldinho free kick which sailed over the head of goalkeeper David Seaman, was something of a fluke but England could have few complaints, failing to create any decent chances even after the scorer was sent off with over half an hour to play.

8) England 0 USSR 1, group stage play-off, 17 June 1958
After finishing joint-second with the USSR in their group,

England faced the Russians in a play-off in Gothenburg with a quarter-final place up for grabs. The original match between the sides had ended 2-2, and this was another tight encounter. England were unlucky not to take the lead when Chelsea right-winger Peter Brabrook, who had earlier hit a post, had a goal disallowed for handball in the second half, and a few minutes later Russian left-winger Anatoli Ilyin struck the winner off a post.

9) England 1 Uruguay 2, group stage, 19 June 2014
Liverpool striker Luis Suárez, the Premier League's top scorer in the 2013/14 season with 31 goals, scored twice for Uruguay in São Paulo to all but end England's interest in the tournament after just two games. The lively frontman opened the scoring for the South Americans late in the first half with a header from Edinson Cavani's cross. Wayne Rooney levelled for Roy Hodgson's men with a quarter of an hour to play, but with just five minutes left Steven Gerrard's attempted headed clearance only diverted the ball into the path of Suárez, who gleefully smashed home the winner.

10) England 0 Portugal 1, group stage, 3 June 1986
England got off to a bad start at the 1986 World Cup in Mexico, missing a host of decent chances against Portugal in Monterrey before falling to a sucker punch in the 75th minute. Arsenal left-back Kenny Sansom was at fault, allowing Portuguese winger Diamantino to skip past before crossing to the far post where the unmarked Carlos Manuel tapped in from close range.

TOP 10 PUNDITS

The most impressive of the many former England internationals who now make a living talking about the game on TV and the radio:

1) Gary Neville
A regular on Sky Sports since 2011, Gary Neville is widely regarded as the best pundit in the business, whether delivering his analysis in the studio or in the commentary box. A highly decorated right-back with Manchester United who also won 85

caps for England, Neville is especially strong when pinpointing the small defensive errors which lead to goals, while his impassioned outbursts on issues which go to the very core of the game – such as the proposed formation of a European Super League – have only served to increase his popularity among fans of all clubs.

2) Glenn Hoddle

With a long career in international football as both a player and manager, Glenn Hoddle exudes an authority and gravitas which few can match, yet his amiable and friendly manner makes him an extremely welcoming presence to the viewer. Now happily recovered from a near-fatal heart attack in October 2018, the Tottenham legend is a football purist who can be relied upon to purr approvingly when a defender 'plays out from the back' rather than aimlessly hoofs the ball clear.

3) Alan Shearer

After retiring as a player with a record 260 Premier League goals to his name, Alan Shearer was immediately snapped up as a pundit by *Match of the Day*. His early appearances were criticised for being boring cliche-fests but the former England captain has upped his game over the years, and now delivers his views in an engagingly forthright style without recourse to the usual platitudes. As you'd expect of one of the greatest strikers to have played the game, his analysis of how forwards are able to get away from their markers and into goalscoring positions is always enlightening.

4) Jamie Carragher

Although he was never a regular in the England team, Jamie Carragher has established himself as one of the top pundits in the country, his partnership with Gary Neville on Sky Sports being especially watchable, underpinned as it is by their former on-field rivalry. However, the former Liverpool defender's TV career almost ended in disgrace in March 2018 when a video emerged of him spitting at a car carrying a man and his daughter after Carragher had covered a Manchester United victory over his beloved Reds at Old Trafford. A remorseful Carragher was suspended by Sky for several months, before resuming his role at the start of the following season.

5) Rio Ferdinand

Rio Ferdinand was an elegant centre-back who read the game superbly as a player with Manchester United and England, so it is not surprising that he has seamlessly adapted to his new role as a pundit for BT Sport, covering both the Premier League and Champions League. Never afraid to tackle difficult or challenging subjects, he won a BAFTA in 2017 for a BBC documentary about bereavement, made two years after his first wife, Rebecca, died of breast cancer aged just 34.

6) Joe Cole

A fairly new addition to BT Sport's punditry team, the former England winger has already made a mark on the small screen and is one to watch for the future. His simple, boyish enthusiasm for the game is infectious but is accompanied by an ability to explain and analyse incidents on the pitch in a clear, insightful manner. Although his support for former club Chelsea is obvious, notably when he wildly celebrated the Blues' Champions League triumph in 2021, Cole is his own man and is prepared to criticise the Stamford Bridge outfit when he deems fit.

7) Chris Sutton

Capped just once by England during Glenn Hoddle's reign, the former Norwich and Blackburn striker didn't have much of an international career but his impassioned rants, deadpan humour and barbed comments have made him an in-demand pundit. Paired with Robbie Savage on Radio 5 Live's popular *606* phone-in, he delights in goading the Welshman in their debates, often with comical results.

8) Karen Carney

Just as comfortable covering men's or women's football for the BBC or BT, the former England winger has built up an impressive punditry CV since retiring from the game in 2019. A perceptive analyst, Carney is also extremely hard-working and it's a rare day indeed when she isn't sitting in a press box somewhere with a mic in her hand.

9) Lee Dixon

The former Arsenal and England right-back was an uncomplicated, play-it-safe sort of player and is equally reliable as a pundit or co-commentator for ITV. Rarely seen in winter without a cloth cap, Dixon delivers his views in a succinct, no-nonsense style – an advantage on a station where regular ad breaks interrupt the flow of football chit-chat.

10) Ian Wright

An experienced TV presenter in his own right, Ian Wright's exuberant personality makes him highly watchable. In punditry terms he perhaps lacks the tactical acumen of some of his peers, but, as a prolific striker in his playing days, he is always worth listening to when it comes to the art of goalscoring. Although his international career was a tad disappointing – none of his 33 caps were earned at a tournament finals – Wright is a massive cheerleader for the men's and women's national sides, his voice sometimes cracking with genuine emotion when he talks about the England team.

TOP 10 ONE-GOAL WONDERS

The long-serving England players who got on the scoresheet just once in their international careers:

1) Sol Campbell

Rugged centre-half Sol Campbell was desperately unlucky to have potentially match-winning goals for England ruled out at the 1998 World Cup against Argentina and at the 2004 Euros against hosts Portugal. However, the 73-cap man was on target for the Three Lions in the group stage of the 2002 World Cup against Sweden in Saitama, Japan, powerfully heading in David Beckham's in-swinging corner to give England the lead in a match which eventually ended in a 1-1 draw.

2) Kenny Sansom

No outfield player has won more than Kenny Sansom's 86 caps and scored just one goal for England – although, to be fair to the former Arsenal left-back, both Ashley Cole (no goals in 107 games) and Gary Neville (none in 85) had even worse goalscoring records. Sansom's big moment came in a World Cup qualifier against Finland at Wembley in October 1984 when he rounded off a comfortable 5-0 victory with a smart left-footer into the bottom corner.

3) Emlyn Hughes

Liverpool defender Emlyn Hughes represented England 62 times in the 1970s, captaining the side on 23 occasions. His one goal for the Three Lions was a tap-in against Wales in a 3-0 win at Ninian Park in May 1972. However, Hughes's father, a former Welsh rugby league international, was less than delighted with his son's success. 'I saw my Dad in the car park afterwards and thought I would get a hug and congratulations from him,' Emlyn recalled. 'Instead, he bellowed, "Oh, boyo, anybody but Wales!"'

4) Kieran Trippier

Kieran Trippier couldn't have chosen a better moment to score his first – and, so far, only – goal for England, curling a beautiful free kick over Croatia's wall and into the top corner to put the Three Lions 1-0 up in the 2018 World Cup semi-final in Moscow. However, England eventually lost the match 2-1 after extra time and Trippier went off injured in the final minutes, leaving Gareth Southgate's team down to ten men as all their subs had been used.

5) James Milner

Hardworking midfielder James Milner played 61 times for England between 2009 and 2016 but only managed a single goal in that time, in a routine 5-0 win in a World Cup qualifier against Moldova in Chișinău in September 2012. Mind you, his low right-footed shot into the bottom corner from the edge of the box was the pick of England's goals on the night.

6) Mark Wright

In an England career spanning 12 years, during which he played 45 times, lanky centre-half Mark Wright only scored once – but it was a vital goal at the 1990 World Cup which took Bobby Robson's team through to the knockout stages. England were struggling to break down an ultra-defensive Egypt in their final group game in Sardinia when Paul Gascoigne swung in a deep free kick from near the left touchline, Wright rising highest to nod home the only goal of a scrappy game.

7) Graeme Le Saux
A left-back who loved to get forward, Graeme Le Saux was capped 36 times by England while with Blackburn and Chelsea between 1994 and 2000. His only goal for his country came in the Umbro Cup – a four-team international tournament held in England in 1995. Having beaten Japan and drawn with Sweden, Terry Venables' team needed to beat reigning world champions Brazil at Wembley to claim the trophy and that seemed possible when Le Saux gave them the lead with an exquisite left-footed lob volley after he had chested down a defensive clearance. However, the South Americans hit back with three second-half goals to win 3-1.

8) Glen Johnson
In England's final home friendly match before the 2010 World Cup finals in South Africa, Liverpool right-back Glen Johnson scored a stunning goal in a 3-1 win against Mexico. Receiving the ball on the right wing, Johnson cut inside past a couple of defenders before unleashing a spectacular left-footed curler into the top corner. It was a goal to remember for the man who won 54 caps.

9) Nobby Stiles
In what was to be a dress rehearsal for the 1966 World Cup Final, England beat West Germany 1-0 at Wembley in a friendly in February of that year. The goalscorer was Nobby Stiles, wearing the number nine shirt but playing in the usual defensive midfield role which he performed for his club, Manchester United. Famously short-sighted, it was probably lucky that Stiles, who made 28 international appearances, was less than a yard out as he tapped in the winner after German goalkeeper Hans Tilkowski had spilled Roger Hunt's header.

10) Alan Mullery
Another player to net his only goal for England at the World Cup, Tottenham midfielder Alan Mullery opened the scoring for the reigning world champions against West Germany in the

1970 quarter-final in Léon, Mexico. Making a rare foray forward, Mullery turned in Keith Newton's low cross from close range on the half-hour mark but the Three Lions' hopes of holding on to their trophy were shattered when the Germans hit back from two down to win 3-2 after extra time. A regular for England between 1967 and 1971, Mullery won 35 caps in total, captaining the side once.

TOP 10 WOMEN

The players who have made the biggest impact with the England Women's team:

1) Lucy Bronze

An attacking right-back who packs one of the hardest shots in the women's game, Lucy Bronze made her England debut in 2013 and two years later was one of the team's outstanding performers at the World Cup in Canada, her vibrant displays earning her a place in the FIFA All-Star squad. UEFA Women's Player of the Year in 2019 and the Best FIFA Women's Player in 2020, Bronze was an ever-present when England won the 2022 Euros, the same year she moved from Manchester City to European titans Barcelona.

2) Kelly Smith

England's main attacking threat for nearly two decades, Arsenal Ladies striker Kelly Smith scored a then record 46 goals for England in 117 appearances between 1995 and 2014. 'Kelly is one of those players who only come along once or twice in a lifetime,' former England manager Hope Powell once said. 'In the men's game you'd think of Diego Maradona or Messi, players with a unique talent, and that's what Kelly has.' Smith's heyday was between 2006 and 2009 when she finished in the top five in the FIFA Women's World Player of the Year rankings in four consecutive seasons.

3) Steph Houghton

England captain between 2014 and 2022, Steph Houghton has recovered from two serious injuries to win more than 100 caps for her country as well as starring for Great Britain at the 2012

London Olympics, when she scored three goals in four games. A tough defender who reads the game well and is also a threat at set pieces, the Manchester City star is one of the best-known faces in the women's game and holds the distinction of being the first female player to appear on the cover of *Shoot!* magazine.

4) Fara Williams

A talented midfielder with a superb range of passing, Fara Williams is England's most-capped player after appearing an incredible 172 times for the Lionesses between 2001 and 2019. A deadly penalty taker, Williams scored three times from the spot at the 2015 World Cup in Canada, including the winner in the third-place play-off against Germany that secured England their best showing at the finals.

5) Ellen White

England's all-time top goalscorer with 52 goals in 113 appearances for the Lionesses by the end of the 2022 Euros, Manchester City striker Ellen White is a natural finisher who is strong on the ground and in the air. She has represented her country at three World Cups, starring at the 2019 tournament in France when she scored six goals – the same as Americans Megan Rapinoe and Alex Morgan, but she was denied the Golden Boot due to a lack of assists. In 2022 she started every match as the Lionesses won the Euros for the first time in their history.

6) Eni Aluko

The sister of Ipswich striker Sone Aluko, the former Chelsea and Juventus forward was once described as 'the Wayne Rooney of women's football'. An excellent dribbler, the pacy Aluko scored 33 times for England in her 102 appearances, but her international career ended on a sour note in 2016 when she alleged that she had been the victim of racist comments by then-Lionesses' coach Mark Sampson and other staff members.

7) Karen Carney

Now a regular TV and radio pundit, Karen Carney had a dream start to her England career, coming off the bench to score on her debut in a 4-1 win against Italy in 2005. The talented Arsenal, Birmingham City and Chelsea winger went on to win an impressive 144 caps for the Lionesses, scoring 32 goals, and she also played in all four games for Great Britain at the 2012 Olympics in London.

8) Rachel Yankey

A true legend of the women's game, Rachel Yankey was just 17 when she made her England debut, scoring in a 4-0 win against Scotland in 1997. The skilful Arsenal Ladies winger ended her international career with 129 caps, becoming the first female player to pass Peter Shilton's men's record of 125 caps. Very much a trailblazer for women in football, Yankey was often selected to model England's new kit, appearing at photoshoots alongside icons such as David Beckham and Michael Owen.

9) Gillian Coultard

In 1997 Gillian Coultard became the first female player to win a century of caps for England, receiving a silver cap from 1966 World Cup-winning hero Geoff Hurst in honour of her achievement. A tireless midfielder for Doncaster Rovers Belles, the diminutive Coultard also captained the Lionesses for four years and holds the distinction of scoring the first England goal at the World Cup, a penalty in a 3-2 win against Canada in 1995.

10) Jill Scott

A tall midfielder who is known as 'Crouchy' after former England striker Peter Crouch, Jill Scott has appeared 161 times for England – a tally only bettered by Fara Williams. Her aerial threat has helped her score 26 goals for the Lionesses but she is also more than capable on the deck, being adept at winning tackles and driving forward with the ball. An FA Women's Cup winner with both Everton and Manchester City, Scott was named FA International Player of the Year in 2011, five years after her England debut. In 2022 she was part of the Lionesses squad which won the Euros for the first time, making several appearances off the bench.

TOP 10 DRAWS

Americans say that a draw is 'like kissing your sister', but England fans who witnessed these tied encounters were happy enough:

1) England 2 Greece 2, World Cup qualifier, 6 October 2001
In this final World Cup qualifier at Old Trafford, England needed to match or better Germany's result at home to Finland to top their group and avoid a tricky play-off with Ukraine. With Greece merely playing for pride, the Three Lions were expected to win comfortably but a jittery first-half display saw them fall behind to Angelos Charisteas's low drive. A minute after coming on as a sub midway through the second half, Teddy Sheringham equalised with a flicked header from David Beckham's free kick but Greece regained the lead immediately through Demis Nikolaidis. England laid siege to the Greek goal to no avail and news of Germany's draw in Gelsenkirchen had filtered through when they saved themselves in dramatic fashion, Beckham firing in a majestic curling free kick from 25 yards deep into injury time. A draw, yes, but to every England fan in the country it felt like a fantastic win!

2) Italy 0 England 0, World Cup qualifier, 11 October 1997
Despite having lost at home to the Italians earlier in the year, England only needed a draw in this final qualifier in Rome to book their passage to France '98 after the *Azzurri* surprisingly dropped points against both Poland and Georgia. A superb team performance – defensively sound but carrying a genuine threat on the counter attack – ensured the Three Lions secured the result they required, although there was a nervy moment right at the end when Christian Vieri's header sailed just wide. England skipper Paul Ince, who had to be patched up after sustaining a nasty head injury in the first half, summed up the feeling in the England camp afterwards when saying, 'I've played in cup finals and in big European matches, but this was right up there with anything I've achieved – possibly the greatest moment of my career.'

3) England 1 Colombia 1 (England won 4-3 on penalties), World Cup last 16, 3 July 2018
The better side on the night in Moscow, England put their fans through the wringer before eventually winning on penalties for the first time in a World Cup match. Up against a tough, physical Colombia side who collected six yellow cards, it was no surprise

that England took the lead from 12 yards, Harry Kane shooting home after he had been bundled over at a corner. Colombia equalised deep into injury time through Yerry Mina's header but it was England who held their nerve better in the shoot-out, Jordan Pickford saving brilliantly from Carlos Bacca before Eric Dier emphatically drilled in the winner.

4) England 0 Spain 0 (England won 4-2 on penalties), European Championship quarter-final, 22 June 1996

England were fortunate to take this quarter-final at Wembley to penalties after David Seaman made some excellent saves and the Spanish were unlucky to have an apparently legitimate goal ruled out for offside. The Arsenal goalkeeper was also the Three Lions' hero in the shoot-out, sealing England's victory by diving to his right to parry Miguel Ángel Nadal's spot-kick after Alan Shearer, David Platt, Stuart Pearce and Paul Gascoigne had all netted from 12 yards.

5) Poland 0 England 0, World Cup qualifier, 11 October 1989

Bobby Robson's England team needed a point from their final World Cup qualifier against Poland in Chorzów to ensure they would book their place at the finals the following year. They achieved their aim thanks mainly to veteran goalkeeper Peter Shilton, who made some fine saves, although even he was left helpless when Polish midfielder Ryszard Tarasiewicz crashed a 30-yard shot against the crossbar in the last minute. The hard-fought draw enabled England to qualify for Italia '90 as one of the best runners-up after finishing a point behind Sweden in the group.

6) England 4 Rest of the World XI 4, friendly, 21 October 1953

A hugely entertaining game at Wembley to mark the 90th anniversary of the Football Association saw England share eight goals with a Rest of the World XI made of players from just five European countries: Austria, Germany, Italy, Spain and Yugoslavia. The Three Lions were 3-1 down at one stage, but fought back to 3-3 thanks to two goals by Wolves winger Jimmy Mullen. Hungarian-born Spanish international László Kubala then made it 4-3 to the visitors with a cracking shot before Alf

Ramsey blasted home a last-minute penalty to maintain England's unbeaten home record against opposition from outside the British Isles.

7) Scotland 1 England 1, European Championship qualifier, 24 February 1968

The British Home Internationals in 1967 and 1968 doubled up as qualifiers for the knockout rounds of the European Championship and, having lost 3-2 to Scotland at Wembley the previous year, England needed to avoid defeat against the Auld Enemy in the return at Hampden Park to reach the quarter-finals. Martin Peters put Sir Alf Ramsey's men ahead on 20 minutes with a fierce drive but Scotland levelled shortly before half-time when Gordon Banks couldn't quite reach John Hughes's looping header. The home fans in the massive crowd of over 130,000 roared Scotland on in the second half, but England held out to claim a vital point.

8) England 0 Brazil 0, World Cup group stage, 11 June 1958

After a 2-2 draw in their opening World Cup fixture against the USSR, England did well to pick up another point in a tightly contested match with eventual champions Brazil in Gothenburg. The Wolves trio of Billy Wright, Bill Slater and Eddie Clamp were outstanding in a dogged defensive display which largely reduced the talented South Americans to long-range efforts, with only Vavá's 20-yarder which struck the crossbar causing any real alarms.

9) England 0 West Germany 0, World Cup second group stage, 29 June 1982

After wins against France, Czechoslovakia and Kuwait, England easily qualified for the second group stage of the 1982 World Cup in Spain. Their first opponents were reigning European champions West Germany, and Ron Greenwood's team were reasonably satisfied to take a point from a cagey match in Madrid which they came close to losing late on when Karl-Heinz Rummenigge's long-range shot rattled the crossbar. The draw meant England needed to beat the hosts by two clear goals to reach the semi-finals, but they could only manage another 0-0 stalemate and so were eliminated.

10) England 0 Switzerland 0 (England won 6-5 on penalties), UEFA Nations League third-place play-off, 9 June 2019
Having lost 3-1 to the Netherlands in the semi-final of the inaugural Nations League finals, England took on Switzerland in Guimarães, Portugal, with the chance to claim third place in the tournament. The Three Lions had the better of the game, striking the woodwork through Harry Kane and Raheem Sterling, while a late Callum Wilson goal was ruled out by the VAR officials after a foul. In the penalty shoot-out that followed the 0-0 draw, goalkeeper Jordan Pickford was the hero, scoring one of England's six successful spot-kicks before making the match-winning save from Josip Drmić.

TOP 10 GRIM ENGLAND NEWSPAPER HEADLINES

Turnips, planks, wallies; you wouldn't want to be an England player or manager after an especially disappointing defeat when the tabloid headline writers have you in their sights:

1) 'Swedes 2 Turnips 1', *The Sun*, 18 June 1992
A 2-1 defeat to hosts Sweden ended England's hopes of progress in the 1992 European Championship and prompted this famous headline. Poor Graham Taylor, a thoroughly decent man who was out of his depth managing in international football, was subsequently rather cruelly dubbed 'The Turnip'.

2) 'A Wally With A Brolly', *Daily Mail*, 23 November 2007
Steve McClaren was put in the stocks by the *Mail* after watching his side lose 3-2 to Croatia in a vital European Championship qualifier at Wembley while protecting himself from a torrential downpour under a giant red and blue FA umbrella. The 'Wally with a Brolly' tag was one McClaren could never quite rid himself of, long after he had departed the England scene.

3) 'Norse Manure!', *The Sun*, 3 June 1993
It's fair to say that a humiliating 2-0 defeat for Graham Taylor's England in a World Cup qualifier against Norway in Oslo did not impress the sports subs at 'The Currant Bun'.

4) 'Ice Wallies', *The Sun*, 28 June 2016

A shocking 2-1 defeat to minnows Iceland spelt the end of England's Euro ambitions and also saw boss Roy Hodgson head for the door. *The Sun* was not in sympathetic mood, putting the boot in with its main headline while also running the banner 'Poundland 1 Iceland 2' above its match report.

5) 'Goulashed', *The Sun*, 15 June 2022

A shocking 4-0 defeat at Molineux to Hungary in the Nations League – England's worst reverse at home for 94 years – resulted in Gareth Southgate's men being booed off and led *The Sun* to wittily reference the Magyars' famous national dish.

6) 'Yanks 2 Planks 0', *The Sun*, 10 June 1993

With England's World Cup qualifying campaign coming off the rails, a 2-0 defeat to the USA in the US Cup in Boston meant *The Sun*'s headline writers weren't going to pull any punches and they revelled in putting the boot into Graham Taylor's under-performing team once more.

7) 'A Gutless Spineless Shower', *The Sun*, 20 June 1988

Two days after England lost 3-1 to the Soviet Union at the European Championship in Germany, *The Sun* was still lambasting the players and boss Bobby Robson, who was pictured with a cone-shaped dunce's hat superimposed on his head.

8) 'In The Name Of Allah, Go!', *The Mirror*, 17 November 1988

After a dismal showing at the 1988 European Championship in Germany, the Daily Mirror had called on England boss Bobby Robson to go 'in the name of God'. Now, following an embarrassing 1-1 draw with Saudi Arabia in Riyadh, the same paper invoked another deity in its ongoing anti-Robson campaign.

9) 'Danish Pasting', *The Mirror*, 18 August 2005

Along with thousands of fans across the country, the sports team at the *Daily Mirror* was distinctly unimpressed with a 4-1 friendly defeat to Denmark in Copenhagen at the start of the 2005/06 season, England's heaviest loss for 25 years.

10) 'Spanish 1 Onions 0', *The Sun*, 10 September 1992
Another amusing headline from *The Sun* during the Graham Taylor era, this time after England lost a friendly to Spain in Santander. And, yes, you've guessed it, the score was 1-0 to Spain.

TOP 10 OWN GOALS

The opposition players who helped England's cause by scoring past their own goalkeepers – thank you, guys!

1) Simon Kjær
The most significant own goal in England's history by some distance was scored by AC Milan defender Simon Kjær in the Euro 2020 semi-final against Denmark at Wembley on 7 July 2021. The Three Lions were trailing to Mikkel Damsgaard's superb free kick when, six minutes before the break, Harry Kane fed Bukayo Saka with a cute pass. The Arsenal man crossed low into the six-yard box and, aware that Raheem Sterling had an easy chance to score, Kjær slid in to block but only managed to knock the ball past Denmark goalkeeper Kasper Schmeichel for the equaliser. The goal proved to be a vital one as England went on to win the match 2-1 after extra time.

2) Carlos Gamarra
In their opening match at the 2006 World Cup in Germany, Sven-Göran Eriksson's England got off to a great start when they took the lead against Paraguay after just three minutes on a boiling-hot day in Frankfurt. David Beckham whipped in a deep free kick from out on the left and the ball flicked off the head of veteran defender Carlos Gamarra before nestling in the bottom corner of the net. The early strike proved to be the only goal of the game, leaving England thankful for the unexpected Paraguayan present.

3) Jozef Barmoš
In their second game at the 1982 World Cup in Spain, England were leading Czechoslovakia by a Trevor Francis goal in Bilbao midway through the second half when Paul Mariner collected the ball on the right-hand side. The Ipswich forward chipped a cross

into the box only for Czech defender Jozef Barmoš to stretch out a leg and divert the ball past Stanislav Seman in goal. The slightly fortunate goal wrapped up a 2-0 win for Ron Greenwood's team and put them through to the second round with a match still to play.

4) Arkadiusz Głowacki
Having started their World Cup qualification campaign with a disappointing 2-2 draw in Austria four days earlier, England needed a win when they faced Poland in Chorzów in September 2004. With the scores tied at 1-1 approaching the hour, Ashley Cole fired in a low cross from the left which Polish central defender Arkadiusz Głowacki attempted to clear, but only succeeded in turning into his own net under pressure from Michael Owen. The goal turned out to be the winner, helping England to eventually top the group just one point ahead of the Poles.

5) Markus Tanner
Following a 2-1 loss in Romania the previous month, England could not afford another slip-up when they faced Switzerland in a World Cup qualifier at Wembley in November 1980. In the event Ron Greenwood's men managed a nervy 2-1 win, after being given a helping hand – or, rather, foot – by Swiss midfielder Markus Tanner who diverted a hard, low cross from England right-winger Steve Coppell into his own net for the opening goal. To complete a miserable night for the 26-year-old FC Basel player, he was subbed off at half-time.

6) Branko Bošković
Requiring two wins from their final pair of qualifiers to be sure of reaching the 2014 World Cup in Brazil, England were leading Montenegro 1-0 at Wembley just past the hour when they were gifted a bizarre own goal by Rapid Vienna midfielder Branko Bošković. Daniel Sturridge's clever back-heel put Danny Welbeck through on the left and although Bošković was first to reach the Manchester United forward's low cross, he miscued his clearance from 12 yards out and could only watch in horror as it bobbled into the net. England went on to win the match 4-1, and then secured their place at the finals with a 2-0 victory over Poland four days later.

7) Anton Weibel

After twice taking the lead, England were drawing 2-2 against Switzerland in a European Championship qualifier in Basel in October 1971 as the clock ticked towards the final ten minutes. A draw would not have been a disaster for Sir Alf Ramsey's men, but they nicked a late victory when Martin Chivers fired in a cross and the ball flicked off Swiss defender Anton Weibel and into the net for the winning goal. Over the next six weeks the Three Lions would go on to book their place in the quarter-finals with a 1-1 draw against the Swiss at Wembley and a 2-0 win in Greece.

8) Taavi Rähn

England were already leading Estonia 2-0 in a Euro 2008 qualifier at Wembley shortly after the half-hour mark when Ashley Cole fired in a left-wing cross from deep. Standing just outside his own penalty area, Estonian midfielder Taavi Rähn flung himself at the ball but got his clearance all wrong, sending a powerful, low header past the dive of Watford goalkeeper Mart Poom and in off a post for the most spectacular of own goals. Surprisingly, it turned out to be the final goal in a routine 3-0 win for England.

9) Aleksandr Kuchma

In a World Cup qualifier at Wembley in October 2008, England were making heavy weather of beating minnows Kazakhstan and were only leading by Rio Ferdinand's header midway through the second half. Then Frank Lampard whipped in a free kick from the left and the ball flicked off the head of Kazakhstan defender Aleksandr Kuchma and into the net, as he attempted to clear under pressure from Wayne Rooney. The lucky break seemed to energise Fabio Capello's team, who went on to cruise to a 5-1 win.

10) Alessandro Della Valle

The hapless San Marino defender is the only player to have scored two own goals against England. Della Valle opened his account for the Three Lions in a home World Cup qualifier in March 2013, side-footing in a Leighton Baines cross for the opening goal in his team's 8-0 eventual defeat. The following year he was on target – or, should that be 'off target' – again in a European Championship qualifier at Wembley, deflecting in a Wayne Rooney cross off his chest for the final goal in a 5-0 thrashing. Sadly for the Three Lions, he retired from international football in 2017.

TOP 10 CAPTAINS

The most inspirational players to have worn the armband for the Three Lions:

1) Bobby Moore

Alf Ramsey first made Bobby Moore his skipper for a 4-2 win against Czechoslovakia in May 1963, although the armband reverted to Blackpool full-back Jimmy Armfield for the following season. However, Moore's composed displays in the heart of the England defence made him the obvious choice as captain and he soon took on the skipper's role on a permanent basis, famously leading his country to World Cup glory in 1966. 'He was the supreme professional, the best I ever worked with,' was Ramsey's assessment of Moore's leadership qualities. 'Without him England would never have won the World Cup.' The West Ham legend also captained the Three Lions at the 1970 World Cup in Mexico, going on to wear the armband a joint record 90 times in his 108 international appearances.

2) Billy Wright

The first man to win a century of caps for England, Billy Wright also captained his country 90 times. The Wolves defender was first given the armband by Walter Winterbottom for a 6-2 thrashing of Northern Ireland in Belfast in October 1948 and held the captaincy for another 11 years, only missing three games through injury when Alf Ramsey deputised as skipper. Captain at the 1950, 1954 and 1958 World Cups, Wright is the only player to have led England at three finals. Remarkably, in his last game as a professional footballer he skippered England to an 8-1 defeat of the USA in a friendly in Los Angeles, bringing down the curtain on an international career which brought him a then-record 105 caps.

3) Bryan Robson

After initially vying with Ray Wilkins for the captaincy under new boss Bobby Robson, Manchester United dynamo Bryan

Robson was soon installed as the Three Lions' regular skipper – although his regular absences through injury meant either Wilkins or goalkeeper Peter Shilton filled the role fairly often. After limping out of the 1986 World Cup, Robbo led England at the 1988 Euros and again at the 1990 World Cup in Italy – although, sadly, his tournament was soon ended by an achilles tendon injury, with Terry Butcher taking the armband in his place. Yet Robson still managed to captain England 65 times in a long international career in which he earned 90 caps.

4) David Beckham

The Manchester United midfielder was first made England captain by caretaker manager Peter Taylor for a friendly against Italy in November 2000 and was installed as the permanent skipper by Sven-Göran Eriksson the following year. Despite initial concerns that he was not a natural leader, Beckham soon grew into the role and led his team-mates by example, no more so than when a brilliant performance against Greece secured the Three Lions' place at the 2002 World Cup. He went on to skipper the side at three tournaments before being surprisingly jettisoned by new boss Steve McClaren after the 2006 World Cup. Capped 115 times, he wore the armband on 59 of those occasions.

5) Harry Kane

Gareth Southgate first made Harry Kane his England skipper against Scotland in June 2017, the Tottenham forward marking the occasion with a goal in a 2-2 draw. Kane has gone on to lead his country nearly 50 times, including at the 2018 World Cup in Russia – when his six goals won him the Golden Boot – and the delayed 2020 European Championship when he became the first Englishman since Bobby Moore in 1966 to captain the Three Lions in a major international final.

6) Kevin Keegan

The Liverpool striker first captained his country in a 2-1 win against Wales in March 1976 and later that year replaced Gerry Francis as the regular England skipper. However, when Ron Greenwood became Three Lions' boss in the summer of 1977 he initially preferred Emlyn Hughes in the role, before returning the armband to Keegan for the 1980 European Championship in Italy. The diminutive forward was also squad captain at the 1982 World Cup in Spain, but, sidelined by injury, the on-pitch skipper was Ipswich full-back Mick Mills. Nonetheless, Keegan captained the Three Lions an impressive 31 times in his 63 appearances.

7) Alan Shearer

Shortly after signing for Newcastle from Blackburn for a world record £15m in July 1996, Alan Shearer was appointed England captain by new boss Glenn Hoddle. Over the next two seasons his appearances for his country were limited by injury, with Tony Adams, Paul Ince, Stuart Pearce and David Seaman all wearing the armband in his absence. However, the prolific striker was fit to captain the Three Lions at the 1998 World Cup in France and continued in the role until announcing his retirement from international football after the 2000 European Championship in Belgium and the Netherlands. In total, he skippered England 34 times in his 63 appearances.

8) Johnny Haynes

After Billy Wright retired in 1959, Blackburn's Ronnie Clayton skippered the Three Lions for five games before being dropped. Walter Winterbottom then passed the armband to Fulham midfield maestro Johnny Haynes, an established international with 34 caps already to his name. Haynes enjoyed a tremendous first season as skipper – a free-scoring England side banging in 46 goals in just nine games in 1960/61 – and then led his country to the quarter-finals of the 1962 World Cup in Chile. Sadly, injuries to his legs sustained in a car crash later that year ended his international career, his 56 caps including 22 as captain.

9) Eddie Hapgood

The tough-tackling Arsenal left-back was first made England captain for the infamous 'Battle of Highbury' clash with world champions Italy in November 1934. He skippered the side for two seasons before losing his place in the side, his Gunners team-mate George Male taking over the armband. Hapgood returned to the Three Lions' line-up in the spring of 1938 and was immediately re-installed as skipper, a role he held until England's very last match before the outbreak of World War II. In all, he captained the side in 21 of the 30 internationals he appeared in.

10) John Terry

The Chelsea centre-back was first made England captain by new boss Steve McClaren in 2006 and went on to skipper his country 34 times. Terry's consistent displays and big personality made him a tremendous leader on the pitch, but his captaincy was marked by two major controversies. First, he was stripped of the armband by Fabio Capello in February 2010 following newspaper reports about his private life; then, after regaining the captaincy in 2011, the FA removed it from him once again a year later when Terry was due to stand trial on allegations of making a racist comment to QPR's Anton Ferdinand – a decision which prompted Capello to resign in protest.

TOP 10 JAILBIRDS

The England players who were sent to prison at some point in their lives:

1) Peter Storey

A Double winner with Arsenal in 1971, hatchet man midfielder Peter Storey won 19 caps for England under Sir Alf Ramsey. When his career ended in 1977 he soon became involved in various criminal enterprises after befriending a couple of local gangsters while running a pub in Islington. In December 1979 he was fined £700 and given a six-month suspended sentence for running a brothel in east London, and the following year he was jailed for three years for his role in a counterfeit money scam. In April 1982 Storey was handed a 12-month suspended sentence for stealing two cars he had on hire purchase for his minicab firm, and in 1990 he spent another 28 days in prison for attempting to import pornographic videos from Europe. He later turned his back on his criminal past, going to live in southern France with his fourth wife.

2) Adam Johnson

Capped 12 times by England between 2010 and 2012 in his Manchester City days, Sunderland winger Adam Johnson was arrested in March 2015 on suspicion of having sexual activity with a 15-year-old girl. The following year at Bradford Crown Court Johnson pleaded guilty to 'one count of sexual activity with a child and one count of grooming'. He denied two further counts of underage sex, but was found guilty of one and was sentenced to six years' imprisonment. He served his time at HMP Moorland near Doncaster and was released in March 2019 but has not returned to football.

3) Graham Rix
Creative midfielder Graham Rix won 17 caps for England while with Arsenal, representing his country at the 1982 World Cup in Spain. In March 1999, while working as assistant manager at Chelsea, Rix was sentenced to 12 months' imprisonment at Knightsbridge Crown Court after pleading guilty to two counts of unlawful sex with a 15-year-old girl and indecently assaulting her. He served six months in Wandsworth Prison before returning to his job at Stamford Bridge.

4) Tony Adams
In May 1990, Arsenal and England defender Tony Adams crashed his Ford Sierra into a wall in Rayleigh, Essex and when breathalysed he was found to be more than four times over the legal drink-drive limit. In December that year he was imprisoned for four months at Southend Crown Court, serving two months in Chelmsford Prison. However, he bounced back to skipper Arsenal to numerous trophies, including two Doubles, and to captain England at Euro '96. Two years later he wrote a best-selling autobiography, dealing with his battle with alcoholism during his playing career.

5) Peter Swan
Sheffield Wednesday defender Peter Swan was capped 19 times by England and was a member of the squad which travelled to Chile for the 1962 World Cup, although illness prevented him from making an appearance at the finals. In April 1964 he was one of three Wednesday players named in a match-fixing scandal, and the following year he was sent to HMP Lincoln for four months as well as receiving a life ban from football. After working as a

car salesman and pub landlord the ban was lifted in 1972 and he returned to professional football for two years, playing for Wednesday and Bury.

6) Tony Kay

Capped once for England in an 8-1 win in Switzerland in June 1963, half-back Tony Kay was implicated in the same betting scandal as Peter Swan the following year. Found guilty of conspiracy to defraud, Kay was sentenced to four months in prison and banned from football for life. Although he was nearly a year younger than Swan, Kay never returned to pro football, working later as a groundsman in south-east London.

7) Gary Charles

Capped twice by England in 1991, full-back Gary Charles struggled with alcoholism after his career ended and in January 2004 was imprisoned for four months after admitting drink-driving offences at Derby Magistrates' Court. Nearly three years later, while serving a suspended sentence for attacking a woman at a taxi rank, he admitted a public order offence after he drunkenly threatened a bouncer with an imaginary knife and was sentenced to 12 months in prison at Derby Crown Court. He has since set up a business helping people with depression and addiction issues.

8) Joey Barton

Fiery midfielder Joey Barton won a single cap for England, coming on as a late sub in a 1-0 defeat to Spain in February 2007. On Boxing Day that year he was arrested in Liverpool city centre after becoming involved in a fight, CCTV footage showing him punching a man 20 times and also attacking a teenager. In May 2008 Barton pleaded guilty to common assault and affray at Liverpool Crown Court and he was sentenced to six months' imprisonment, serving 74 days behind bars.

9) Kerry Dixon

Chelsea striker Kerry Dixon was capped eight times by England in the mid-1980s, scoring four goals. In June 2015 the Blues legend was jailed for nine months after being found guilty of actual bodily harm following an incident in a Dunstable pub in which he punched and kicked a man who had insulted him. Dixon served four months in Bedford prison, an experience he later described as 'lonely, boring, scary and harrowing'. He has since rebuilt his life, working as a heating engineer and writing an autobiography.

10) Ian Wright

As a 19-year-old lad hoping to make it as a pro footballer, Ian Wright had two cars but no licence, tax or insurance. After failing to pay his fines he was convicted of various driving offences and sent to Chelmsford Prison for two weeks. 'The sound of those prison doors closing and the nutters inside taught me: I can't live my life like this,' he later recalled. To his credit, the teenage tearaway turned his life around, winning 33 caps for England before becoming a successful TV personality.

TOP 10 GOLDEN OLDIES

The England players who were still turning out for the Three Lions aged 36 – or even older!

1) Stanley Matthews

'The Wizard of the Dribble' was aged 42 years and 103 days when he played his final game for England against Denmark on 15 May 1957, rounding off an international career which stretched back to 1934. Matthews bowed out in style, too, as Walter Winterbottom's team cruised to a 4-1 win in Copenhagen and his consistently outstanding performances on the wing for Blackpool led many to believe he should have been selected for the 1958 World Cup in Sweden. However, England's oldest ever player continued to defy Father Time, turning out for Stoke City in the top flight five days after his 50th birthday.

2) Peter Shilton

The veteran goalkeeper made the last of his record 125 appearances for England in the third-place play-off against hosts Italy at the 1990 World Cup, aged 40 years and 292 days. However, it was not an especially happy occasion for Shilton in Bari as he was at fault for the Italians' opener in a 2-1 defeat. Although it was probably the right moment to call time on his international career, Shilton carried on playing club football for another seven years, finally retiring with more than 1,000 league games under his belt when aged 47.

3) Alec Morten

Goalkeeper for amateur side Crystal Palace, Alec Morten would have played in England's first match, against Scotland in November 1872, but for injury. Instead he had to wait until the following March to make his international debut when he captained the Three Lions to a 4-2 victory over the Scots at Kennington Oval aged 41 years and 113 days – the second-oldest player to represent England. As the first match had finished 0-0, Morten holds the unwanted distinction of being the first England goalkeeper to concede a goal. The following year he acted as an umpire in England's 2-1 defeat to Scotland at Partick.

4) David James

After starting the 2010 World Cup in South Africa as the reserve goalkeeper, Portsmouth's David James was recalled to the team by England boss Fabio Capello after a calamitous error by Rob Green in the Three Lions' opener against the USA. James kept clean sheets against Algeria and Slovenia, helping England to qualify for the knockout stages, but fared less well in the disastrous 4-1 defeat to Germany in the last 16 in Bloemfontein. Aged 39 years and 330 days, it turned out to be the last of his 53 caps in an international career which had begun in 1997.

5) Ted Taylor

Having started out with Oldham and seen his career interrupted by World War I, goalkeeper Ted Taylor enjoyed a glorious Indian Summer with Huddersfield in his 30s, helping the Terriers win three consecutive league titles between 1924 and 1926. His fine form saw him called up by England, making a debut against Northern Ireland aged 35, and he went on to win eight caps, the last coming in a 1-0 defeat to Scotland at Old Trafford in April 1926 when he was aged 39 years and 41 days.

6) David Seaman

QPR and Arsenal goalkeeper David Seaman had a superb international career, conceding just 44 goals in 75 matches and starring for his country as England reached the semi-finals of

Euro '96. However he won't remember his last appearance for the Three Lions with much pleasure, as he conceded a goal straight from a corner in a 2-2 draw with Macedonia at Southampton in October 2002. Aged 39 years and 27 days at the time, it was clear to all watching that Seaman's best days were behind him and he was promptly dropped by Sven-Göran Eriksson in favour of David James.

7) Leslie Compton

A few months after helping Arsenal win the FA Cup in 1950, half-back Leslie Compton made his international bow in a 4-2 win against Wales at Sunderland. Aged 38 years and 64 days, he remains the oldest outfield player ever to make his debut for England. A week later Compton won his second and last cap, rather blotting his copybook by scoring an own goal in a 2-2 draw with Yugoslavia at his club ground, Highbury. His brother, Denis, also represented the Three Lions in 12 wartime internationals, but was better known for his cricketing career as a dashing middle-order batsman for Middlesex and England.

8) Stuart Pearce

Known throughout the football world as 'Psycho' for his relentlessly committed approach to the art of defending, Stuart Pearce's England career looked to be over after he was discarded by Glenn Hoddle following the Three Lions' success at Le Tournoi in France in 1997. However, two years later he was recalled by Kevin Keegan for a pair of European Championship qualifiers, and the West Ham left-back took his caps total to 78 with appearances against Luxembourg and Poland in September 1999, the latter coming when he was aged 37 years and 137 days.

9) Sam Hardy

One of a handful of players to represent England both before and after World War I, Aston Villa goalkeeper Sam Hardy made his final appearance for the Three Lions against Scotland at Hillsborough aged 37 years and 228 days in April 1920. Dubbed 'Safe and Steady Sam', Hardy didn't quite live up to that moniker on the day, conceding four goals in a thrilling 5-4 win for the home side.

10) Jesse Pennington
A regular for England before World War I, West Brom left-back
Jesse Pennington was recalled to the Three Lions' team for two
games in 1920. The first didn't go so well, as his slip led to Wales's
winner in a 2-1 defeat at Highbury. However, a month later, when
aged 36 years and 230 days, 'Peerless Pennington' was able to
round off his international career in some style, helping England
beat old enemies Scotland 5-4 at Hillsborough.

TOP 10 TV PRESENTERS

Loads of former England internationals have worked as football
pundits on TV, but this lot made the more challenging move into
the presenter's chair:

1) Gary Lineker, *Match of the Day*
England's fourth-highest goalscorer is the longest-serving
presenter of the BBC's flagship football highlights programme,
having taken over from Des Lynam in 1999. Famously, he
presented the first show of the 2016/17 season in just a pair of
shorts after promising the previous campaign to strip to his
undies if his beloved Leicester City won the Premier League. A
highly experienced and capable broadcaster who never appears
ruffled, Lineker has also presented *Football Focus*, the BBC's
coverage of major golf tournaments, BT's Champions League
shows and hosted comedy news programme *Have I Got News For
You?* on several occasions.

2) Jimmy Greaves, *Saint and Greavsie*
After working with former Scottish international Ian St John on
ITV's football preview show *On the Ball*, Jimmy Greaves teamed
up with his old sparring partner again on *Saint and Greavsie*,
which ran on ITV from 1985 to 1992. While 'The Saint' played the
role of the serious football presenter, 'Greavsie' was the perfect foil,
invariably focusing on the lighter side of the game and annoying
viewers north of the border with his disparaging comments about
Scottish goalkeepers. Greaves also worked as a presenter on the
short-lived regional chat show *Jimmy Greaves*, ITV children's

programme *The Saturday Show* and as a TV reviewer on breakfast show *TV-am*.

3) Ian Wright, *Moneyball*

Arsenal striker Ian Wright began his TV career while still playing in the top flight, occasionally presenting *Top of the Pops* and then hosting a chat show on ITV, *Friday Night's All Wright*. After retiring from the game, the ebullient Londoner was a team captain on the BBC comedy sports quiz *They Think It's All Over*, a presenter for one series of *Gladiators* and then teamed up with former model Melinda Messenger in 2009 to host Channel 5's early evening magazine show *Live from Studio Five*. More often seen on our screens in a pundit role in recent years, Wright returned to presenting to front ITV's primetime game show *Moneyball* in October 2021. Hollie Richardson in *The Guardian* was impressed, describing the former England international as 'football's most affable man' and 'a natural host'.

4) John Fashanu, *Gladiators*

In 1992, three years after he won his two England caps and while he was still playing up front for Premier League side Wimbledon, John Fashanu co-hosted the original series of *Gladiators* on ITV alongside Ulrika Jonsson. He proved to be a popular presenter of the sports entertainment show, delighting fans with his nonsensical catchphrase 'Awooga!', and he continued in the role until 2000 – apart from two series when he was replaced by rugby union star Jeremy Guscott. In 2003 Fashanu fronted an ITV series based on the American show *Man vs. Beast*, but after protests from animal rights groups it was never broadcast.

5) Dion Dublin, *Homes Under the Hammer*

After a football career which saw him win four caps as a battering ram striker in 1998, Dion Dublin moved into punditry before becoming a co-presenter on the BBC house renovation and auction show *Homes Under the Hammer* in 2015. His enthusiastic performances have generally been well-received by viewers, although he has been mocked online for pointing out the 'stairs going up to the bedrooms' virtually every time he visits a different house.

6) Alex Scott, *Football Focus*

After making 140 appearances for the England women's team, Alex Scott moved into TV and in 2018 became the first female football pundit for the BBC at a World Cup. In 2020 she was one of the hosts for the BBC Sports Personality of the Year Awards and the following year she replaced Dan Walker as the presenter of *Football Focus* – the first permanent female host of the long-running BBC Saturday lunchtime football preview show. Thus far, her bubbly personality and empathetic interviewing style has made her a big hit with viewers.

7) Jack Charlton, *Jack's Game*

A World Cup winner with England in 1966, Jack Charlton always enjoyed spending his free time hunting, shooting and fishing in the countryside and in 1983 made a series for Yorkshire Television about field sports. Hare coursing, deer stalking and salmon fishing were among the activities 'Big Jack' was seen taking part in, and his gruff northern persona made him an ideal presenter for the series. However, his involvement sparked protests from the anti-blood sports movement and in October 1984 broken glass was sprinkled on the pitch at Coventry ahead of a visit by Newcastle, then managed by Charlton.

8) Jermaine Jenas, *The One Show*

After cutting his teeth as a TV football pundit, former England midfielder Jermaine Jenas began co-presenting *The One Show* for the BBC in 2020. Reviews for his performance on the live magazine-style show have been mainly positive from viewers, but he has made a few gaffes in the hot seat, on one occasion having to apologise to actor Martin Clunes for getting his name slightly wrong. In April 2022 Jenas presented the World Cup finals draw live from Qatar.

9) Alan Shearer, *Alan Shearer: Football, Dementia and Me*

In November 2017 former England striker Alan Shearer investigated the potential link between heading and dementia in this one-off BBC documentary. 'He is a bit awkward, doesn't have Gary Lineker's ease and wit,' was the verdict of Sam Wollaston in *The Guardian*. 'But he's serious, engaged and engaging, and proves he can make the step up from *Match of the Day* punditry and go it alone.'

10) Peter Crouch, *Crouchy's Year-Late Euros: Live*

The gangly ex-England striker teamed up with DJ Maya Jama and musician and comedian Alex Horne to present this late-night BBC entertainment show during the delayed Euro 2020 tournament. Crouch proved to be an amiable host alongside guests like Jimmy Carr, Harry Redknapp and John Barnes, but the show attracted almost unanimous negative reviews. 'It's just too cringeworthy to watch,' one viewer complained, 'too many unprofessional awkward moments – jokes that don't land and talking over each other. Just awful!'

TOP 10 UNDER-CAPPED PLAYERS

The following players won fewer than five England caps each, despite starring for their clubs on a regular basis and winning a host of honours. Incredibly, between them they played for the Three Lions just 24 times – three fewer appearances than the thoroughly mediocre Phil Jones managed on his own!

1) Tony Brown

Attacking midfielder Tony 'Bomber' Brown is probably West Brom's greatest ever player, scoring a club record 279 goals in 720 appearances. After topping the old First Division scoring charts in 1970/71 with an impressive 28 goals, he was selected by Sir Alf Ramsey to play for England against Wales at Wembley. 'Alf wanted me to play as an out-and-out striker and I never enjoyed that, playing with my back to goal,' he recalled. An experimental England side could only manage a 0-0 draw, with Brown being subbed off after 74 minutes. An outstanding player for the Baggies, he deserved much better than this single cap.

2) Alan Hudson

'Where have England been hiding this player?' was the incredulous reaction of the great Günter Netzer after Stoke midfielder Alan Hudson put on a five-star show on his England debut against reigning world champions West Germany at Wembley in

March 1975. The silky playmaker set up Colin Bell's opener in an impressive 2-0 win and seemed set for a long international career, but the 23-year-old's individualistic style and forthright personality were not to England boss Don Revie's taste and he only featured once more, in a 5-0 thrashing of Cyprus the following month, before being unceremoniously jettisoned. A terrible waste of a prodigious talent.

3) Peter Osgood

The flamboyant Chelsea striker was in the form of his life in 1970 – hitting a career best 31 goals in all competitions and scoring in every round of the FA Cup – and was tipped to make a big impression at that summer's World Cup. However, he only played for a total of 42 minutes in two substitute appearances in Mexico before being discarded by Sir Alf Ramsey until earning a belated recall for a friendly against Italy at Wembley in November 1973. Just four caps seems a measly return for a sublimely skilled player who is still revered at Stamford Bridge, his statue standing outside the West Stand.

4) Stan Collymore

A pacy, powerful and prolific striker, Nottingham Forest's Stan Collymore won two caps under Terry Venables in 1995 for the Umbro Cup matches against Japan and Brazil. Later that summer he moved to Liverpool for a then British record £8.5m, where he formed a deadly attacking partnership with Robbie Fowler, but he didn't figure for England again until September 1997 when a late substitute appearance against Moldova at Wembley turned out to be his last cap.

5) Charlie George

The darling of Arsenal's North Bank had moved on to Derby County when he played for England in a friendly against the Republic of Ireland at Wembley in September 1976. An attacking midfielder known for scoring spectacular goals, George helped to set up Stuart Pearson's opener but at half-time was ordered to move to the left wing by England boss Don Revie. 'I'm not a left-winger, and I told him so,' George revealed to *The Independent* in 2013. 'But I knew when I saw Gordon

Hill warming up that I was coming off, and I told Revie what I thought of him in no uncertain terms. So I had one hour for England and that was it.'

6) Fred Pickering

Shortly after joining Everton from Blackburn Rovers for £85,000 – then a record fee between two English clubs – Fred Pickering made his debut for England in a friendly against the USA in New York in May 1964. He scored a hat-trick in a 10-0 win and later that year played twice more for his country, opening the scoring in a 4-3 victory against Northern Ireland in Belfast and then notching again in a 2-2 draw with Belgium at Wembley. Despite this excellent start to his international career, the Toffees striker never added to those three caps.

7) Alan Hinton

After making his England debut as a 19-year-old against France in October 1962, Nottingham Forest left-winger Alan Hinton was recalled by Alf Ramsey for a friendly against Belgium at Wembley two years later. His deflected cross helped England claim a 2-2 draw and in the next match, at home to Wales, he set up both of his Forest team-mate Frank Wignall's goals in a 2-1 win. However, Hinton never played for England again, despite performing consistently at club level for Forest and Derby County in his trademark white boots.

8) Terry Venables

An imaginative and creative central midfielder with Chelsea, Terry Venables made his England debut in a 2-2 draw with Belgium at Wembley in October 1964. Six weeks later he won his second cap in Amsterdam, setting up Jimmy Greaves for a late equaliser in a 1-1 draw with the Netherlands. Venables' quick-thinking and rapid pass-and-move style would probably have suited Alf Ramsey's wingless system, but the competition from the likes of Martin Peters, Alan Ball and Bobby Charlton proved too stiff and he was not picked again.

9) Fred Tilson

After scoring both goals for Manchester City in their 2-1 defeat of Portsmouth in the 1934 FA Cup Final, striker Fred Tilson made his England debut against Hungary in a friendly in Budapest. He scored in a 2-1 defeat, repeating the feat six days later in another 2-1 loss against Czechoslovakia in Prague. Later that year he netted a brace in a 4-0 win against Wales in Cardiff and, after missing the next four England games, he was again on target in a 3-1 win against Ireland in Belfast in October 1935. However, despite hitting five goals in four games for England, he was not selected again.

10) Steve Perryman
Defensive midfielder Steve Perryman made his only England appearance as a 70th minute substitute in a 1-1 draw against Iceland in Reykjavík in June 1982, a fixture that was originally assigned B team status before being upgraded. A solitary cap seemed poor reward for an ultra-consistent player who helped Tottenham win two FA Cups, two League Cups and the UEFA Cup in both 1972 and 1984 as well as being named the Football Writers' Association Footballer of the Year in 1982.

TOP 10 WINS AGAINST SCOTLAND

The most fondly remembered of England's 48 victories against the 'Auld Enemy':

1) England 9 Scotland 3, British Home Championship, 15 April 1961
On a sunny day at Wembley England thrilled their fans by recording their biggest ever win against Scotland to claim the 1960/61 Home Championship. The Three Lions shared out the goals, with Jimmy Greaves (three), Bobby Smith (two), Johnny Haynes (two), Brian Douglas and future England boss Bobby Robson all getting on the scoresheet. However, they were helped in no small measure by hapless Celtic goalkeeper Frank Haffey who had a nightmare match between the sticks for Scotland. Afterwards, school kids up and down the country delighted in asking each other, 'What's the time?' The correct answer, of course, was, 'Nine past Haffey!'

2) England 2 Scotland 0, European Championship group stage, 15 June 1996

The first meeting between England and Scotland at a major tournament finals was won by the Three Lions after a dramatic second half at Wembley. Following a disappointing 1-1 draw with Switzerland in their opening fixture, England badly needed all three points and took the lead on 52 minutes, Alan Shearer heading in Gary Neville's cross at the far post. Twelve minutes from the end Scotland were awarded a penalty after Tony Adams fouled Gordon Durie, but David Seaman produced a tremendous save to thwart Gary McAllister. Play quickly moved to the other end of the pitch where midfield talisman Paul Gascoigne sealed victory for England with a marvellous goal, flicking the ball over Scottish centre-half Colin Hendry before volleying in from 12 yards.

3) England 7 Scotland 2, British Home Championship, 2 April 1955

England hadn't beaten Scotland at home since 1934 but ended the 21-year hoodoo in superb style at Wembley to clinch the 1954/55 British Home Championship.. Wolves striker Dennis Wilshaw was the Scots' chief tormentor with four goals, including one in the opening minute. However, 40-year-old wing wizard Stanley Matthews was an equally important figure in England's crushing victory, setting up four of his side's goals with pinpoint crosses. Nat Lofthouse (two) and Don Revie were the other players to find the net for England, for whom 18-year-old midfield powerhouse Duncan Edwards made an impressive debut.

4) Scotland 0 England 2, European Championship qualifying play-off first leg, 13 November 1999

In a 'Battle of Britain' clash with a place at the Euro 2000 finals at stake, England gained a first-leg advantage thanks to two goals by Manchester United midfielder Paul Scholes. The first came on 21 minutes when he chested down Sol Campbell's pass before shooting past Scotland goalkeeper Neil Sullivan. Then, three minutes before half-time, Scholes silenced the home fans at Hampden Park for a second time, heading in David Beckham's free kick.

'We played fantastic today,' said England boss Kevin Keegan afterwards, 'I couldn't have asked for more.' However, four days later the Three Lions put their fans through the wringer at Wembley, losing 1-0 to win the two-legged play-off by the narrowest of margins.

5) Scotland 0 England 5, Scottish FA centenary match, 14 February 1973

A match to celebrate the centenary of the Scottish FA turned into a humiliating occasion for the home side and their new boss, Willie Ormond. On a snow-covered pitch, the contest was effectively over after 15 minutes as an own goal from Peter Lorimer and further strikes from Allan Clarke and Mick Channon gave England a 3-0 lead. Long kicks by goalkeeper Peter Shilton set up Martin Chivers and Clarke for two more goals late on in the second half to round off a real St Valentine's Day Massacre by Sir Alf Ramsey's team. However, Scotland had the last laugh, qualifying for the 1974 World Cup later in the year while England were eliminated by Poland.

6) England 3 Scotland 0, World Cup qualifier, 11 November 2016

England made light work of a Scottish side wearing ghastly pink shirts, opening the scoring after 23 minutes when Liverpool striker Daniel Sturridge headed in Kyle Walker's cross. Adam Lallana doubled the Three Lions' lead early in the second half with a well-directed header from Danny Rose's left-wing cross and Gary Cahill wrapped up a comfortable England win with another header from Wayne Rooney's corner on 63 minutes.

7) Scotland 0 England 1, World Cup qualifier/British Home Championship, 15 April 1950

The British Home Championship in 1949/50 also doubled as a qualifying group for the 1950 World Cup in Brazil. With the top two teams guaranteed qualification by FIFA, both England and Scotland had already booked their passage by the time they met at Hampden Park in the last game of the series. England, though, had a point to make and clinched victory midway through the second half when Chelsea striker Roy Bentley scored on his debut from a pass by Bolton winger Bobby Langton. Miffed at coming second behind their oldest rival, Scotland turned down the invitation to South America.

8) Scotland 0 England 5, British Home Championship, 17 March 1888

England had lost six and drawn two of their previous eight meetings with Scotland, but the Three Lions ended that dismal run in fine style with an emphatic victory at Hampden Park. In a tremendous attacking display by the whole team, Preston North End's Fred Dewhurst took many of the plaudits with two excellent goals: the first a header and the second a fierce shot. Victory clinched the British Home Championship for England, their first outright triumph in the five-year-old competition.

9) England 5 Scotland 1, British Home Championship, 24 May 1975

England clinched the British Home Championship with a crushing victory over the Scots at Wembley, QPR midfielder Gerry Francis starting the rout after five minutes with a superb swerving shot from 25 yards. Just two minutes later a brilliant England counter attack ended with left-back Kevin Beattie heading in Kevin Keegan's right-wing cross. After Colin Bell made it three with a low drive from the edge of the box, Scotland pulled one back just before half-time through a Bruce Rioch penalty. However, there was to be no comeback as England piled on the misery for shellshocked Scottish goalkeeper Stewart Kennedy in the second half with further goals from Francis and Ipswich striker David Johnson.

10) England 5 Scotland 4, British Home Championship, 10 April 1920

The small matter of World War I meant the two countries had not met for six years, but they made up for lost time with a thrilling encounter in front of 35,000 fans at Hillsborough. Having taken an early lead through Chelsea striker Jack Cock, England were trailing 4-2 at the break and looking in some disarray. However, a superb second half display saw England score three times without reply, debutants Bob Kelly (two) and Fred Morris grabbing the goals.

TOP 10 ENGLAND WOMEN QUOTES

Some of the most famous names from the women's game have their say:

1) 'The celebrations are going to be big and I don't think I'm going to sleep this week!'
Jill Scott, after England won the 2022 Euros

2) 'Women's football is a prettier game to watch to men's football because there is no cheating going on.'
Kelly Smith, 2015

3) 'It's the proudest moment of my life until I have kids, I suppose.'
England captain Leah Williamson after the Lionesses beat Germany in the final of Euro 2022

4) 'I've played for England and in World Cups and Olympics, but I've never been as nervous as I am during the results show.'
Alex Scott on competing in *Strictly Come Dancing* in 2019

5) 'I made my England debut against Japan in 2013. Hope Powell, our manager at the time, always demanded the best. She had quite a stern approach ... she'd look at you over her glasses sometimes.'
Lucy Bronze, 2019

6) 'I like City and England having a female kit – because little girls will watch us and say, "I want the women's tracksuit or kit."'
Alex Greenwood, 2021

7) 'Women's football was growing when I was a kid kicking a ball around the parks of north-west London, but I didn't even know England had a women's team.'
Rachel Yankey, 2019

8) 'I've never, ever set my sights on getting 100 – it's more my family. My dad's been counting down the caps for every single

home game, and he's been to every single one I've played for England.'

Former England captain Steph Houghton, after winning her 100th cap in 2018

9) 'Probably a career highlight would be when I told my mum when I was 11 I would play for England, and then at 17 doing it.'

Karen Carney, 2019

10) 'When I was at City, there was this thing about me going out with Sergio Agüero and I was like, "This is news to me."'

Toni Duggan, 2019

TOP 10 BORN-ABROAD

These players were all born outside England but they were still extremely proud to wear the Three Lions on their chest:

1) Raheem Sterling (Jamaica)

Just like the 1980s Watford and England duo Luther Blissett and John Barnes, Raheem Sterling was born in Jamaica before coming to England as a child. After starting out with QPR he joined Liverpool when he was still 15 in 2010, and just over two years later he made his England debut in a friendly away to Sweden. A nippy, skilful and quick-thinking winger who was central to Manchester City's recent successes before moving to Chelsea in the summer of 2022, Sterling has gone on to play over 70 times for his country, appearing in four major international tournaments, most notably the delayed 2020 Euros when he scored vital goals for England in wins against Croatia, the Czech Republic and Germany.

2) Terry Butcher (Singapore)

Although he was born in Singapore, where his father was commissioned with the Royal Navy, Terry Butcher spent most of his childhood in Lowestoft. He joined Ipswich Town, the club he supported, as a 17-year-old in 1976 and four years later made his England debut in a friendly against Australia in Sydney. Over the next decade the tough-tackling centre-back was pretty much a fixture in the Three Lions' defence, playing in three World Cups, winning 77 caps and captaining the side on seven occasions. He later moved into management, holding the reins at Coventry, Sunderland, Motherwell and Hibs among other clubs.

3) Owen Hargreaves (Canada)

Owen Hargreaves was born in Calgary, Alberta, to British parents who had emigrated to Canada at the start of the 1980s. After growing up watching and playing basketball, ice hockey and American football he didn't start playing football seriously until he was 15, but his talent was such that he was soon scouted by Bayern Munich. A year after breaking into the Bayern first team, Hargreaves made his England debut in a 2-0 defeat against the Netherlands in August 2001, despite having previously played three games for the Wales under-19 side. A tireless defensive midfielder who was an expert at retrieving possession, he went on to win 42 caps for England.

4) Tony Dorigo (Australia)

Born in Melbourne to an Italian father and Australian mother, Tony Dorigo was signed up by Aston Villa in 1983 after writing to 14 top-flight English clubs asking for a trial. Australia wanted the attack-minded left-back to play in the 1986 World Cup qualifiers but Villa manager Tony Barton refused him permission to travel, believing that the games against Pacific Island minnows would be a waste of Dorigo's time. However, after moving to Chelsea the now-British citizen made his England debut against Yugoslavia in 1989. Dorigo was part of England's squad at Italia '90 and won the last of his 15 caps while with Leeds in 1993.

5) Cyrille Regis (French Guiana)

Born in French Guiana in South America, Cyrille Regis moved to England aged five and grew up in Harlesden. He played for non-league Hayes before joining West Brom in 1977, where his surging runs and powerful shooting soon made him a cult hero. With dual French and British nationality, Regis could have chosen to represent either France or England, but opted for the Three Lions, making his under-21 debut in September 1978. He made his senior debut as a sub in 4-0 defeat of Northern Ireland at Wembley in February 1982. Later that year he was injured in his first start away to Iceland, ruling him out of contention for the World Cup in Spain. He ended his international career with just five caps – a disappointing return for such an exciting attacking talent.

6) William Kenyon-Slaney (India)

One of eight players born in India to represent England, William Kenyon-Slaney's father was a captain in the Second Bombay Light Cavalry in the East Indian Company. After attending Eton College, Kenyon-Slaney joined the Grenadier Guards while also playing first-class cricket for MCC and Shropshire. He excelled too at football, and on 8 March 1873 became the first player to score in an international match, netting twice in England's 4-2 win against Scotland at the Surrey County Cricket ground, Kennington. Surprisingly, this turned out to be his only cap.

7) John Salako (Nigeria)

Born in Ibadan, Nigeria, John Salako came to England as a ten-year-old with his mother after his father died. A flying winger, he attracted international attention after helping Crystal Palace reach the 1990 FA Cup Final. 'Nigeria called me up first of all and then Wales wanted to call me up,' he told the Eagles' website in 2019. However, Salako's heart was set on playing for England and in 1991 he appeared four times on a post-season tour of Australia, New Zealand and Malaysia before winning a final cap in a 1-0 defeat to Germany at Wembley.

8) Colin Viljoen (South Africa)

One of seven South African-born players to be capped by England, Colin Viljoen was signed by Ipswich from Johannesburg Rangers in 1966 when he was just 18. The neat-passing midfielder spent most of his career at Portman Road, helping Town win the FA Cup in 1978 although he was not selected for the final against Arsenal by future Three Lions' boss Bobby Robson. Three years earlier he played twice for England at the start of Don Revie's tenure, starting in draws against Northern Ireland and Wales.

9) Wilfried Zaha (Ivory Coast)

The talented Crystal Palace winger was born in Abidjan, Ivory Coast, and came to England aged four. After representing England at under-19 and under-21 level, he was one of six players to make his senior debut in a 4-2 friendly loss to Sweden in November 2012, coming on as a late sub for Raheem Sterling, The following August, at the start of an unsuccessful spell with Manchester United, Zaha replaced Theo Walcott for the last 15 minutes of an exciting 3-2 win against Scotland at Wembley. In November 2016, however, he decided to switch his international allegiance to his birth country in a move which disappointed England manager Gareth Southgate.

10) John Bain (Scotland)

Born in Bothwell, Lanarkshire to Scottish parents, John Bain was educated at Sherborne School and Winchester College before going up to Oxford. He helped the university team reach the FA Cup Final in 1877 and in the same year was selected as a forward against Scotland in a much-changed home line-up at the Kennington Oval. England lost the match 3-1 and Bain was not selected again, but he remains the only Scottish-born player to have appeared for the Three Lions.

TOP 10 INTERWAR PLAYERS

Although England declined to participate in the first three World Cups in the 1930s, the Three Lions were a major force in the global game in the period between the two world wars thanks, in no small part, to the players who feature on this list:

1) Eddie Hapgood

Captain of the Arsenal side which dominated English football in the 1930s, Eddie Hapgood led the Gunners to five league titles and two FA Cup triumphs in a glorious decade for the north London club. An elegant and composed left-back, Hapgood also skippered England 21 times in his 30 internationals, leading his country for the first time in the notorious 'Battle of Highbury' against Italy in November 1934, a match in which he suffered a broken nose and had to leave the pitch for 15 minutes. His career was prematurely ended by World War II, after which he had spells managing Blackburn Rovers, Watford and Bath City.

2) Cliff Bastin

Arsenal's third-highest goalscorer of all time behind Thierry Henry and Ian Wright, Cliff Bastin banged in 178 goals in all competitions while helping the Gunners win seven major trophies in the 1930s. The tricky left-winger made his England debut aged just 19 in a 3-1 win against Wales at Anfield in November 1931 and won a total of 21 caps, scoring 12 goals, including a well-placed volley in the famous 6-3 win against Germany in Berlin in May 1938. His career was effectively ended aged 27 with the start of World War II, during which he served as an ARP warden stationed on top of Highbury stadium. After the war, Bastin ran a pub in his native Exeter.

3) William 'Dixie' Dean

Famed for his heading ability, Dixie Dean scored an all-time single-season record of 60 league goals for Everton as the Toffees won the title in 1927/28 and went on to bag an incredible total of 379 league goals – a tally only bettered by Arthur Rowley. First capped by England in a 3-3 draw with Wales in February 1927, he scored an impressive 12 goals in his first five internationals, including hat-tricks against Belgium and Luxembourg. However, he couldn't match that lightning start and his England career was over by 1932 when he was still only 25. In all, he won 16 caps, scoring 18 times.

4) Stanley Matthews

'The Wizard of the Dribble' played 17 times for England before his career was interrupted by World War II and scored eight goals, including a hat-trick in a thrilling 5-4 win against Czechoslovakia at White Hart Lane in December 1937. Ironically, at the same venue two years earlier Matthews had been jeered by England fans after a poor display in a 3-0 victory against Germany, after which he was ignored by the selectors for 16 months. However, the Stoke winger's talents were such that, along with striker Tommy Lawton and creative midfielder Raich Carter, he was one of just three players to feature for England both before and after the conflict, appearing in his last game for the Three Lions aged 42 in 1957.

5) Harry Hibbs

An unspectacular but reliable goalkeeper, Harry Hibbs was a one-club man who made over 350 league appearances for Birmingham City. After impressing on an FA tour of South Africa, he was selected for England for a 6-0 drubbing of Wales at Stamford Bridge in November 1929. Over the next seven years he made a total of 25 appearances for the Three Lions – a record for an England goalkeeper which stood until beaten by Ron Springett in 1962. In 1944 Hibbs became manager of Walsall, a role he held for seven years.

6) George Camsell

An ex-miner, George Camsell scored a phenomenal 59 league goals in the 1926/27 season as Middlesbrough stormed to the Second Division title, and he finished his career with a club record 325 league goals for the Teessiders. He was equally prolific for England, scoring an extraordinary 18 goals in just nine games, including four goals against Belgium in May 1929 and a hat-trick against Wales later that same year. His average of exactly two goals per game for the Three Lions is better than any player who played in more than a single match.

7) Sammy Crooks

A Derby County stalwart for almost two decades, Sammy Crooks was a gifted right-sided winger or inside-forward. In 1930, while helping the Rams finish runners-up in the old First Division to champions Sheffield Wednesday, Crooks made his England debut in a 5-2 win against Scotland at Wembley. He went on to play 26 times for the Three Lions, scoring seven goals including a brace in a tremendous 7-1 rout of Spain at Highbury in December 1931. After his playing career ended he managed Shrewsbury Town for four years before later working as Derby's chief scout.

8) Eric Brook

A left-winger who was known for his powerful runs and fierce shot, Eric Brook was part of the Manchester City side which won the FA Cup in 1934, the league title in 1937 and then, incredibly, was relegated the following season despite being the division's top scorers. His England career was not quite as dramatic, but he served his country well in 18 appearances between 1929 and 1937, scoring ten times. Two of those goals came in the first 12 minutes of the infamous 'Battle of Highbury' against Italy in November 1934 when he also missed a first-minute penalty in an eventual 3-2 win. After retiring from the game, he worked as a coach driver, barman and crane operator.

9) Billy Walker

An Aston Villa legend, Billy Walker scored a club record 244 goals in all competitions for the Brummie outfit. He won the FA Cup in 1920 and later lifted the trophy again as a manager with both Sheffield Wednesday in 1935 and Nottingham Forest in 1959 – the 24-year gap remaining a record to this day. A tall inside-forward who was dangerous in the air, he scored on his England debut against Ireland in a 2-0 win at Sunderland in 1920 and four years later bagged the Three Lions' first goal at Wembley, the equaliser in a 1-1 draw with Scotland. After a near six-year gap, he was recalled to captain England in a 4-3 win against Austria at Stamford Bridge in December 1932, the last of his 18 caps.

10) Ernie Blenkinsop

Consistent Sheffield Wednesday left-back Ernie Blenkinsop won consecutive league titles with the Owls in 1929 and 1930 and made nearly 400 league appearances for the Yorkshire outfit before joining Liverpool in 1934. His England career only lasted for five years but saw him play in a then-record 26 consecutive internationals, the last coming when he captained the side for the fourth time, in a 2-1 defeat against Scotland at Hampden Park in April 1933. After retiring from the game, he was the licensee of a pub in Sheffield until his death aged 67 in 1969.

TOP 10 GOALS BY SUBSTITUTES

The players who have come off the bench to make a difference for the Three Lions:

1) David Platt, England 1 Belgium 0, World Cup last 16, 26 June 1990

A tight World Cup tie with Belgium in Bologna was still goalless when England boss Bobby Robson decided to make a positive change with 18 minutes to play, bringing on attacking midfielder David Platt of Aston Villa for the more defensively minded Steve McMahon. The gamble paid off in the last minute of extra time when, with a penalty shoot-out seemingly inevitable, Paul Gascoigne chipped a free kick towards the far post where Platt swivelled to guide a superb volley into the far corner. Without doubt the most important goal by an England sub, and probably the best too.

2) Teddy Sheringham, England 2 Greece 2, World Cup qualifier, 6 October 2001

Needing to at least match Germany's result against Finland to secure automatic qualification to the finals of the 2002 World Cup, England were trailing 1-0 to Greece at Old Trafford when Three Lions' boss Sven-Göran Eriksson subbed off Robbie Fowler for veteran Tottenham striker Teddy Sheringham. Incredibly, just 15 seconds later the 35-year-old scored, flicking on David Beckham's beautifully delivered free kick from the left with his head, the ball nestling in the bottom corner.

3) Daniel Sturridge, England 2 Wales 1, European Championship group stage, 16 June 2016

In the second minute of injury time England won their 'Battle of Britain' Euro 2016 clash with Wales in Lens thanks to a brilliant piece of opportunism from Daniel Sturridge. Introduced as a half-time substitute for Raheem Sterling, the Liverpool striker picked up the ball outside the penalty area before playing a pass into Jamie Vardy. The Leicester man flicked it off to Dele Alli, who in turn touched it into the path of Sturridge who, in a crowded six-yard box, somehow managed to squeeze a low shot in at the near post past Wales goalkeeper Wayne Hennessey.

4) Theo Walcott, England 3 Sweden 2, European Championship group stage, 15 June 2012

In a see-saw Euro 2012 match in Kyiv, England boss Roy Hodgson reacted to Sweden taking a 2-1 lead on the hour by replacing James Milner with Theo Walcott. The attacking change paid dividends two minutes later when the Arsenal striker controlled a headed clearance from a corner and fired in a swerving shot which completely bamboozled Sweden goalkeeper Andreas Isaksson and flew into the middle of the goal. Even better, the Three Lions went on to grab a late winner through Danny Welbeck.

5) Jamie Vardy, England 2 Wales 1, European Championship group stage, 16 June 2016
On as a half-time substitute for Harry Kane, Jamie Vardy scored the most important of his seven England goals 11 minutes into the second half in a Euro 2016 match in Lens to cancel out Gareth Bale's long-range free kick for Wales. The Leicester striker looked to be offside when he spun to slam the ball in from three yards, but Daniel Sturridge's cross had flicked off the head of Wales defender Ashley Williams so the goal was correctly awarded by the German referee.

6) Steven Gerrard, England 2 Sweden 2, World Cup group stage, 20 June 2006
After victories against Paraguay and Trinidad and Tobago at the 2006 World Cup in Germany, England completed their group stage with a match against Sweden in Cologne. With the scores tied at 1-1 midfielder Steven Gerrard, on as a 69th-minute sub for Wayne Rooney, appeared to have clinched all three points when he nodded in Joe Cole's cross at the far post with just five minutes left on the clock. However, the Three Lions had to settle for a draw when Barcelona striker Henrik Larsson poked home in the last minute of normal time.

7) Jermain Defoe, England 2 Italy 1, friendly, 15 August 2012
England gained some revenge for their Euro 2012 penalty shoot-out defeat by Italy with a friendly win over the *Azzurri* in Bern. On as a half-time substitute for Andy Carroll, Tottenham striker Jermain Defoe scored a superb winner in the 79th minute, collecting a pass from James Milner before cutting inside his marker and then unleashing a powerful shot from the edge of the box into the far top corner. This was the last of the record seven goals Defoe scored for his country as a substitute.

8) Peter Crouch, England 2 Uruguay 1, friendly, 1 March 2006

England were trailing at Anfield to a spectacular long-range strike by Uruguay's Omar Pouso when lanky striker Peter Crouch replaced Wayne Rooney soon after the hour. Just 11 minutes later the Liverpool target man met a Joe Cole cross from the left with a textbook downward header into the bottom corner to level the scores. Crouch's goal inspired the Three Lions to continue bombarding the South Americans' penalty area, and Cole grabbed a last-minute winner.

9) Jimmy Mullen, Belgium 1 England 4, friendly, 18 May 1950
Wolves left-winger Jimmy Mullen made history in this warm up match in Brussels for the 1950 World Cup, becoming England's first substitute when he replaced the injured Jackie Milburn in the tenth minute. Just 16 seconds into the second half Mullen netted the equaliser in an eventual 4-1 win with a low left-foot shot from a tight angle, setting an even more impressive record as the Three Lions' first scorer from off the bench.

10) Harry Kane, England 4 Lithuania 0, European Championship qualifier, 27 March 2015
On as a 72nd-minute substitute for skipper Wayne Rooney, Tottenham striker Harry Kane marked his England debut with a goal just 79 seconds later. Raheem Sterling was the provider, chipping a delightful ball to the far post which Kane met with a firm downward header palmed over the line by the Lithuania goalkeeper. The well-taken goal wrapped up a routine 4-0 Wembley win for England in what proved to be a successful Euro 2016 qualifying campaign.

TOP 10 OUTFIELD PLAYER BLOOPERS

The times when England players just wanted the ground to swallow them up – surprisingly, perhaps, this list includes monumental mistakes by some of the biggest names to represent the Three Lions:

1) Stuart Pearce, San Marino 1 England 7, World Cup qualifier, 17 November 1993
A tragicomic qualification campaign under hapless England manager Graham Taylor was given a fittingly ridiculous epilogue

in Bologna when left-back Stuart Pearce under-hit his back-pass to goalkeeper David Seaman right after kick-off, allowing San Marino winger Davide Gualtieri to nip in and score with a neatly placed low shot. The unexpected goal for the mountain-top minnows was timed at just 8.3 seconds – the fastest in World Cup history at the time.

2) David Beckham, Turkey 0 England 0, European Championship qualifier, 11 October 2003

England looked set to take the lead in a tricky fixture in Istanbul when Steven Gerrard was chopped down in the box. David Beckham stepped up to take the penalty but his standing foot gave way as he approached the ball, resulting in a shot that blazed yards over the bar. Beckham looked mortified, and his mood wasn't helped when a couple of Turkish players began taunting him about the appalling miss.

3) Bobby Moore, Poland 2 England 0, World Cup qualifier, 6 June 1973

Bobby Moore, England's legendary World Cup-winning captain of 1966, was some way past his best by the time of this vital match against Poland in Chorzów – and, unfortunately, it showed. Shortly after half-time, with the Three Lions trailing 1-0, the West Ham defender attempted to dribble past Włodzimierz Lubański but was dispossessed, the speedy Polish striker racing forward to shoot low past Peter Shilton with the 32-year-old Moore trailing in his wake.

4) Geoff Thomas, England 2 France 0, friendly, 19 February 1992

When Geoff Thomas went clean through on goal it looked as though the Crystal Palace midfielder might get off the mark in international football a year after making his England debut. Spotting that France goalkeeper Gilles Rousset had advanced to the edge of his area, Thomas attempted to chip him but badly mishit his shot, the ball bobbling off in the vague direction of the corner flag to the groans of the fans at Wembley. The thoroughly inept effort proved to be one of his last actions in an England shirt, as the Eagles journeyman was never picked for the Three Lions again.

5) Norman Hunter, England 1 Poland 1, World Cup qualifier, 17 October 1973

One of the hardest players in English football history, Norman Hunter looked odds on to win the ball when Poland launched a counter attack down the left in this crucial qualifier at Wembley. However, for once 'Bites Yer Legs' went in for the challenge rather tentatively and lost out to winger Grzegorz Lato, who ran on with the ball before passing to Jan Domarski, whose low shot from just inside the area beat England goalkeeper Peter Shilton. Although the Three Lions hit back to equalise through Allan Clarke it was not enough to take Sir Alf Ramsey's men to the finals in West Germany.

6) Kevin Keegan, Spain 0 England 0, World Cup second group stage, 5 July 1982

England needed to win this match against hosts Spain in Madrid by two clear goals to reach the World Cup semi-final and, in a last throw of the dice, Three Lions' boss Ron Greenwood brought on star players Kevin Keegan and Trevor Brooking, both of whom had missed the earlier matches through injury. Brooking soon had a fierce shot well saved and then Keegan was served up a glorious opportunity, Bryan Robson crossing from the left only for the Hamburg striker to head wide from six yards with the goal gaping.

7) Gary Lineker, England 1 Brazil 1, friendly, 17 May 1992

Just one short of Bobby Charlton's then-England record goals tally of 49, Gary Lineker had a golden opportunity to level with the 1966 World Cup legend when the Three Lions were awarded an early penalty in this friendly against Brazil. Normally, Lineker would blast his penalties but on this occasion, for some unfathomable reason, he decided to try a delicate 'Panenka' chip. The plan backfired disastrously as Brazil goalkeeper Carlos pounced on the woeful shot, and Lineker would remain stuck on 48 goals for the rest of his England career.

8) Steven Gerrard, England 1 France 2, European Championship group stage, 13 June 2004

England were holding out for a decent 1-1 draw against reigning European champs France when, deep into injury time, Steven

Gerrard needlessly tried to pass the ball back to David James. However, his pass was too short and pacy French striker Thierry Henry got there first, a split-second before he collided with the England goalkeeper. It was a clear penalty and Zinedine Zidane, who just two minutes earlier had scored France's equaliser with a majestic free kick, made no mistake from the spot.

9) Eric Dier, England 2 Australia 1, friendly, 27 May 2016
Two minutes after coming on as a sub at Sunderland's Stadium of Light against Australia, Tottenham defender Eric Dier got on the scoresheet, but it's not a goal he will want to remember. Australia sub Miloš Degenek crossed from the right and, in attempting to clear, Dier only succeeded in heading the ball low through goalkeeper Fraser Forster's legs. The comical own goal halved England's lead but Roy Hodgson's men hung on to win 2-1 in this warm-up friendly ahead of Euro 2016.

10) Jeff Astle, England 0 Brazil 1, World Cup group stage, 7 June 1970
England were trailing 1-0 in this absorbing match against eventual world champions Brazil in Guadalajara, Mexico, when Jeff Astle, just on as a 63rd-minute substitute for Francis Lee, was gifted a glorious chance to equalise. The Brazilian defence failed to clear a high cross from the left and the ball fell invitingly to the West Brom striker, standing near the penalty spot. Considering that Astle had just topped the old First Division scoring charts, the opportunity could not have fallen to a better man, but he rather rushed his left-footed shot and put the ball narrowly wide of the post.

TOP 10 FRIENDLY WINS

The best of the matches England have won against top opposition outside of major tournaments:

1) Brazil 0 England 2, 10 June 1984
After failing to qualify for the 1984 Euros in France, England instead went off on a three-match South American tour, kicking off with a first – and, so far, only – win away to Brazil. Watford

winger John Barnes was the star of the show in the Maracanã Stadium in Rio, scoring a wonderful solo goal shortly before half-time when he dribbled past four defenders before coolly planting the ball into the net. Then, on the hour, Barnes crossed to the far post for Portsmouth striker Mark Hateley to score with a towering header and clinch a famous triumph.

2) Germany 3 England 6, 14 May 1938
A German side which included several top Austrian players following the annexation of their country by the Nazis earlier in the year proved no match for a Stanley Matthews-inspired England. The Stoke winger scored the goal of the game, dribbling from inside his own half before shooting home, to help the Three Lions take a 4-2 lead at the break. Then, in the second half, he turned provider, setting up West Ham's Len Goulden for a ferocious shot which ripped the net from the crossbar to seal an impressive 6-3 victory.

3) England 3 Argentina 1, 13 May 1980
World champions in 1978, Argentina arrived at Wembley with a new star in their ranks, 19-year-old attacking midfielder Diego Maradona. The teenage prodigy tormented England's defence throughout and, after a quickfire brace from Liverpool striker David Johnson, got his side back into the game when he was chopped down by Kenny Sansom, Argentina captain Daniel Passarella smashing home the resulting penalty. However, Three Lions skipper Kevin Keegan wrapped up an excellent win for Ron Greenwood's men with 20 minutes to play, rifling in a low shot from just inside the box.

4) England 2 West Germany 0, 12 March 1975
Having failed to qualify for the 1974 World Cup, England had a point to prove when they took on world champions West Germany on a wet night at Wembley. Impressing on his international debut, Stoke midfielder Alan Hudson fired in a free kick which Colin Bell converted with the help of a deflection midway through the first half. Then, halfway through the second half, England skipper Alan Ball crossed to the far post for Newcastle striker Malcolm Macdonald to head in his first goal for his country.

5) Italy 0 England 4, 16 May 1948

Having won the last pre-war World Cup in 1938, Italy were still technically the holders of the trophy when England visited Turin in 1948. In one of their best away performances, Walter Winterbottom's side made light work of the *Azzurri* and took the lead after just three minutes when Stan Mortensen crashed in a shot from a tight angle. The Blackpool forward then set up Tommy Lawton for number two midway through the first half, and two well-taken goals by Preston winger Tom Finney completed the rout in the final 20 minutes.

6) England 4 Brazil 2, 9 May 1956

In the first meeting of the sides, England came out on top against Brazil in a highly entertaining match at Wembley. Early goals from Manchester United striker Tommy Taylor and Sheffield United winger Colin Grainger put the Three Lions in control, but the South Americans hit back with two goals of their own at the start of the second half, the second a shot by Didi that Coventry goalkeeper Reg Matthews spilt over the line. The final half hour, though, was all England: Brazil goalkeeper Gilmar saved two penalties, but he could do nothing about headers from Taylor and Grainger, the latter converting a pinpoint cross by the outstanding Stanley Matthews.

7) England 3 Italy 2, 14 November 1934

World champions Italy came to north London determined to win, not least because their players had each been promised £150, an Alfa Romeo car and exemption from military service should they triumph. Despite missing a first-minute penalty, England came out on top thanks to two fine goals by Manchester City winger Eric Brook and another from Arsenal centre-forward Ted Drake. The match, though, is best remembered for the violence of the tackling which resulted in Italian defender Luis Monti suffering a broken foot and England captain Eddie Hapgood a broken nose, later leading to the infamous encounter being dubbed 'The Battle of Highbury'.

8) England 3 Argentina 2, 12 November 2005

In a thrilling match in Geneva, England twice came from behind to beat old rivals Argentina in dramatic style. Chelsea striker

Hernán Crespo tapped in to give the South Americans the lead on 34 minutes but Wayne Rooney soon levelled for Sven-Göran Eriksson's men with a composed finish. Argentina regained the lead early in the second half through a Walter Samuel header, but were pegged back with just three minutes to play when Michael Owen headed in Steven Gerrard's right-wing cross. Then, in injury time, Owen grabbed a sensational winner, meeting Joe Cole's centre with a firm downward header into the bottom corner.

9) England 2 Rest of the World 1 XI, 23 October 1963
A prestigious friendly celebrating the centenary of the Football Association saw England take on a Rest of the World side containing greats like Alfredo Di Stéfano, Ferenc Puskás and Eusébio at Wembley. The Three Lions had the upper hand in the first half, only to be denied by some fine saves by Russian goalkeeper Lev Yashin. Alf Ramsey's side eventually took the lead on 70 minutes, Southampton winger Terry Paine scoring from close range, but the visitors soon hit back with an opportunistic goal from Scottish striker Denis Law. Three minutes from time Jimmy Greaves grabbed the winner for England, pouncing on a rebound after Bobby Charlton's shot had been saved.

10) England 1 Spain 0, 12 November 2011
Reigning World and European champions Spain dominated possession at Wembley, but it was Fabio Capello's England who came out on top to the delight of the home fans. Skipper Frank Lampard stooped low to nod in the only goal of the game on 49 minutes after Darren Bent's header from James Milner's free kick had struck a post. Spain upped the tempo in search of an equaliser and twice came close, David Villa hitting the post and Cesc Fàbregas shooting narrowly wide, but England held on for a famous win.

TOP 10 GOAL CELEBRATIONS

The England goal celebrations which live long in the memory:

1) Paul Gascoigne
After sealing England's victory over Scotland at Euro '96 with a superb individual strike, Paul Gascoigne ran to the side of the

goal and lay down with his mouth wide open. Team-mate Teddy Sheringham then squirted liquid from an energy drink into his mouth in a tongue-in-cheek reference to the 'dentist's chair' boozing episode in Hong Kong which had generated negative media headlines before the start of the tournament. Funny and imaginative, the celebration was almost as good as Gazza's magical goal.

2) Stuart Pearce
Having missed his spot-kick in England's World Cup semi-final shoot-out defeat against Germany six years earlier, Stuart Pearce bravely stepped up to take another penalty in a Euro '96 quarter-final against Spain at Wembley. This time 'Psycho' drilled his shot into the corner and raced towards the fans, eyes bulging while yelling a torrent of swear words. Haunted by his failure in 1990, Pearce had finally found 'closure'.

3) Chloe Kelly
On as a sub against Germany at Wembley in the final of the Women's 2022 Euros, Chloe Kelly poked the ball over the line in extra time to restore England's lead and then raced off towards the touchline, tearing off her shirt and twirling it in triumph above her head. Chloe's exuberant celebration earned her a yellow card, but she didn't care as her goal proved to be the winner in a tense and dramatic match that had the nation gripped from start to finish.

4) Peter Crouch
After scoring his second goal for England – in a 3-1 win against Hungary at Old Trafford in May 2006 – lanky striker Peter Crouch celebrated with a few jerky dance moves. Four days later the Liverpool star revived the 'robot' at the same venue while notching a hat-trick in a 6-0 demolition of Jamaica. The unusual celebration captured the imagination of fans around the country, making Crouch something of a cult figure.

5) David Beckham
After scoring a fantastic last-minute long-range free kick against Greece at Old Trafford to clinch England's place at the 2002 World Cup, David Beckham's first thought was to celebrate with the

fans rather than his delighted team-mates. Adrenaline coursing through his veins, the England skipper rushed towards the Stretford End to bask in the acclaim of the supporters, his arms outstretched like a victorious gladiator.

6) Raheem Sterling and Declan Rice
Celebrating his opening goal in a World Cup qualifier against Hungary in Budapest in September 2021, Raheem Sterling ran off to a corner where he took off his shirt to reveal a tribute on a T-shirt to a friend who had just died. As the England players congratulated the Manchester City winger they were bombarded with plastic drinking cups by the home fans, but rather than taking evasive action Declan Rice cheekily picked up one of the cups, raised it to his lips and pretended to take a swig.

7) Wayne Rooney
Wayne Rooney had several goal celebrations in his locker, but when he was especially happy enjoyed a spot of eye-catching acrobatics. So when he scored a late goal to seal a 3-1 win for England against Scotland at Celtic Park in November 2014 he milked the moment with a Simone Biles-style cartwheel somersault.

8) Harry Kane
After scoring at the second attempt against Denmark in the semi-final of Euro 2020, England captain Harry Kane sped off to the corner flag before diving full length. It was a celebration which demonstrated his joy at scoring on such an important occasion, but also contained a touch of relief after Kasper Schmeichel had initially saved Kane's penalty.

9) Alan Shearer
Alan Shearer was so excited about scoring against Germany in the semi-final of Euro '96 at Wembley that he forgot all about his trademark 'arm in the air' goal celebration and, instead, raced off along the touchline pursued by his delighted team-mates.

10) Michael Owen
After completing his hat-trick in England's famous 5-1 win against Germany in Munich in September 2001, Michael Owen celebrated with a simple forward roll of the type seen in many

a school gymnastics class. It was as if the Liverpool striker was saying, 'Yes, it really was as easy as that!'

TOP 10 WORST KITS

Even diehard England fans thought twice before forking out for replicas of these monstrosities:

1) Third, 1992
Traditionalists were horrified when Umbro brought out a pale blue third strip in 1992 with three huge lions in darker blue across the upper arm and chest. The tacky design, which seemed to mock England's proud heritage, was slammed by critics who claimed the lions were almost cartoon-like. Fortunately, the unloved kit was only worn twice in friendlies against Czechoslovakia and Spain before being unceremoniously binned.

2) Away, 2016–2017
First worn in an excellent 3-2 win against Germany in March 2016, this red Nike away shirt featured maroon sleeves, red shorts and, unusually, blue socks. Fans were unimpressed and Three Lions legend Gary Lineker also gave the ugly kit the thumbs down, tweeting, 'Can't think of a worse England strip.' However, in the six matches the team wore the outfit they were undefeated.

3) Away, 1996
The most controversial England shirt ever was described by kit manufacturers Umbro as being in two tones of 'indigo blue' but to fans and media alike it was simply grey – and a dull grey, at that. Designed to look good with jeans, the shirt sold reasonably well but was only worn three times – most famously, in the Euro '96 semi-final against Germany at Wembley. England's defeat in a dramatic penalty shoot-out spelt the end for a kit fans felt was unlucky, and it was retired sooner than originally planned.

4) Home, 1997–1999
England's 1998 World Cup campaign provided a memorable moment when Michael Owen scored one of his country's greatest ever goals, but the kit he was wearing was one of the worst in the

Three Lions' history. The Umbro-designed white shirt boasted broad navy blue and red panels and a large collar in the same colours, but the overall look was spoilt by a horribly cluttered middle section which featured no fewer than five different elements: the manufacturer Umbro, the Three Lions crest, the word England, tournament details and the player's number. As they say, too much information!

5) Away, 1973
In a complete break with tradition, England wore a new Aertex lightweight kit of yellow shirts, blue shorts and yellow socks for their European summer tour in 1973. The outfit, which was similar to away kits worn by Everton and Chelsea around that time, didn't look bad but, on the other hand, it didn't exactly scream 'England' either. Two defeats, including a catastrophic one against Poland in a World Cup qualifier, and a draw from the three matches was not a great return, and the Three Lions have never worn yellow again.

6) Away, 1970
England wore a sky blue change kit for their 1970 World Cup group game against Czechoslovakia in Mexico in 1970, Sir Alf Ramsey believing that light colours would keep his players cool in the scorching conditions. However, for the millions watching at home on black-and-white TV sets there was a distinct lack of contrast with the all-white of the Czechs. After England's 1-0 win Ramsey admitted, 'I think the choice, and it was my choice, of pale blue as a second colour, was a bad one. Where I sat looking from the shade into the sun, it was very difficult to distinguish the players.' The kit was never worn by England again.

7) Away, 1994–1995
Umbro introduced this 'wine-coloured' strip in 1994 – the first time England had worn all-red for nearly a quarter of a century. The dark blue winged collar and cuffs were especially unappealing aspects of a shirt which was only sported by the Three Lions three times, with one of those games being the infamous friendly against the Republic of Ireland in February 1995 which was abandoned after just 27 minutes because of serious crowd trouble.

8) Home, 2016–2017
This Nike-designed kit proved unpopular with fans who didn't especially care for the pale blue sleeves or the clashing red socks – a supposed tribute to the outfit England wore when famously beating Brazil in a friendly in Rio back in 1984. Notoriously, Roy Hodgson's Three Lions sported this outfit when losing 2-1 to Iceland at the 2016 Euros in France – one of the most humiliating defeats in England's history.

9) Away, 2008
England wore this red shirt with blue and white bands on both sides of the collar for Fabio Capello's first match in charge of the Three Lions, a 2-1 friendly win against Switzerland at Wembley in February 2008. The design was reminiscent of the Admiral away kit of the early 1980s, but many fans felt that the shirt looked more like a training top than a proper England jersey.

10) Home, 2013–2014
Nike's first kit for England had an unusual launch when midfielder Jack Wilshere went back to his old school in Hitchin and selected 16-year-old Jason Kelly to model the outfit. The strip was attractive enough but, thanks to the very dark blue crew neck collar and shorts, many fans felt it was too much like a West German one from the 1960s or 1970s. First worn in a 1-1 draw at Wembley against the Republic of Ireland in May 2013, the outfit was only sported eight times before being replaced ahead of the 2014 World Cup.

TOP 10 CELEBRITY FAN QUOTES

Stars from the worlds of music, politics and TV reveal their love for the England team:

1) 'In the last few moments of the match I found myself kneeling in front of the TV, shrieking and foaming at the mouth.'
TV presenter Michael Aspel, recalling England's victory in the 1966 World Cup Final

2) 'They might have beaten us at our national sport, but we managed to beat them at their national sport twice in the 20th century.'
Prime Minister Margaret Thatcher after England lost on penalties to West Germany in the 1990 World Cup semi-final

3) 'We are out of the World Cup, the sun has gone in and Trump is coming to town. Shall we all just get on the gin?'
TV presenter Fearne Cotton after England lost to Croatia in the semi-final of the 2018 World Cup

4) 'Your success goes far beyond the trophy you have so deservedly earned. You have all set an example that will be an inspiration for girls and women today, and for future generations.'
The Queen, congratulating the England Women's team after their victory at the 2022 Euros

5) 'This is a moment London will never forget. I can't remember the last time I saw our city so alive. An England final in London Wembley's Stadium – does it get much better?'
London mayor Sadiq Khan after England beat Denmark in the semi-final of Euro 2020

6) 'By the time of the game against Germany, we'd moved up the river and we couldn't get the [BBC] World Service so we had to listen to a French commentary and it was like listening to someone describe a flower display, no excitement at all.'
TV presenter Michael Palin, on following England's Euro '96 semi-final while filming in the Andes

7) 'I can't really believe this is happening. So exciting and I just wish you the very best of luck. You bring out the very best of England and we are all behind you. The whole country is behind you. So bring it home.'
Prince William, the president of the FA, before the Euro 2020 final between England and Italy at Wembley

8) 'British ferries have stopped transporting live animals to the continent. This has made it very difficult for England fans to get to away matches.'
Comedienne Jo Brand

9) 'As always the England fans have been fantastic. They have been let down by the team and let down by people earning £125,000 a week. It's a disgrace.'
Elton John, letting off steam after England were eliminated from the 2006 World Cup

10) 'This is the most deflated I've felt after an England game. I feel like a very, very big beach ball with a hole in it.'
Comedian Tim Vine after England were knocked out of Euro 2016 by minnows Iceland